Scenes from

THE LIVES
OF THE SAINTS

Relics and Blessed Objects
& Some Other Persons Described

A.C. Emmerick

SCENES FROM THE LIVES OF THE SAINTS

Also Relics, Blessed Objects
&
Some Other Persons Described

From the Visions of
ANNE CATHERINE EMMERICH

Selected, Edited & Arranged
With Extensive New Translations from
the Original Notes of Clemens Brentano by
JAMES R. WETMORE

Volume 9 of 12
of the Series: *New Light on the*
Visions of Anne Catherine Emmerich

(With 9 Illustrations)

✿ Angelico Press

For information, address:
Angelico Press
169 Monitor St.
Brooklyn, NY 11222
angelicopress.com

ISBN 978-1-62138-375-8 (pbk)
ISBN 978-1-62138-376-5 (cloth)
ISBN 978-1-62138-388-8 (ebook)

Cover Image:
J. James Tissot (French, 1836–1902)
The Ascension from Below (detail), Brooklyn Museum,
purchased by public subscription: 00.159.349
Reproduced by permission of the Brooklyn Museum
Cover Design: Michael Schrauzer

CONTENTS

Preface i

Saints

Agatha 1

Agnes and Emerentiana 5

Anthony of Padua 11

Apollonia 14

Thomas Aquinas 15

Augustine 17

    Augustine Appears to Anne Catherine 17

    Scenes from the Life of Augustine 19

    Theater Life in Carthage 21

    Augustine is Baptized 23

Benedict and Scholastica 26

Benedict, Rita of Cascia, Bobadillo 30

Boniface 31

Catherine 32

Cecilia and Valerian 39

    During the Investigation of Anne Catherine's Stigmata 43

Clare 44

    Working in the Vineyard 46

Clare of Montefalco 46

Clement 48

Cunegundes 51

Dionysius the Areopagite 54

    Dionysius and Anne Catherine in a Heavenly Garden 55

    The Fulfillment of the Vision of the Feast of St. Dionysius 57

Dorothea 57

Engelbert of Cologne 59

Ermelinda 59

Eulalia 60

Francis of Assisi 61
    During the Forced Investigation of Her Stigmata 63

Francis Borgia 64

Francis de Sales • Jane de Chantal 64

Gertrude of Nivelles 68

Gregory 69

Hermann Joseph 69

Hubert 70

Ignatius of Loyola and Others of His Order 72
    Ignatius of Loyola 72
    Aloysius 78

Isidore 79

Justina and Cyprian 81

Louis of France 83

Madeline of Hadamar and Colomba Schanold of
    Bamberg (Two Stigmatics) 84

Marcella 87

Marcellus and Lucina 88

Margaret of Antioch 89

Nicholas of Flüe 91

Nicostratus 95

Odilia 96

Paschal and Cyprian 98

Paula 100

Perpetua and Felicity 101

Placidus 109

Stephen, Lawrence, and Hippolytus 110

Susanna, Holy Martyr 115

Thekla 118

Theoctista 125

Ursula 126

Viliulphus and Chrysostomus 132

Walburga 133

Zephyrinus 136

Relics and Blessed Objects

Anne Catherine's Gift of Recognizing Relics and
    Blessed Objects 139

Feast of Holy Relics, 1820 142

History of a Reliquary 162

An Infant-Martyr of Sachsenhausen 167

Relics Belonging to Churches in Münster 170

Longinus and the Effects of the Sacred Lance 176

A Particle of the True Cross 177

Relics of Mary 178
    Relics of the Blessed Virgin's Clothing 178
    Other Relics of Mary and the Holy House of Loreto 181
    Spurious Relics of Mary's Hair 184

Blessed Objects 185
    St. Benedict's Medal 186
    Petrified Bone: A Glance at Paradise 187

Some Other Persons Described

Datula and Pontianus 191
    Vignettes From Datula's Journey to Jerusalem 204
    Regarding Datula's Island 205
    Datula's Passing 206
    Some Further Glimpses 208
    Datula's Daughter 210

Judith of Africa 213

Mary of Agreda 222

Preface

ANNE Catherine Emmerich was born on September 8, 1774, at Flamske, near Coesfeld, Germany. From early childhood she was blessed with the gift of spiritual sight and lived almost constantly in inner vision of scenes of the Old and New Testaments. As a child, her visions were mostly of pre-Christian events, but these grew less frequent with the passing years, and by the time she had become, at twenty-nine, an Augustinian nun at the Order's convent in Dülmen, Germany, her visions had become concerned primarily with the life of Jesus Christ, although they encompassed also the lives of many saints and other personages (some unknown as yet to history) as well as far-reaching insights into the creation, the fall, a mysterious mountain of the prophets, the spiritual hierarchies, paradise and purgatory, the heavenly Jerusalem, and much besides.

In the context of Anne Catherine's visions, and related conversations, much was said also of spiritual labors, described symbolically as work in the "nuptial house," the "inner chamber," the "garden," and the "vineyard." In this way many teachings on the inner life and prayer came forward, along with detailed accounts of healing work and journeys for "poor souls" in purgatory or in past epochs. Anne Catherine also showed considerable concern for the souls of those around her, especially her later amanuensis Clemens Brentano, in connection with his initial lack of faith.

Owing to difficult political circumstances, Anne Catherine's convent was disbanded on December 3, 1811, and one by one the nuns in residence were obliged to leave. Anne Catherine—already very ill—withdrew to a small room in a house in Dülmen. By November, 1812, her illness had grown so severe that she was permanently confined to bed. Shortly thereafter, on December 29, 1812, she received the stigmata, a manifesting of the wounds suffered by Christ on the cross, and the highest outward sign of inner union with him. Unable to assimilate any form of nourishment, for the rest of her life she was sustained almost exclusively by water and the eucharist.

As news spread that she bore the stigmata (which bled on Fridays), more and more people came to see her. For us, the most significant of these was Clemens Brentano, who first visited her on Thursday morning, September 24, 1818. He was so impressed by the radiance of her being that he decided to relocate nearby in order to record her visions. Anne Catherine had already had a presentiment that someone—whom she called "the pilgrim"— would one day come to preserve her revelations. The moment Clemens Brentano entered her room, she recognized him as this pilgrim.

Brentano, a novelist and Romantic poet then living in Berlin, was associated with leading members of the Romantic Movement in Germany. He settled his affairs and moved from Berlin to Dülmen early in 1819. Thereafter he visited Anne Catherine every morning, noting down briefly all she related to him. After writing out a full report at home, he returned later the same day to read it back to her. She would then often expand upon certain points, or, if necessary, correct details.

On July 29, 1820, Anne Catherine began to communicate visions concerning the day-by-day life of Jesus. These visions encompassed the better part of his ministry, and she was able to describe in extraordinary detail the places he visited, his miracles and healings, his teaching activity in the synagogues and elsewhere, and the people around him. She not only named and described many of these people with astonishing concreteness, but spoke also of their families, their occupations, and other intimate biographical details.

It seems clear that Anne Catherine was called to relate these day-by-day details of the life and ministry of Jesus, and that Clemens Brentano was called to record all she communicated of her visions. They worked together daily until her death on February 9, 1824, except for one period of six months, during which Brentano was away, and several shorter periods when, mainly due to illness, it was impossible for Anne Catherine to communicate her visions.

⊕

ENCOUNTERING the visions of Anne Catherine Emmerich can raise the question: how is it possible that this woman, who never left the German region in which she was born and had very little education, could describe in such detail not only the story of creation; heaven, hell, and purgatory; the fall of angels and humanity; the spiritual hierarchies and saints; the Promise and the Ark of the Covenant; the apocalypse; spiritual warfare; and the heavenly Jerusalem—but *also* the geography and topography of Palestine and the customs and habits of people living there at the time of Jesus Christ? To at least partially answer this, the researcher upon whose work the *chronological* aspects of this new edition is largely based, Dr. Robert Powell, undertook an exhaustive analysis of her work, gradually laying bare the historical reality underlying the life of Jesus (see "Chronology" below). But his work was not done in isolation, for others had earlier laid some groundwork.

For example the French priest Abbé Julien Gouyet of Paris, after reading an account of Anne Catherine's visions concerning the death of the Virgin Mary near Ephesus, traveled there and searched the region. On October 18, 1881, guided by various particulars in her account, he discovered the ruins of a small stone building on a mountain (Bulbul Dag, "Mount Nightingale") overlooking the Aegean Sea with a view across to the remains of the ancient city of Ephesus. Abbé Gouyet was convinced that this was the house described in Anne Catherine's visions as the dwelling of the Virgin Mary during the last years of her life. He was at first ridiculed, but several years later the ruins were independently rediscovered by two Lazarist missionaries who had undertaken a similar search on the basis of Anne Catherine's visions. They determined that the building had been a place of pilgrimage in earlier times for Christians descended from the church of Ephesus, the community referred to by St. John (Rev. 2:1–7). The building had been known in those days as Panaya Kapulu, the house of the Blessed Virgin, and was revered as the place where she had died. Traditionally, the date of her death, August 15, was the *very day* of the annual pilgrimage to Panaya Kapulu.

That Anne Catherine's visions provide spiritual nourishment had long been the experience of many spiritual seekers, but the discovery of Panaya Kapulu confirmed that her visions could also (at least in part) be corroborated along conventional lines of research.

Sources

THE visions of Anne Catherine Emmerich have been published in English translation in various editions since late in the nineteenth century. These editions focused primarily on the visions of the life of Jesus Christ and of Mary, with some material drawn from Old Testament times also. However the *original* notes of Clemens Brentano contained material on many other fascinating subjects. Much of this material has not been readily available before now, either in German or in English translation, a gap that this twelve-volume *New Light on the Visions Anne Catherine Emmerich* series is meant at least to begin filling.

Until now the only translations available of some of this latter material appeared in the two-volume biography of Anne Catherine by Rev. Carl E. Schmöger, first published in English in 1885. Rev. Schmöger, who was also instrumental in the selection and arrangement of the visions related to the life of Jesus Christ upon which later English translations were based, included in the biography a selection of the supplemental material mentioned above —but his selection was necessarily limited.

Clemens Brentano himself was only able to compile from his notes a few volumes for publication, and upon his death the notes passed to his brother Christian, who had been an interested participant in Clemens's work with Anne Catherine from the start (in fact, Christian had arranged his brother's first meeting with the visionary). Christian, however, proved unable to coordinate the notes any further. And so the first phase of this seemingly insurmountable task fell in due course to Rev. Schmöger.

Then, in the last decades of the twentieth century, the German publisher Kohlhammer commenced publishing, under the auspices of the *Frankfurter Brentano Ausgabe*, an intended complete edition of Brentano's works, projected to number as many as sixty volumes. Part of this project was the publication of facsimiles of the thirty-eight notebooks of Brentano's notes of the visions of Anne Catherine. (Brentano also noted down details of their conversations in other contexts, as well as his own experiences while attending her.) With the Kohlhammer edition, a wider public would finally gain access to the originals upon which later compilations and translations of the visions had been based. However, this noble project has not been completed, and at present there is no indication whether it will recommence. An additional impediment for researchers in dealing with the facsimiles is the fact that Brentano's notes were penned in a now archaic German script that only specialists can read.

Thus matters stood until Jozef De Raedemaeker, a dedicated Belgian researcher, undertook the enormous task of transcribing the full body of notes from the archaic script into modern German—making it available in printed and digital form in 2009. The combined 38 notebooks exceed 7,300 pages and include many hand-drawn illustrations as well as typographic conventions to identify the contributions of others present at Anne Catherine's bedside, who sometimes took notes or added comments, and sometimes drawings.

⊕

ANYONE who does even minimal research on the visions of Anne Catherine Emmerich as depicted in the works attributed to Brentano's notes will soon discover that there are conflicting opinions regarding their fidelity to the words of Anne Catherine herself. This would be a subject in itself, but some remarks may be offered here. First, Anne Catherine, who had little formal education, spoke in a Low-German dialect that even Brentano, at the outset, had some difficulty understanding. Secondly, the material that was eventually fit together into a connected account in the published versions often represents a collation of as many as a dozen or more passages gleaned from visions separated sometimes by months, or even years. This can be partially explained by the fact that the visions were often related to events in the ecclesiastical year, to feasts of saints, to individuals with specific needs or requests, or to the presence of relics.

And so a great deal of work had to be done to organize and knit together related segments of visions, and to then arrange them in a meaningful sequence. Then again, it was deemed necessary to refine the language sufficiently to render it in a more contemporary idiom. There is, then, a legitimate concern that so famous and gifted a literary figure as Clemens Brentano might, even if unintentionally, have introduced some of his own impressions, interpretations, and sensitivities into his renditions. And a similar concern could be raised concerning Rev. Schmöger's subsequent arrangements, as well as those of later editors and translators working at yet a further remove.

Much of the debate on this subject, however, took place without ready access to the original notes, a defect that has now been remedied. At certain points in his transcriptions De Raedemaeker addresses this issue by comparing fragments of the original notes with versions of these same fragments as they appear in Rev. Schmöger's edition, after he in turn had worked, in some instances, with Brentano's own compilations from his original notes—and in some cases there are non-trivial discrepancies. This is an area that requires further research.

Perhaps I myself may be permitted to chime in here, as there are not many who have entered into this vast field, and I can at least appeal to many years of engagement with the visions of Anne Catherine, *including* examining De Raedemaeker's transcriptions of all thirty-eight notebooks. While thus occupied, I inevitably began to identify for myself many of the original sources upon which Rev. Schmöger based his versions well over a century ago, and in such cases could assess the fidelity of the latter to the former. Although such details do not lie within the scope of this series, I can say that, with very rare exceptions—especially allowing for the frequent need to splice together disparate fragments—Rev. Schmöger's renderings remain remarkably true to the original, and any minimal divergences are for the most part quite trivial, insofar as I have been able to investigate.

During this process, however, I *was* struck by the fact that considerable material had been *omitted*. This may well have been owing to the enormity of the task, as also to pagination limits set by the publisher; or also, partly a measure of Rev. Schmöger's personal judgment and concerns. Perhaps some of the excluded material seemed unintelligible to him, or even scandalous. However that may be, in this current series as much as possible of this neglected material has been extracted, translated, and incorporated in the relevant volumes.

It needs to be said also, in response to assertions (made mostly without benefit of access to his actual notes) that Brentano misrepresented Anne Catherine, or, even worse, took advantage of his notes to compile an independent literary work that might embellish his reputation, that in fact, in his notes, Brentano *candidly* reports *exactly* what he heard Anne Catherine say, *no matter* how extraordinary, puzzling, or even apparently contradictory. He himself offers many instances where only later—sometimes years after Anne Catherine had died—he (often with the help of academic experts) finally began to understand previously incomprehensible passages in the visions. He steadfastly refused—according to his own account and that of others—to edit out "difficulties," feeling himself, rather, under a sacred obligation to preserve his record intact and unaltered for posterity. And when the notes passed to his brother Christian, the latter adhered to the same policy.

Even without the benefit of access to the original notes on the part of most researchers, and even in face of an undercurrent of scepticism as to the authenticity of the visions, it may be worthwhile, in drawing this matter to a close for our present purposes, to note that on October 3, 2004, Anne Catherine was beatified by Pope John Paul II, who remarked: "Her example opened the hearts of poor and rich alike, of simple and cultured persons, whom she instructed in loving dedication to Jesus Christ." And in the Vatican's biography of Anne Catherine we read: "Her words, which have reached innumerable people in many languages from her modest room in Dülmen through the writings of Clemens Brentano are an outstanding proclamation of the gospel in service to salvation right up to the present day."

Chronology

PERHAPS the most surprising feature of this new series on Anne Catherine Emmerich will be the inclusion of *historical dates*—and so a brief discussion of this feature is offered below.

As described earlier, Anne Catherine was so attuned to the life of Jesus Christ as a mystical-historical reality that her comprehensive visions encompassed even minute details of time and place—testable "coordinates" in fact. This degree of precision was made possible by the many temporal as well as geographical descriptions and references contained in the visions—as mentioned earlier in connection with the discovery of the house of the Blessed Virgin.

Many chronologies of the life of Jesus Christ have been put forward over the centuries, but the dates offered in this current series differ from previous efforts in that they derive from the application of modern chronological and astro-chronological science to the whole of Anne Catherine's visions—which latter constitute a vast body of data internally consistent as to time and place to an extraordinary degree, so that, taking the generally agreed upon time period of Jesus's life, results of a high degree of reliability can be determined.

Naturally, the overriding value of the visions lies in the additional insight they offer into the life of Jesus Christ, so that for some the dating may represent no more than a convenient framework for study and meditation. Such readers need not trouble themselves about the specific dates, although they may nonetheless find that the chronology offers a useful way to maintain their orientation within any given volume, as also when referring to events in volumes already read. Some, however, will wish to assess for themselves the method by which specific dates have been thought reliable enough to include here. They may read elsewhere[1] the story of the determination of the chronology of the life of Jesus Christ included in these volumes.

---

[1] *The Visions of Anne Catherine Emmerich*, Book III, Appendix I (Kettering, OH: Angelico Press, 2015), which is based on the work of Dr. Robert Powell.

The New Light on the Visions
of Anne Catherine Emmerich Series

THE present book is one of the twelve volumes of the "New Light on the Visions of Anne Catherine Emmerich" series published by Angelico Press. This series supplements two earlier Angelico publications: *The Visions of Anne Catherine Emmerich*, Books I–III (1,700 pages in large format, with 600 illustrations and forty-three maps); and the smaller-format, slightly abridged edition: *Life, Passion, Death, & Resurrection of Jesus Christ (A Chronicle from the Visions of Anne Catherine Emmerich)*, Books I–IV (1,770 pages with 150 illustrations and 43 maps). As described earlier, in 2009 Clemens Brentano's original notes of Anne Catherine's visions became readily available for reference. At that time the above texts were already nearing completion. With the appearance of these notes, however, the editor resolved to pause, and, to the extent possible, research this vast body of notes to ascertain what further light they might shed on what had by then been prepared for publication. While the better part of another decade was devoted to the task, much research, of course, remains to be done (see "Future Prospects" below). But at some point one must call a halt, and so, after the insertion of relevant new translations into the two sets mentioned above and their publication in 2015–2016, the present series was conceived as a means to present in various contexts such new material as has since then been selected and translated from the notes.

In general, the content of each volume of this series consists (1) of material selected by individual or theme from earlier translations—reviewed, supplemented, and revised where necessary, especially for consistency of usage; and (2) of newly selected and translated material germane to the content of that volume. With regard to both individuals and themes, the procedure was to extract every reference thus far located in the notes and in prior translations and weave them together into a connected account. The reader can thus find in one place almost all of what Anne Catherine had to say about any given individual or theme.

Virtually every individual in the biblical visions (approximately 250 in total) is referenced in the five *People of the New Testament* volumes (which include also some figures from earlier and later times). A separate volume, *The Life of the Virgin Mary*, is dedicated to Mary and her ancestry (including much on the Essenes); and another volume, *Scenes from the Lives of the Saints*, treats of fifty-nine saints. Separate volumes cover events prior to the appearance of the holy family: *First Beginnings* and *Mysteries of the Old Testament*. Two further volumes cover a multitude of separate themes: *Inner Life and Worlds of Soul & Spirit* and *Spiritual Works and Journeys*. A final volume represents a condensed, edited, rearranged, supplemented, and retypeset edition of Rev. Carl E. Schmöger's exhaustive biography of Anne Catherine, first published in English in 1885. For clarity of organization, much of this biography in its original form has been redistributed among other volumes of this series. What remains has also been enriched with newly-translated material. A list of all twelve volumes of this series appears at the conclusion of this preface.

Practical Considerations

IN view of the sometimes extensive wealth of material presented concerning certain individuals—especially major characters—a judicious essentializing of scenes has sometimes been resorted to. In some cases, especially those of closely related apostles and disciples (or others regularly treated together in the visions), rather than duplicating material, the expedient adopted was to disentangle scenes to the extent possible, so that the full story could be garnered gradually by reading the separate accounts of each. Nonetheless, since readers may jump around in their selection of individuals to study, some repetition was unavoidable in order to provide enough context to keep the separate accounts reasonably sequential and unified. Put another way, these volumes are conceived primarily as reference works to which one turns for particulars on specific persons or themes rather than as connected narratives to be read cover to cover. Of course, the volumes may be read in the latter fashion also, in which case the occasional repeated material will be more noticeable.

Another consideration was that some individuals play so great a role in the visions (e.g., John the Baptist, St. Joseph, Peter, Matthew, Judas, and the Virgin Mary) that it would be impractical to include every mention in a chronological itinerary. Emphasis in such cases has been placed primarily on more general and newly-translated material. Inquisitive readers can of course turn to the index of the large-format, three-volume *The Visions of Anne Catherine Emmerich* to expand their research on such individuals.

It must be well understood that all the editor could do was work with what Anne Catherine actually said. Some little-known (or even totally unknown) individuals may enjoy longer accounts in these volumes than other, very well known, figures from the gospels or later Christian tradition! There can be no question of assigning relative importance to any individual based solely upon how extensive Anne Catherine's visions of that person may have been. Likewise, stories may have gaps, or sometimes end abruptly. It is indeed unfortunate that (as Brentano repeatedly laments in his notes) so much was lost owing to Anne Catherine's considerable suffering, household distractions, and the many obligations laid upon her—all of which interfered with her visions and her capacity to recall them. And yet withal, how much we have to be grateful for!

To streamline as far as possible a complex text, these usages were established: The voice of the narrator (Rev. Schmöger) is put in italics. Direct citations from Brentano (and a few others) are put in quotes. Anne Catherine's text bears no quotation indicators *except* where references to her words are embedded in the two contexts just mentioned. Parentheses enclose supplemental material from Anne Catherine or Brentano; brackets enclose material from Rev. Schmöger or the present editor. Footnotes from the hand of Brentano are followed by CB; those consisting of further visionary content from Anne Catherine are—for clarity in this context—enclosed in quotation marks; all other unattributed footnotes have been supplied by the present editor, sometimes incorporating what seemed worth retaining from notes by others in earlier editions.[1]

---

[1] The most useful material of this sort has been integrated from notes to a version of *The Life of the Virgin Mary* provided by Rev. Sebastian Bullough, O.P., to whom we express our gratitude.

For convenience, especially in itineraries of individuals, dates are incorporated in what is otherwise purely Anne Catherine's visionary text. It must, however, be well understood that these dates are derivative, as mentioned in "Chronology" above, *not* from the hand of Anne Catherine. As another help, for many major figures, summaries are provided at the outset. These are often in the third person—as they represent a condensation by the editor—but are nonetheless derived directly from the visions.

In such a context as these visions represent, capitalization (a topic upon which there are many and various usages, and often passionate opinions) represented a particular challenge. In the end, after experimenting with progressively increasing degrees of simplification, it was determined—in order not to overly fatigue the reader of what essentially amounts to an extended narrative rather than devotional reading properly speaking—to implement a very spare policy indeed, reserving capitalization to the Deity, and to certain terms that in Anne Catherine's visions assume a unique significance, such as the Ark of the Covenant, and what she calls the Promise, or sometimes the Holy Thing, the Mystery or Sacrament (in this special sense), or even the Germ or Seed. Finally, in cases where more general considerations are followed by chronological extracts forming a connected itinerary, the break is signaled by a row of five typographic crosses.

Prospects for the Future

AS editor of this series I am only too aware of my limitations in the face of the awe-inspiring magnitude of the task. My initial inspiration was solely the *spiritual value* of Anne Catherine's visions as a means to help seekers find their way *back* to a faithful connection with Jesus Christ; or, in the case of so many in our time, find their way *for the first time* to a dawning awareness of what they may thus far have failed to see. Further, there are great, resonant depths in the visions, like choirs of symbolism. As time went on I could only go deeper, entering upon the work that has led now, finally, to completing this series. Along with spiritual benefits and guidance, it was and will ever remain also a thrilling journey of discovery. Now, with Brentano's original notes available thanks to the efforts of Jozef De Raedemaeker, there are further depths to explore, as alas—despite so many years of work—the rich sod has only been broken.

In the visions will be found fascinating indications and hints for archeologists, historians, linguists, theologians, students of comparative religion, chronologists, specialists in symbolism, and more. Over and above the *primary element* of spiritual inspiration, it is my hope that such specialists may in due course take up these visions (including the entire corpus of Brentano's notes) and press further forward. How one would love to see a foundation, a university, a religious sodality, or some private individual or group sponsor so important and propitious a project. If the largely solitary results presented here serve to advance such future research, if hearts and souls are moved and enriched by *The Anne Catherine Emmerich Series* as a whole, the effort will have achieved its primary purpose.

JAMES RICHARD WETMORE

Acknowledgments

IT is difficult to sift out elements from earlier translators of these visions, but our main debt of gratitude for much of the English text taken as a foundation in the current work is owed to Sir Michael Palairet. Incalculable thanks are owed to Jozef De Raedemaeker for his past and present work with the original handwritten notes of Clemens Brentano. Occasional assistance with translation was received from Mado Spiegler, James Morgante, and especially Harrie Salman. A special thanks goes to Robert Powell, who has been a companion at every stage of this journey owing to his dedication to Anne Catherine in every respect: researching, translating when necessary, and, preeminently, applying his skills to the task of establishing the chronology that has been incorporated in this edition (in which connection Fr. Helmut Fahsel should also be mentioned). Most line drawings in the volumes are taken from Brentano's notes; the occasional paintings included are from the hand of James J. Tissot, as are all but one of the cover illustrations.

The New Light on the Visions
of Anne Catherine Emmerich Series

1 FIRST BEGINNINGS: *From the Creation to the Mountain of the Prophets & From Adam and Eve to Job and the Patriarchs*

2 MYSTERIES OF THE OLD TESTAMENT: *From Joseph and Asenath to the Prophet Malachi & The Ark of the Covenant and the Mystery of the Promise*

3 PEOPLE OF THE NEW TESTAMENT, BOOK I: *Joseph, The Three Kings, John the Baptist, & Four Apostles (Andrew, Peter, James the Greater, and John)*

4 PEOPLE OF THE NEW TESTAMENT, BOOK II: *Nine Apostles (Philip, Bartholomew, James the Less, Thomas, Judas Iscariot, Matthew [Levi], Judas Thaddeus, Simon the Zealot & Matthias), Paul, and Lazarus & the Secret Disciples*

5 PEOPLE OF THE NEW TESTAMENT, BOOK III: *Major Disciples of Jesus & Other Followers and Friends*

6 PEOPLE OF THE NEW TESTAMENT, BOOK IV: *Early Friends and Minor Disciples of Jesus, and Those Who Opposed Him*

7 PEOPLE OF THE NEW TESTAMENT, BOOK V: *The Primary Holy Women, Major Female Disciples and Relations of Jesus, Minor Disciples & Others*

8 THE LIFE OF THE VIRGIN MARY: *Ancestors, Essenes, Anne & Joachim, Elizabeth & Zechariah, Immaculate Conception, Birth, Temple Life, Wedding, Annunciation, Visitation, Shepherds, Three Kings, Flight into Egypt, Life in Egypt and Return, Death, Assumption, The Mystical Virgin*

9 SCENES FROM THE LIVES OF THE SAINTS: *Also Relics, Blessed Objects & Some Other Persons Described*

10 THE INNER LIFE AND WORLDS OF SOUL & SPIRIT: *Prayer, Parables, Purgatory, The Heavenly Jerusalem, Revelations, Holy Places, Gospels, &c.*

11 SPIRITUAL WORKS & JOURNEYS: *The Nuptial House, Vineyard, Sufferings for Others, the Church, and the Neighbor*

12 THE LIFE OF ANNE CATHERINE EMMERICH: *With Introductory Biographical Glimpses and Appendix on the Ecclesiastical Investigations, Arrest, and Captivity (A revised, abridged edition of works by Rev. Carl E. Schmöger and Fr. Helmut Fahsel, with new translations).*

Saints

Agatha

LAST night I was in that city in which I saw the "great insurrection" (Palermo). The churches and houses still bear the marks of it. I saw a grand and wonderful festival. The church was hung with tapestry, and in the middle of it was a curtain like our Lenten curtain, our *Hungertuch*. In one place I saw a great fire like our St. John's fires, to which the priests all went in procession carrying a veil. It was a grand festival, great pomp and parade. The people seem to join in it eagerly, and brawls are of frequent occurrence. The church was magnificent, and during the ceremonies I saw Agatha and other saints.

I saw that Agatha was martyred in another city, Catana, though her parents lived in Palermo. Her mother, a Christian in secret, had instructed her child in the faith; but the father was a pagan. Agatha had two nurses. From her earliest years she enjoyed most familiar intercourse with Jesus. I often saw her sitting in the garden, and by her, a shining beautiful boy playing and conversing with her—it seemed as if they were growing up together. I saw her make a seat for him in the grass and listen to him thoughtfully, her hands in her lap. Sometimes they played with flowers and little sticks. He seemed to grow as she grew, but he only came when she was alone. I think she saw him, for her actions indicated awareness of his presence.

I saw her increase wonderfully in interior purity and strength of soul. It is impossible to say how one sees such things. It is as if some object continually became more magnificent, like gold being purified, a spark becoming a star, a fire becoming a sun! I saw Agatha's extraordinary fidelity to grace. I saw her constant turning away from every shadow of impurity, from every little imperfection, for which she punished herself severely. When she would have wished to lie down in the evening, her guardian

1

angel often stood visibly by her side reminding her of something, some forgotten duty perhaps, that she would then hasten to perform: some prayer, some alms, something relating to charity, purity, humility, obedience, mercy, or some effort to prevent sin.

I often saw Agatha as a child gliding along unknown to her mother with alms and food for the poor. She was so noble, so dear to Jesus—and yet she lived in a constant struggle! I often saw her pinch and strike herself for the least faults, the slightest inclinations; but with it all, she was so open, so frank, so courageous!

I saw her in her eighth year taken in a carriage with several other maidens to Catana. This was by her father's orders, for he wanted her reared in all the liberty of paganism. She was placed in the house of a shameless woman who had five daughters. I cannot say that she kept a public house of infamy such as I have often seen in those times; she seemed rather to be a bold, worldly woman of high position. Her house was beautifully situated, everything about it sumptuous. Here Agatha remained a long time, but she was never allowed to go out. I generally saw her with other little girls in a handsome room before which lay a lake that reflected in its waters the whole house; the other sides of the dwelling were guarded.

The lady and her five daughters gave themselves the greatest trouble imaginable to form Agatha to their kind of virtue. I saw them walking with her in the beautiful gardens and showing her all kinds of elegant clothes; but she turned away indifferently from such things. And here too I often saw the heavenly boy at her side, while she daily became more serious, more courageous. Agatha was a very beautiful child, not tall, but perfectly formed. She had dark hair, great black eyes, a beautiful nose, round face, a very mild but firm manner, and an expression indicative of extraordinary strength of soul. Her mother died of grief during her child's absence.

I saw Agatha in this house constantly and courageously overcoming herself and her natural inclinations, resisting every seduction. Quintianus, who afterward condemned her to death, often visited the house. He was a married man but he could not endure his wife. He was a disagreeable, very vulgar, and insolent man, and used to go prowling around the city spying out everything, annoying and tormenting the inhabitants. I used to see him with the lady of the house. He often looked at Agatha as one might gaze on a beautiful child, but he never offered her any improper attentions. I saw her heavenly bridegroom standing by her, visible to her alone, and I heard him say to her: "Our bride is little, she has no breasts. When she will have them, they will be cut off; for none shall ever drink thereof!"[1] The youth spoke these words to Agatha in vision, and they mean that but few Christians, few priests, were then in her country (Sicily).[2] I saw that the instruments of her martyrdom were shown her by her bridegroom; indeed, I think they played with them.

Later I saw Agatha again in her native city, after her father's death, when she was about thirteen years old. She made an open profession of Christianity and had only good people around her. Then I saw her dragged from her house by men sent by Quintianus from Catana to arrest her. In passing out of the city gate she stooped to fasten her shoe, and looking back she perceived that all her friends had abandoned her and were hurrying back to the city. Agatha begged God to set up some sign as a memorial of their ingratitude, when instantly there arose on the spot a sterile olive tree.

I saw Agatha again with the wicked woman and her heavenly bridegroom by her. He said: "When the serpent, formerly mute, began to speak, Eve should have known it was the devil." The woman tried again in every way to seduce her by flattery and amusements but I heard Agatha applying to her the teachings of her bridegroom. When she urged her to wantonness, Agatha replied: "Your flesh and blood are, like the serpent, creatures of God; but he who speaks through them is the devil!" I saw Quintianus's communications with this woman, and I knew very well two of his other friends there.

Then I saw Agatha thrown into prison, interrogated, beaten,

---

[1] Canticle 8:8.

[2] Agatha was "The Bride," the Church of Sicily, as yet young. Her martyrdom was here foretold, by which she was to become the spiritual mother of innumerable souls, to whom the milk of her breasts—that is, the rich blessings flowing from her martyrdom—was to procure the grace of salvation.

and finally, her breasts cut off. One man held her while a second took off the breasts with an instrument shaped like a poppy pod. It opened in three parts like a mouth, and bit off the breast in one piece. The executioners had the revolting cruelty to hold them up mockingly before the maiden and then throw them on the ground at her feet.

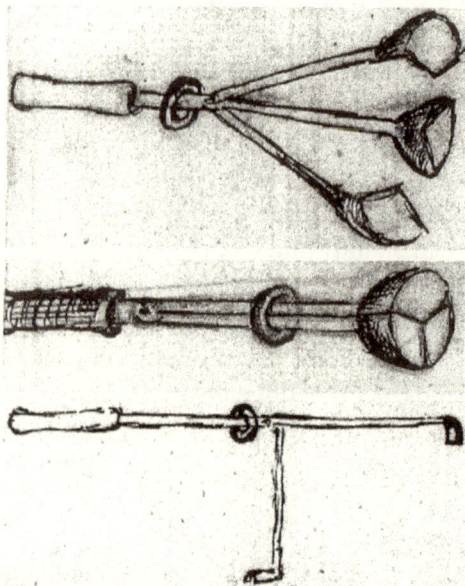

During the torture Agatha said to Quintianus: "Do you not shudder to tear from a woman that from which thy own mother once fed you?" She stood firm, self-possessed, and once she exclaimed: "My soul has breasts more noble than those you can take from me!" Agatha was scarcely more than a child, and her bosom was far from being developed. The wound was perfectly round; it was not lacerated, the blood gushed out in little streams. I often saw that same instrument used in torturing the martyrs. They used to tear off whole pieces of flesh from their person with it. How wonderful were the help and strength the martyrs received from Jesus Christ! I often see him by them strengthening them for the combat; they faint not where another would die.

Then I saw Agatha in prison where an aged man appeared to her, offering to heal her wounds. She thanked him but replied that she had never had recourse to medicine; that she had her Lord Jesus Christ who could heal her if he so willed. "I am a Christian and a gray-haired old man," said he, "be not ashamed of me!" She replied: "My wounds have nothing about them revolting to modesty! But Jesus will heal me, if he sees fit. He created the whole world, and he can also restore my breasts!" Then the old man laughed and said: "I am his servant Peter! Behold! Thy breasts are healed!" and he disappeared. I saw that an angel fastened to the roof of her prison something like a ticket on which was writing, but I do not now remember what it was. Agatha's breasts were perfectly restored. It was not merely a healing of the skin, it was a new, a perfect bosom. Around each breast I saw circles of light, the inner one composed of rainbow-colored rays.

Again was Agatha led forth to martyrdom. In a vault were rows of furnaces like deep chests, stuck full of sharp points and potsherds; under them burned fires. There was room to pass between the chests, and many poor victims were roasted at the same time. As Agatha was thrown into one of these furnaces the earth quaked and a falling wall crushed the two friends of Quintianus. The latter had fled during a revolt of the people. Agatha was led back again to her prison, where she died. I saw Quintianus, when on his way to seize Agatha's property, drowning miserably in a river. I afterward saw a mountain vomiting forth fire and people fleeing before the fiery wave. It rolled as far as Agatha's tomb, where it was extinguished.

Agnes and Emerentiana

I SAW a very lovely, delicate maiden dragged through the streets by rude soldiers. She was wrapped in a long brown woolen mantle, her braided hair concealed under a veil. The soldiers seized her mantle by the sides and dragged her so violently forward that they tore it apart. They were followed by a crowd, among them a few women. She was led through a high gateway, across a square court, and into an apartment destitute of furniture, saving some long, cushioned chests. They pushed her in, dragged her from side to side, and tore from her both mantle and veil. Agnes was like an innocent patient lamb in their hands, and light and airy as a bird; she seemed to fly as they pulled her here and there. They took her mantle and left her.

Agnes, in a white, sleeveless undergarment open at the sides, now stood back in the corner of the room praying calmly with outstretched hands and face upturned. The women who had followed her were not admitted into the courtyard. All sorts of men stood around the doors, as if the saint were their common prey. I saw her white tunic bloody around the neck from a wound received, perhaps on the way.

First, two or three youths entered and fell upon her, furiously dragging her hither and thither and tearing from her person the open garment. I saw blood on her neck and breast. She did not attempt to defend herself, for on the instant they deprived her of her garments, her long hair fell down around her and I saw a shining figure just above her in the air, who spread over her, like a garment, a stream of light. The wretches who had assaulted her fled terror-stricken. They encountered her insolent lover outside, who began to mock their cowardice. He rushed in himself to seize her, but Agnes grasped him firmly by the hands and held him back. He fell to the ground, but arose quickly, and again rushed madly upon her. Again did the virgin drive him back as far as the door, and again did he fall; but this time motionless. She stood calm as before, praying, shining, blooming, her face like a brilliant rose.

A loud cry was raised and several distinguished personages hastily entered the room. One of them seemed to be the youth's father. He was furious, indignant. He spoke of sorcery. But when Agnes told him she would pray for his son's restoration if he would ask it in the name of Jesus, he grew calm and begged her to do so. Then Agnes turned toward the dead youth and addressed a few words to him. He arose and was led away still weak and tottering. And now came other men toward Agnes, but like the first they too retired in fright.

Then I saw the soldiers go into the room. They took with them a brown robe, open at the side and fastened by a clasp, and an old veil such as were generally given to the martyrs. Agnes put the robe on, twisted her hair under the veil, and accompanied the soldiers to the judgment hall. This was a square place, surrounded by a wall in which were prisons, or chambers—one could stand on it and watch what was going on below. There were spectators on it at the time of which I speak.

Many Christians were led to the tribunal from a prison that seemed not far from the place in which Agnes had been so ill-used. I think they were a grandfather, his two sons-in-law, and their children, all bound together with cords. They were led before the judge, who was seated on a high stone seat in the square courtyard, and Agnes with them. The judge spoke to them kindly, questioned them, and warned them; but it was soon evident that the prisoners had been brought out only to be present at Agnes's death.

Three times was she summoned before the tribunal. At last she was condemned to be burned alive. She was led to a stake, made to mount three steps, and the faggots piled around her. They wanted to bind her, but this she would not allow. And now the torch was applied, and again I saw the shining youth shedding over her streams of light that enveloped her as with a screen, while at the same time the flames turned upon her executioner, leaving Agnes untouched. She was then taken down and led before the judge, at whose command she was placed upon a block, or stone. Again they wanted to bind her hands, but again she refused and crossed them on her bosom. The executioner seized her by the hair and cut off her head which, like Cecilia's, remained hanging upon one shoulder. Her body was thrown, clothed as it was, upon the funeral pyre, and the other Christians were led back to their prisons.

During the trial I saw Agnes's friends standing afar off weeping. I often wondered that nothing was ever done to the friends who showed so much sympathy, assisting and consoling the martyrs. Agnes's body was not burned, nor her clothing either, I think. Her soul went forth from her body white as the moon, and flew toward heaven. Her execution took place in the forenoon, I think, for it was still day when her friends took the body from the funeral pile and reverently buried it. Many were present, but enveloped in mantles, to avoid being known, I think. I saw at the tribunal the youth whom Agnes restored to life, but who was not yet converted.

I saw Agnes also apart from this vision, as an apparition near me, radiant and sparkling with light, a palm in her hand. The aureola that surrounded her whole person was rosy in the center, the rays changing to blue. She was full of joy; she consoled me in my sharp pains, saying: "With Jesus to suffer, in Jesus to suffer, is sweet!"

I cannot describe the great difference there is between these Romans and people of the present day. There was no mixture in them; they were wholly one thing or another. With us all is so indifferent, so complicated! It is as if there were in us a thousand compartments within a thousand compartments.

I had another vision. I saw a maiden prostrate in prayer at Agnes's tomb, whither she often went by night, wrapped in a long mantle, gliding along like Magdalene to the tomb of our Lord. I saw the enemies of the Christians lying in wait for her; they fell upon her and dragged her off. Then I saw a little church, a perfect octagon, and over its altar a feast among the saints, apparently a patronal feast, very simple, innocent, and yet solemn. A lovely young martyr sat on a throne, while other Roman martyrs, youths and maidens of the early times, wreathed her with garlands. I saw St. Agnes, and by her a little lamb.

Here the pilgrim handed Anne Catherine a relic under which, in legible characters, appeared the name of the apostle Matthew, but which she had already designated as belonging to Emerentiana. Scarcely had he touched it when she exclaimed:

O what a lovely child! Whence comes that beautiful child? And see, there's a woman with another child!

Next morning she related what follows: Last night I saw two lovely children with a nurse. First, one about four years old came out through a gate in a portico, followed by an old woman, like a Jewess. She was dressed in a flowing garment, a scalloped collar, and lappets like maniples on her arms. She led another little girl of about five and a half years.

The old nurse walked up and down under the portico while the children played. The center columns of the portico were round, capped by curled heads crowned with crisped leaves, and entwined by sculptured serpents with beautiful human faces that stretched out from the columns. The corner ones were square with huge masks cut on the inner side, like oxen's heads, below which were hollowed out three round holes one under the other. At certain distances in the inner wall stood pillars; above it was a platform to which steps led on either side. In the middle was an arrangement like a tabernacle by which something could be turned out from the wall. All around were seats sculptured like the lower part of the columns; below them were compartments in which the children could put their toys. Here the nurse sat and watched them. The two lovely children wore little knit or woven slips like shirts, confined by a belt.

Some other children from the neighborhood joined them and they played very nicely together, mostly near the tabernacle that they drew out and in which they put their toys—little puppets on wires, very artistically made. They skipped around the steps by the tabernacle and ran up and down to the platform. They had also some little vessels with which they played by the seats with the semicircular boxes. I took a peevish little thing up into my lap, but she struggled and would not stay with me. This made me feel sad, for I thought it was because of my unworthiness.

Then the strange children went home, and the servant, or nurse, took her two charges in through the gate, across a court-yard, and up a flight of steps to an apartment in which the mother of one was seated, apparently reading from a book. She was a large woman, wore a robe with folds, walked heavily and lan-guidly, had a grave air, and took little notice of the children. She did not caress them, although she gave them little cakes of differ-ent shapes and colors. She took still less notice of the strange child than of her own. The seats in this room were like cushions, some leather, others worsted, and they had something by which to lift them. The ceiling and walls were covered with paintings. The windows were not glass, but furnished with nets embroidered in all sorts of figures. In the corners of the room stood statues on pedestals.

Then I saw the nurse and children in a garden that lay like a courtyard in the middle of the building, with rooms all around it and a fountain in the center. Here the children played and ate fruit. I saw not the father.

And now I had another picture. I saw the two children a few years later alone and in prayer, and I felt that their nurse was a

Christian in secret and that she directed their steps. I saw them going by night stealthily with other maidens to one of the small houses next the large mansion. I also saw persons cautiously approaching by night the house in which they lived and giving the residents a sign through a hole in the wall, whereupon the latter arose and came out. The nurse used to lead the children out by a back passage and then return. I saw them wrapped in mantles and gliding with others by an old wall to a subterranean apartment in which many people were assembled. There were two such rooms. In one was an altar on which all on entering deposited an offering. In the other was no altar; it appeared to be used only for prayer and instruction. To these secret underground reunions I saw the children going by night.

Again I stood before the house in which I had seen the little ones at play, and I felt an eager desire for them to come out. I saw one of their playmates, and I sent her in to coax the nurse to bring the children out. She did so, with Agnes in her arms, an infant of about eighteen months. She said that the other child was not there. I replied that she would certainly come soon, and we went together to a great shade tree like a linden. Sure enough, here came the other child in the arms of a young girl from a small, neighboring house. But the nurses could not stay; they had something to do. I begged them to leave the children with me a little while, which they did. I took them both on my knees, kissed and caressed them, but they soon grew uneasy and began to cry. I had nothing to give them, and in my perplexity laid them on my breast, and they became quiet. I threw around them my large mantle when suddenly, to my surprise and alarm, I felt that they were really receiving nourishment from me. And so I handed them to their nurses, who soon returned, followed by the children's mothers. Emerentiana's mother was the smaller, the more active, the more pleasing of the two. She carried her child home herself, while Agnes's mother let the nurse carry her.

But now, to my great alarm, I noticed something strange about my breasts, as if by the children's suckling they had become swollen, full of nourishment, and I felt an oppression, a burning in them that gave me great anxiety. I was hardly halfway home when two poor children of our neighborhood came and drained my breast, causing me much pain. Several others did the same. I noticed on these poor little ones swarms of vermin, which I removed, so that they were fed and cleaned at the same time. I was relieved of the oppression in my breast; but, as I thought it had all happened in consequence of the relics, I put them away in the closet.

The following day as Anne Catherine lay in ecstasy, the pilgrim approached her bed with the relics of Sts. Agnes and Emerentiana. She turned quickly away, exclaiming:

No, No! I cannot! I love those children, but I cannot again!

Anthony of Padua

ONE *night, Anne Catherine was consoled by visions of the life of St. Anthony of Padua.*[1] *She said*: I saw the dear saint, very handsome and noble-looking, quick and active in his movements like Xavier. He had black hair, a nose long and beautiful, dark, soft eyes, and a well-shaped chin with a short, forked beard. His complexion was very fair and pale. He was clothed in brown and wore a small mantle, but not exactly in the style of the Franciscans of the

---

[1] Saint Anthony of Padua, born Fernando Martins de Bulhões (1195–13 June 1231), was a Portuguese Catholic priest and friar of the Franciscan Order. He was born and raised by a wealthy family in Lisbon, Portugal, and died in Padua, Italy. He was noted by his contemporaries for his forceful preaching, expert knowledge of scripture, and undying love and devotion to the poor and the sick. Fernando was strongly attracted to the simple, evangelical lifestyle of the Franciscan friars, whose order had been founded only eleven years prior. News arrived that five Franciscans had been beheaded in Morocco, the first of their order to be killed. Inspired by their example, Fernando obtained permission from Church authorities to join the new Franciscan Order. Upon his admission to the life of the friars he adopted the name Anthony (from the name of the chapel located there, dedicated to Saint Anthony the Great), by which he was to be known. He soon came to the attention of Francis of Assisi, who had held a strong distrust of the place of theological studies in the life of his brotherhood, fearing that it might lead to an abandonment of their commitment to a life of real poverty. In Anthony, however, he found a kindred spirit for his vision, who was also able to provide the teaching needed by young members of the order who might seek ordination. In 1224 he entrusted the pursuit of studies for any of his friars to the care of Anthony.

present day. He was very energetic, full of fire, yet full of sweetness too.

I saw him eagerly entering a little wood on the seashore and climbing a tree whose lower branches extended over the water. He sprang from bough to bough. He had hardly seated himself when the sea suddenly rose and inundated the thicket, and an incredible number of fishes and marine animals of all kinds were borne in on the waves. They raised their heads, looked quietly at the saint, and listened to him as he addressed them. After a little while he raised his hand and blessed them, when the sea receded, carrying them back to the deep. Some remained on the shore. The saint put them back carefully into the waters, which bore them off. I felt as if I were lying in the wood on a soft bed of moss. By me lay a wonderful marine animal, flat and broad. The head was round as a battle-axe, with the mouth underneath; the back was green streaked with gold. It had golden eyes, and golden spots on the lower part of the body. There it lay floundering from side to side. I tried to drive it away by striking it on the back with my handkerchief, and I also chased off an enormous spider that was running after it. The thicket and the whole country around lay in darkness. Anthony alone was bathed in light.[1]

Again I saw Anthony in the little thicket by the sea. He knelt facing a distant church, and his whole soul turned toward the blessed sacrament. At the same moment I saw the church, the blessed sacrament on the altar, and the saint's prayer arising before it. Then I saw a little old hunchback with an ugly face running up behind Anthony. He carried a beautiful white basket (the edges, colored above and below, made perhaps of brown osiers) full of lovely flowers prettily arranged. The old man wanted to give them to the saint. He shook him to attract his attention, but Anthony neither saw nor heard anything. He was kneeling in ecstatic prayer, his eyes fixed on the blessed sacrament. Then the old man set the basket down and withdrew.

Then I saw the church drawing nearer and nearer to Anthony while he prayed. From the blessed sacrament there issued, as it

---

[1] The darkness of unbelief, hard-heartedness, and heresy. CB

were, a little monstrance which, attracted by his burning prayer, approached him in a stream of light and hovered in the air above him. From it came forth a lovely little Jesus dazzling, sparkling with glory, and rested on the saint's shoulder, tenderly caressing him. After a little while the child re-entered the monstrance, which went back again into the blessed sacrament on the altar of the far-off church that had drawn near. Then I saw the saint returning to the city, but the flowers remained where the old man had put them.

Again I saw Anthony in a field outside a city near the sea, disputing with several persons. One in particular, a violent, passionate man, argued against the saint in bitter terms. Then I saw that they all agreed on some point, and Anthony—fired with holy zeal—stepped forward, his arms under his little mantle, as if affirming something. After this he pushed his way through the crowd and left the place. It was a large meadow planted with trees and surrounded by a wall. It extended from the city to the shore, and was full of people walking about or listening to the saint.

Then I had another vision: Anthony saying mass in a church, the broad road leading to it from the city gate filled with an expectant crowd, and the man who had disputed so hotly with him driving up to the city an immense ox with long horns. Meanwhile, the saint, having finished mass, walked solemnly to the church door, bearing in his hands a consecrated host. Instantly the ox began to struggle; it freed itself from its master and ran rapidly up the street toward the church. The owner and several others pursued it, the tumult became general, women and children fell one over the other, but the ox could not be caught. When at last it reached the church, down it knelt, stretched out its neck, and bowed humbly before the blessed sacrament, which Anthony, standing at the door, held up before it. Its master offered it hay, but the animal noticed it not, changed not its position; whereupon the whole crowd, including the owner, prostrated humbly, praising and adoring the blessed sacrament. Anthony re-entered the church followed by the people. Then only did the ox arise and allow itself to be led back to the city gate, where it ate the food presented it.

I saw a man accusing himself to Anthony of having kicked his mother, and in another scene I saw the same man so contrite in consequence of the saint's exhortations that he was about to cut off the foot that had done the wicked deed. But Anthony suddenly appeared before him and restrained his arm.

Apollonia

I HAD the saint's relic by me, and I saw the city in which she was martyred. It stands on a cape not far from the mouth of the Nile; it is a large and beautiful city. The house of Apollonia's parents stood on an elevated spot surrounded by courtyards and gardens. Apollonia was, at the time of her martyrdom, an aged widow, very tall. Her parents were pagans. But she had been converted in childhood by her nurse, a Christian in secret, and had married a pagan in obedience to her parents, with whom she lived at home.

She had much to suffer; married life was for her a rude penance. I have seen her lying on the ground, praying, weeping, her head covered with ashes. Her husband was very thin and pale, and he died long before her, leaving her childless. She survived him thirty years. Apollonia was extremely compassionate to the poor persecuted Christians; she was the hope and consolation of all in suffering. Her nurse also suffered martyrdom shortly before her in an insurrection during which the dwellings of Christians were plundered and burned and many of the occupants put to death.

Later on I saw Apollonia herself arrested in her house by the judge's orders, led before the tribunal, and cast into prison. Again I saw her brought before the judge and horribly maltreated on account of her severe and resolute answers. It was a heart-rending sight, and I cried bitterly, although I had witnessed with less emotion even more cruel punishments. Perhaps it was her age and dignified bearing that touched me. They beat her with clubs, and struck her on the face and head with stones until her nose was broken. Blood flowed from her head, her cheeks and chin were all torn, and her teeth shattered in her gums. She wore the open white robe in which I have so often seen the martyrs, and under it a colored woolen tunic. The executioners placed her on a stone seat without a back, her hands chained behind her to the stone,

14

her feet in fetters. Her veil was torn off, and her long hair hung around her face, which by now was quite disfigured and covered with blood. One executioner stood behind and violently forced back her head, while another opened wide her torn mouth and pressed into it a small block of lead. Then with great pincers he drew out the broken teeth one after the other, tearing away with each a piece of the jawbone. Apollonia almost fainted under this torture, but I saw angels, souls of other martyrs, and Jesus himself strengthening and consoling her. At her own request, the power was conferred upon her of relieving all pains of the teeth, head, or face.

As she still continued to glorify Jesus and insult the idols, the judge ordered her to be thrown on the funeral pyre. She could not walk alone, she was half dead; consequently, two executioners had to support her under the arms to a high place where a fire burned in a pit. As she stood a moment before it, she appeared to pray for something; she could no longer hold up her head. The pagans thought she was about to deny Jesus, that she was wavering, and so they released their hold upon her. She sank on the ground as if dying, lay there a moment, and then suddenly arose praying and leaped into the flames. During the whole time of her martyrdom I saw crowds of the poor whom she had befriended wringing their hands, weeping, and lamenting.

Apollonia could never have leaped into the fire by herself. Strength came to her with the inspiration from God. She was not consumed, but only scorched. When she was dead, the pagans withdrew; and the Christians, approaching stealthily, took the holy body and buried it in a vault.

Thomas Aquinas

MY sister received from a poor woman the present of a relic in a case. She put it away in her chest, but I felt its presence and gave her in exchange for it a picture of the saint. The relic shone with a beautiful light, and I laid it in my little closet. Now, last night after having endured all the pains, all the tortures that a human body can undergo, I had a vision of Thomas. I saw a large mansion in which was a nurse with a child in her arms, to whom she

15

gave a scrap of paper on which was written *Ave Maria*. The little fellow held it fast, put it to his lips, and would not give it up. His mother entered the room and tried to take the writing from him, but the child struggled. He cried bitterly when she succeeded in opening his little hand and getting the paper. At last, however, seeing him so distressed, she gave it back to him, when he quickly swallowed it.

Then I heard an interior voice saying: "That is Thomas Aquinas!"—and the saint appeared to me several times from the little closet, but each time at a different period of his life. He told me that he would cure me of the pain in my side, and the thought struck me: "My confessor belongs to his order! Now, if I can only tell him that Thomas cured me, he will readily believe that that is his relic!"—whereupon the saint replied, in answer to my thought: "You may tell him. I will cure you!" and he laid his girdle on my head.

The confessor relates on this point the following:

"Anne Catherine spoke of Thomas. She said that he was by her, that he would certainly cure her, if I thought well of it. I ordered her to look for the relic. She did so and handed it to me; but the pain in her side was so intense that she could, so to speak, neither live nor die. I touched the relic to her side, telling her to pray and to have confidence in Jesus Christ. I prayed with her thinking, if it really were St. Thomas, she might indeed rise quite cured. Suddenly she sprang lightly to her feet and wanted to leave her bed: 'I feel no pain, no pain in my side! The saint has cured it; but he says I must bear my other sufferings!'

"Then she went on: 'I have seen various incidents of his life. Even as a little child, he loved to turn over the leaves of a book; he was unwilling to relinquish it even during his bath. I have seen that this relic was presented to our convent by an Augustinian, its first superior, of whose life I also saw many incidents. He had all the relics belonging to the convent rearranged and freshly ornamented. There lived at that time in our convent a very holy young lady whom I have often seen.'"

Once again that day, Anne Catherine, being in ecstasy, wanted to rise and take the relic to the pilgrim. She appeared to be very much preoccupied with the saint:

I saw St. Thomas writing in his cell one morning. Several religious entered his room, disputing vehemently what he was writing. He took firm hold of his writing paper and repulsed the disputants. Then he entered a church alone, lay the paper, or book, upon the altar, and withdraw from a compartment under the tabernacle a candle that was about the length of his hand. This he placed upon his writings, and then prostrated himself in fervent prayer before the altar, whereupon he heard the voice of God affirming that Thomas's writings were good and true. After this, the saint gathered his writings and returned to his cell.

Augustine

Augustine Appears to Anne Catherine
(A Wondrous Healing)

JUST *after Pentecost 1820, Anne Catherine said*: I saw St. Augustine in his episcopal robes, and he was so kind! What seemed strange to me was that I thought I saw his holy relics in a curiously twisted house, like a snail's shell, and indeed there was some singular creature therein. I could not imagine what it meant, when suddenly I saw the house under a more beautiful form. The creature was no longer present, and the house smooth like stone, and in a portion thereof I saw a relic, a bone, of the saint, and a sort of label, not in Latin, but in some angular characters, spelling out "Augustinus." It was a wonder to me that I could make out his name.

In the blink of an eye the saint himself stood there before me clear as day, by his relic, and said to me "This bone is of me." I was rejoiced to see him and I accused myself of never especially honoring him.[1] He replied: "Still I know you. You are my child!" When I asked him to relieve my pain, he presented me a nosegay in which was a blue flower—and a feeling of strength and relief instantly pervaded my whole person. The saint said to me: "You will never be entirely well, for your way is that of suffering. But, when in need of help and consolation, think of me. I shall always

---

[1] Anne Catherine had lived as a nun in an Augustinian convent at Agnetenberg, in Dülmen, prior to its suppression.

give them to you. Now rise and say the *Te Deum* to thank the Most Holy Trinity for your cure." Then I arose and prayed. I was perfectly strong and my joy was very great.

Afterward I saw Augustine in his heavenly glory. First, I beheld the Most Holy Trinity and the Blessed Virgin—I can hardly say how. I seemed to see an old man on a throne. From his forehead and breast streamed rays of light thus, △ joining together before him then in the form of a cross from which, in turn, shot numerous other rays over the choirs and orders of angels and saints. At some distance, surrounded by blessed spirits, I saw Augustine's celestial glory. He was seated on a throne, receiving from the cross of the Holy Trinity streams of light that he imparted to the surrounding choirs. Around him were priests in various costumes, and on one side—rising like a mountain one above the other and floating like clouds in the sky—were numerous churches, all of which had emanated from the saint. This was a picture of his heavenly greatness. The light received from the Trinity symbolized his own personal illumination. The choirs around him were the different vessels, the different souls, that received light through him. They, in their turn, poured it upon others while receiving, also, rays directly from God. The sight of such things is unspeakably beautiful and consoling, and so natural—yes, more natural, more intelligible, than the sight of a tree or flower upon earth.

In the choirs around the saint were all the priests and doctors, all the orders and communities that had emanated from him, inasmuch as they are blessed, inasmuch as they have become vessels of God, gushing fountains of living waters whose source is in him. After this I saw him in a heavenly garden, but this picture was a little lower down. The first was a vision of his glory, his place in the starry heaven of the Holy Trinity; the second was rather a picture of his actual influence upon earth, his assistance to the Church Militant, to living men. All pictures of the celestial gardens appear lower than those of the saints in God, in glory.

I beheld him then in a beautiful garden full of the most wonderful trees, shrubs, and flowers. There were many others with him, among whom I remember particularly Francis Xavier and Francis de Sales. They were not seated in order as for a feast, but

18

going around, distributing the flowers and fruits of the garden, which represent the graces and good works of their life. I saw numbers of the living in the garden, many of whom I knew, and they were receiving gifts in manifold ways.[1]

I saw pictured where the main part of Augustine's body now lies, in a distant, sparsely populated land, stony and unfruitful, surrounded by forest. None there know of his remains, which I see interred in a stone sarcophagus under a vault. Only the ribs are fully intact, much else having been distributed at other times.

Scenes from the Life of Augustine

I SAW Augustine, a boy in his father's house, not far from a tolerably large city. It was built in the Roman style with a courtyard and colonnade, around it other buildings with gardens and fields; it looked to me like a villa. He had a broad forehead, pleasant soft eyes, expansive countenance, and long nose.

The father was a tall, vigorous man with something morose and severe about him. He must have had many orders to give, for I saw him speaking earnestly to people who looked like his inferiors. I saw others kneeling before him as if presenting petitions; they may have been servants or peasants.

In little Augustine's presence he was more affable and gracious toward Monica, his wife, as if he were fond of the boy; he did not seem to have much to do with him, however, for Augustine was generally with his mother and two men.

Monica was a little woman already advanced in years, slightly stooped in her carriage, and of very dark complexion. She was

---

[1] "The apparition of the living is something very special: the counterpart, as it were, of the apparition of saints upon earth. They appear in the garden of the saints like spirits under certain indeterminate forms and receive all kinds of fruits and flowers. I see some who seem to be raised into this sphere of grace by prayer, and others who seem to receive such favors without conscious effort on their part—they are vessels of election. The same difference exists between these two classes as between one who takes the trouble to gather fruit in a garden, and another who sees it falling at his feet as he walks along, or to whom God deigns to send it by this or that saint."

exceedingly gentle and God-fearing and in constant dread and anxiety on Augustine's account. She followed him everywhere, for he was restless and mischievous. I saw him climbing perilous heights and scampering recklessly around on the very edge of the flat roof.

Of the two men, one seemed to be his preceptor, the other his servant. The former used to take him to a school in the neighboring city which many little boys attended and bring him home again.

Augustine was at all sorts of tricks when out of school. I saw him beating animals, throwing stones at them, quarreling with other boys, running into people's houses, ransacking cupboards and eating the good things. Still, there was something very generous in him, for he always divided what he found with his companions; sometimes he even threw it away.

There lived also in his father's house a woman who was perhaps a nurse or servant of some kind. Later on I saw Augustine placed at school in a larger and more distant city, to which he went in a low chariot on small heavy wheels, drawn by two beasts. He was always accompanied by two persons.

Then I saw him in school with many other boys. He slept with several of them in a large hall, their beds separated by a reed, or light wooden partition. The schoolroom was larger than the sleeping hall. It had stone benches all around the wall. On these the scholars sat holding little brown boards on their knees for writing, rolls of parchment and pencils in their hands. The master stood in a little pulpit raised about two steps, behind which was a larger board on which he drew numerous figures. He called his pupils, now this one, now that one, into the middle of the floor, where they stood facing each other and reading from their parchment rolls, gesticulating at the same time as if they were preaching, and again as if disputing.

In school Augustine was well-behaved and almost always stood first; but outdoors he carried on all sorts of pranks with the other boys, damaging and destroying whatever fell in his way. I saw him, out of pure mischief, beating and stoning to death certain long-necked birds, the domestic fowl of that country, and then carrying away the dead bodies with tears of pity. I saw him running and wrestling with other boys in the shady walks of a circular garden, and stealing, injuring, wasting many things.

I saw him return home from this school and give himself up to all kinds of mad pranks and disorders. One night I saw him robbing an orchard with companions like himself, and afterward throwing away a whole mantleful of the fruit. I saw Monica incessantly remonstrating with him, praying, and shedding many tears.

Then I saw him crossing a bridge over a broad river on his way to the great city in which Perpetua was martyred (Carthage). I soon recognized it. On one side arose rocks with walls and towers jutting out into the sea, where lay many ships. A smaller city stood at no great distance from the large one. There were many great buildings as in ancient Rome, and also a large Christian church.

Theater Life in Carthage

I HAD numerous visions of Augustine's follies committed here with other young people. He dwelt alone in a house and held constant disputations with other young men. I used to see him going by himself to visit a certain woman.

But he did not remain long in any one place, he was constantly on the go. I often saw him at public shows, in my eyes, truly diabolical. These shows were held in a great round building. On one side, seats rose one above the other like steps, and below were numerous entrances opening on the stairways that led to the seats. The building had no roof, only a tent-like covering. The place was crowded, and opposite the spectators, on an elevated platform, were enacted abominable scenes. In the background were all sorts of pictures which, at certain times, suddenly disappeared, as if swallowed up by the earth. Once there unfolded a large beautiful place in a great city; and yet, the whole scene occupied in reality but a very small space. Then men and women appeared, two by two, talking together and behaving wantonly. It was all horrible to me! The actors had frightful, colored faces with huge mouths; they wore on their feet broad-soled socks with pointed toes, red, yellow, and other colors. Below these were whole troops, talking and singing alternately with those above. I saw boys, eight or twelve years old, who played on straight and twisted flutes and also upon stringed instruments. Once several of them precipitated themselves head foremost from on high with outspread limbs. They must certainly have been fastened to something, but it looked very frightful. Then again there was a wrestling match in which one of the combatants received two cuts across his face, which a surgeon came and bandaged. I cannot describe the horrors, the confusion of the scene. The women among the actors were men in disguise. Augustine himself used to appear in public, though not in such performances as these.

He entered with zest into all sorts of amusements, indulged in all sorts of sins. He was the leader everywhere, a distinction he seemed to seek out of pure ostentation, for it gave him no real satisfaction—he was always sad and discontented when alone. I saw also that the woman with whom he lived brought a child to his house, which circumstance, however, did not seem to disconcert him in the least. I most frequently beheld him in halls and public places, disputing with others, speaking or listening, unfolding and reading rolls of parchment, etc.

I saw his mother visit him in Carthage. She spoke to him earnestly and shed many tears, but she did not stay with him while in the city. I never saw in Monica's house either cross or holy picture. There were all kinds of pagan statues, but neither she nor her husband took any notice of them. I constantly saw her in some secluded corner of the house or garden, bent in two praying and weeping; and yet, with all this, I saw that she was not without her own faults. While lamenting her son's thefts of sweetmeats, etc., she herself loved dainties; it was from her that he had inherited his inclination. Whenever she went to the cellar to draw wine for her husband, she used to sip a little herself from the cask and eat good things; but she greatly regretted this inclination and struggled against it. Then many of her pious customs were shown me: for instance, at certain seasons she used to take baskets of bread and other provisions to the cemetery, which was surrounded by strong walls. She laid the food on the tombstones with a pious intention; the poor afterward came and took it away.

I saw her once—her son having now attained the age of manhood—journeying on foot with a servant, who carried a small package. She was going to visit a bishop, who spoke to her a long time and encouraged her on the score of her son. She shed abundant tears, but he said something to her that calmed her.

Again, I saw Augustine returned from Carthage after his father's death and teaching in the little city, where his life was as restless and disorderly as ever. I saw him at the bedside of a sick friend who, shortly before death, received baptism, at which Augustine hooted, although deeply afflicted at his friend's death. Then I saw him again at Carthage, living as before.

Augustine is Baptized

ON *the night of May 28–29, 1820, Anne Catherine saw in vision Augustine's baptism at the hand of Ambrose. Unfortunately she had been much beset during the night, and so quite exhausted, so that what follows is all she could remember:*

I saw Augustine, his son, a friend, and his mother Monica. They were not in the city, but had traveled into the countryside. I saw Augustine and Ambrose praying before an altar. Monica was on her knees in another quarter of the church. It was quite early in the day, and many people were still present in the church. Augustine was wearing a long, sleeveless mantle, white, with cloud-like forms in red. The wide, white sleeves of his undergarment could be plainly seen beneath. The mantle was drawn close with a broad belt or girdle attached on two sides and fastened in front with a clasp. The mantle fell in wide folds below. Ambrose wore a mantle of similar color and design, but over the shoulders was an ample cloth in the form of open half-sleeves. And upon his head he wore a bishop's mitre. There was no baptismal font there; instead, there was in the middle of the church a quadrangular opening down which steps led to a small round spring. Over this opening lay a covering of two steps, in form rather like the approach to an altar, upon which one could also sit. The arrangement was like this:

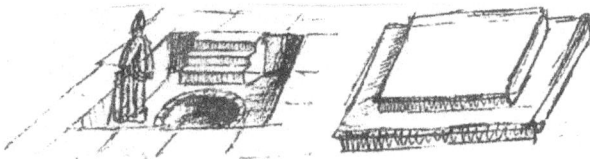

23

This cover was moved aside when a baptism was to be performed; and so also on this occasion of Augustine's baptism it was removed, whereafter Augustine, Ambrose, and two other religious made their way to the spring at the bottom, which lay about half a man's height below floor level. The spring's water seemed as though quick with life. I saw that Augustine held a glowing light in his hand. He did not step into the spring itself, such as I had seen earlier on the occasion of other baptisms, but instead bowed his head over the water while Ambrose raised up water from the spring in a spoon. The two other religious, one of whom was quite old, were apparently the sponsors.

As Augustine was baptized I saw the light of the Holy Spirit descend upon him, as also upon his son and friend when they where baptized in turn. In the vault or arch of the spring a dove was painted.

After the baptism Augustine's mantle with the red, cloud-like designs was removed and he stood only in his white undergarment. Then I saw him standing together again with Ambrose before the altar, singing a sort of call and response. It seemed to me to be the *Te Deum*.

On the eve of the festival of the Most Holy Trinity, Anne Catherine said: When I saw the bad preparation of so many persons who were going to confession, I renewed my petition to God to let me suffer something for their amendment—and then indeed my task began. It seemed as if I were being pierced incessantly by fine darts of pain shot at me like arrows, and in the night they became more intense than I had ever felt before. They began around my heart, which felt like a furnace of pain tightly bound in flames. Waves of fiery pains swept thence through all parts of my body, through the marrow of my bones, to the tips of my fingers, my nails, and my hair. It was like the regular flow of the tide from my heart to my hands, feet, and head and back again, my wounds being the principal centers.

My sufferings increased until midnight, when I awoke steeped in perspiration and unable to move. I had only one consolation— the indistinct idea of the cross formed by the principal centers of my pain, which seemed to be grinding me to powder. At midnight I could bear it no longer, for my stupor made me forget its cause; so I turned like a child to my father, St. Augustine. "Ah! dear father, Augustine, you promised to help me whenever I invoked you! Ah! see my distress!"—and my prayer was instantly heard. The saint stood before me, telling me most kindly why I was suffering so, but that he could not take away my pains since I was to endure them in union with the passion of Jesus Christ. He bade me be comforted, although I was still to suffer three hours more. I was greatly consoled, though in intense agony, knowing that it was for the love of Christ's passion and to satisfy divine justice for sinners.

I rejoiced to be of some use, and I threw my whole heart into my pains. I accepted the grace of expiatory suffering with loving confidence in the mercy of the heavenly Father. Augustine reminded me moreover that three years ago, on the morning of All-Saints, my Lord had appeared to me as I lay at the point of death. He had given me my choice either to die and go to purgatory or to live longer in suffering, and that I had replied: "Lord, in purgatory my sufferings will be of no avail. If then it be not contrary to thy will, let me live and endure all possible torments if thereby I can aid but a single soul!" Then, although I had at first asked for death, my Savior now granted my second request by prolonging my life of suffering. When my holy father Augustine recalled this circumstance, I distinctly remembered it, and from that moment until the end of the three hours I calmly and thankfully endured the most cruel tortures. Pain forced from me the bitterest tears and the sweat of death.

I had another vision then of the Most Holy Trinity under the form of a resplendent old man seated on a throne. From his forehead streamed an indescribably clear, colorless light; from his mouth flowed a luminous stream slightly tinged with yellow, like fire; and from his breast near the heart, another stream of colored light. These streams formed in the air above the old man's breast a cross that sparkled like the rainbow; and it seemed to me that he laid his hands on its arms. Innumerable rays issued from it. They fell first on the heavenly choirs and then down upon the earth, filling and quickening all things.

A little below the Holy Trinity and to the right, I saw Mary's throne. A ray darted to her from the old man and another from her to the cross. All this is quite inexpressible. But in vision—although dazzling and swimming in light—it was perfectly intelligible: one and three, vivifying all, enlightening all, and most wonderfully sufficing for all.

Below the throne were the angels in a world of colorless light; above them the twenty-four Ancients with silver hair, surrounding the Most Holy Trinity. All the rest of the boundless space was filled with saints who were themselves the luminous centers of shining choirs. At the right of the Trinity was Augustine surrounded by his choirs—but much lower than Mary—and all around lay gardens, shining palaces, and churches. I felt as if I were wandering among the starry heavens. These vessels of God are of every variety of form and appearance, but all are filled with Jesus Christ. The same law governs all, the same substance pervades all, though under a different form—and a straight line leads through each into the light of the Father through the cross of the Son.

On the feast of St. Paul's Conversion, Anne Catherine suddenly fell into ecstasy, during which she prayed fervently. That evening she said to the pilgrim:

There has been a thanksgiving feast in the spiritual church. It was filled with glory, and a magnificent throne stood in the middle of it. Paul, Augustine, and other converted saints figured conspicuously. It was a feast in the Church Triumphant, a thanksgiving for a great, though still future, grace—something like a future consecration. It referred to the conversion of a man whom I saw of slight figure and tolerably young, who was one day to be pope.

Benedict and Scholastica

THROUGH the relics of Scholastica I saw many scenes in her life, and that of Benedict. I saw their paternal house in a great city, not far from Rome. It was not built entirely in the Roman style; before it was a paved courtyard whose low wall was surmounted by a red latticework, and behind lay another court with a garden and a fountain. In the garden was a beautiful summerhouse overrun by vines, and here I saw Benedict and his little sister Scholastica, playing as loving, innocent children are wont to amuse themselves. The flat ceiling of the summerhouse was painted all over with figures that I thought, at first, sculptured, so clearly were their outlines defined. The brother and sister were very fond of each other and so nearly of the same age that I thought them twins. The birds flew in familiarly at the windows with flowers and twigs in their beaks and sat gazing at the children, who also were playing with flowers and leaves, planting sticks and making gardens. I saw them writing and cutting all sorts of figures out of colored stuffs.

Occasionally their nurse came to look after them. Their parents seemed to be people of wealth who had much business on hand, for I saw about twenty persons employed in the house; but they did not seem to trouble themselves about their children. The father was a large, powerful man, clothed in the Roman style; he took his meals with his wife and some other members of the family in the lower part of the house, while the children lived entirely upstairs in separate apartments.

Benedict had for preceptor an old ecclesiastic with whom he stayed almost all the time, and Scholastica had a nurse near whom she slept. The brother and sister were not often allowed to be alone together; but whenever they could steal off for awhile they were very gleeful and happy.

I saw Scholastica by her nurse's side, learning some kind of work. In the room next to that in which she slept stood a table on which lay in baskets the materials for her work—various colored stuffs, from which she cut figures of birds, flowers, etc., to be sewed on other larger pieces. When finished they looked as if carved on the groundwork. The ceilings of the rooms, like that of the summerhouse, were covered with different colored pictures. The windows were not glass; they were of some kind of stuff on which were embroidered all sorts of figures, trees, lines, and pointed ornaments.

Scholastica slept on a low bed behind a curtain. I saw her in the morning, when her nurse left the room, spring out of bed and prostrate in prayer before a crucifix on the wall. When she heard the nurse returning she used to slip quickly behind the curtain and be in bed again before she re-entered the room. I saw Benedict and Scholastica separately learning from the former's tutor. They read from great rolls of parchment, and they painted letters in red, gold, and an extraordinarily fine blue. As they wrote they rolled the parchment. They made use of an instrument about as long as one's finger. The older the children grew, the less were they allowed to be together.

I saw Benedict at Rome, when about fourteen years old, in a large building in which there was a corridor with many rooms. It looked like a school or a monastery. There were many young men and some aged ecclesiastics in a large hall, as if at a holiday feast. The ceilings were adorned with the same kind of paintings as those in Benedict's home. The guests did not eat reclining. They sat on round seats so low that they were obliged to stretch out their feet; some sat on one side, back to back, at a very low table. There were holes hollowed in the massive table to receive the yellow plates and dishes; but I did not see much food, only three large plates of flat, yellow cakes in the center of the table.

When all had finished, I saw six females of different ages, relatives of the youths, enter the hall bearing something like sweetmeats and little flasks in baskets on their arms. The young men arose and conversed with their friends at one end of the hall, eating the dainties and drinking from the flasks. There was one woman of about thirty years of age, whom I had once before seen at Benedict's home. She approached the young man with marked affability; but he, perfectly pure and innocent, suspected nothing bad in her. I saw that she hated his purity and entertained a sinful love for him. She gave him a poisoned, an enchanted, drink from a flask. Benedict suspected nothing, but I saw him that evening in his cell restless and tormented. He went at last to a man and asked permission to go down into the courtyard, for he never went out without leave. There he knelt in a corner of the yard, disciplining himself with long thorn branches and nettles. I saw him later on, when a hermit, helping this his would-be seducer, who had fallen into deep distress precisely because she had sought to tempt him. Benedict had been interiorly warned of her guilt.

Afterward I saw Benedict on a high, rocky mountain when, perhaps, in his twentieth year. He had hollowed out a cell for himself in the rock. To this he added a passage and another cell, and then several cells all cut in the rock; but only the first opened outside. Before it he had planted a walk of trees. He arched them and ornamented the vaulted roof with pictures that seemed to be made of many small stones put together. In one cell I saw three such pictures: heaven in the center, the nativity of Christ on one side, the Last Judgment on the other. In the last, Our Lord was represented sitting on an arch, a sword proceeding from his mouth; below, between the elect and the reprobate, stood an angel with a pair of scales. Benedict had, besides, made a representation of a monastery with its abbot, and crowds of monks in the background. He seemed to have had a foresight of his own monastery.

More than once I saw Benedict's sister Scholastica, who lived at home, going on foot to visit her brother. He never allowed her to stay with him overnight. Sometimes she brought him a roll of parchment that she had written. Then he showed her what he had done, and they conversed together on divine things. Benedict was always very grave in his sister's presence, while she in her innocence was all mirth and joy. When she found him too serious, she turned to God in prayer, and he instantly became like herself, bright and gay. Later on I saw her under her brother's direction, establishing a convent on a neighboring mountain distant only a short day's journey. To it flocked numbers of religious women. I saw her teaching them to chant; they had no organs. Organs have been very prejudicial to singing. They make of it only a secondary affair. The nuns prepared all the church ornaments themselves with the same kind of needlework that Scholastica had learned when a child at home. On the refectory table was a large cloth on which were all sorts of figures, pictures, and sentences, so that each religious always had before her that to which she was especially obliged. Scholastica spoke to me of the sweets and consolations of spiritual labor and the labor of ecclesiastics.

I always saw Scholastica and Benedict surrounded by tame birds. While the former was yet in her father's house, I used to see doves flying from her to Benedict in the desert; and in the monastery I saw around her doves and larks bringing her red, white, yellow, and violet-blue flowers. Once I saw a dove bringing her a rose with a leaf. I cannot repeat all the scenes of her life that were shown me, for I am so sick and miserable! Scholastica was purity itself. I see her in heaven as white as snow. With the exception of Mary and Magdalene, I know of no saint so loving.

Benedict, Rita of Cascia, Bobadilla

THE *pilgrim gave Anne Catherine a reliquary enclosing a medal on a scrap of velvet; she said:* This is a blessed medal of St. Benedict, blessed with the benediction Benedict left to his order by virtue of the miracle that took place when his monks presented him a poisoned draught. The glass fell to pieces when he made over it the sign of the cross, which is a preservative against poison, pestilence, sorcery, and the attacks of the devil. The red velvet on which the medal is sewn is also blessed; it once rested on the tomb of Willibald and Walburga, the place where oil flows from the bones of the latter: I saw the priests carrying it there barefoot and then cutting it up for such purposes as this. The medal was blessed in that monastery.

One day the pilgrim laid near Anne Catherine's hand a little picture of Rita of Cascia,[1] *which some time previously had been moistened by a drop of blood from her own stigmata. She took it, saying:*

There, I see a sick nun without flesh or bones! I cannot touch her.

On another occasion, while Anne Catherine was relating something she had seen in vision, the pilgrim quietly slipped into her hand a book opened at a page stained with her own blood. Instantly a bright smile played over her countenance and she exclaimed:

What a beautiful flower! red and white streaked. It has fallen from the book into the palm of my hand.

Again the pilgrim laid the same leaf in her hand with the question:

---

[1] Saint Rita of Cascia, born Margherita Lotti (1381–22 May 1457), was an Italian widow and Augustinian nun venerated as a saint in the Roman Catholic Church. Rita was married at an early age. The marriage lasted for eighteen years, during which she is remembered for her Christian values as a model wife and mother who made efforts to convert her husband from his abusive behavior. Upon the murder of her husband by another feuding family, she sought to dissuade her sons from revenge. She subsequently joined an Augustinian community of religious sisters, where she was known both for practicing mortification of the flesh and for the efficacy of her prayers. Various miracles are attributed to her intercession, and she is often portrayed with a bleeding wound on her forehead, which is understood to indicate a partial stigmata. Canonized with the title Patroness of Impossible Causes, she is more particularly known as patroness of abused wives and heartbroken women.

"Has it touched anything?" She felt it a moment and answered:

Yes, the wounds of Jesus!

Some months later, a lady sent Anne Catherine from Paris a little picture that had touched the bones of St. Bobadilla.[1] She was at the moment suffering from intense headache. She raised the picture to her forehead, when the saint appeared to her, relieved her pain, and she saw the whole scene of his martyrdom.

As she lay in ecstasy one day, the pilgrim offered her a broken silver ring blessed in honor of Nicholas von der Flüe,[2] at his tomb in Sachseln. When returned to consciousness, she said:

I saw how Brother Klaus separated from his family and how, in his conjugal union, by suppressing the material, he rendered the spiritual bond so much the stronger. I saw the mortifying of the flesh figured by the breaking of a ring, and I received an instruction on carnal and spiritual marriage. The ring that brought me this vision was blessed in honor of Brother Klaus.

Boniface

ON *June 5, 1820, Anne Catherine had a vision of St. Boniface:*[3] I knelt before the blessed sacrament in a church in the middle of which were high seats, and there I saw the holy bishop surrounded by

---

[1] Bobadilla was born at Valencia, Spain, 1511; died at Loreto, Italy, September 23, 1590. After having taught philosophy in his native country, he went to Paris to acquire a more perfect knowledge of Greek and Latin. Here he met Ignatius of Loyola, joined him in his plans, and was among the first seven followers of the saint to consecrate themselves to God in the Society of Jesus at Montmartre. See "Ignatius and Some of His Order."

[2] See "Nicholas of Flüe."

[3] Saint Boniface (c. 675–5 June 754), born in the kingdom of Wessex in Anglo-Saxon England, was a leading figure in the Anglo-Saxon mission to the Germanic parts of the Frankish Empire during the eighth century. He established the first organized Christianity in many parts of Germania and was the first archbishop of Mainz. The roles Boniface played made him one of the truly outstanding creators of the first Europe: as the apostle of Germania, the reformer of the Frankish Church, and the chief fomentor of the alliance between the papacy and the Carolingian family. Through his efforts to reorganize and regulate the Church of the Franks, he helped shape Western Christianity, and is regarded as a unifier of Europe.

people of every age in ancient costume, some even in the skins of beasts. They were simple and innocent. They listened open-mouthed to their holy bishop. Around him shone a light, like rays from the Holy Spirit, which fell in various degrees upon his hearers.

Boniface was a tall, strong, enthusiastic man. He was explaining how the Lord marks out his own, imparting to them at an early hour his grace and spirit. "But," said he, "men must cooperate. They must carefully preserve and make use of such graces, for they are only given that their possessors may become instruments in the hand of God. Strength and ability are given to each member that it may act, not only for itself but for the whole body. The Lord gives vocations even in childhood. He who does not labor to maintain the life of grace and make use of it for his own good and that of others, steals from the body of the faithful something that belongs to it, and becomes thereby a robber in the community. Man should reflect that in loving and assisting a member of the Church he is loving and assisting a member of one and the same Body, a chosen instrument of the Holy Spirit. Above all, should parents look thus upon their children. They should not prevent their becoming the instruments of the Lord for the good of his Body, the Church. They should maintain and develop the life of grace in them and aid them to a faithful co-operation, since they can form no idea of the great injury they do the faithful by a contrary line of conduct."

Catherine

ST. Catherine's father was named Costa. He belonged to a royal race and was a descendant of Hazael, whom Elijah, by God's command, anointed king of Syria. I saw the prophet with the box of ointment, crossing the Jordan and anointing Hazael, with whom after that all went well. Costa's immediate ancestors emigrated to Cyprus with the Persians or Medes, and there obtained possessions. They were, like Costa himself, star and fire worshippers and held also to the Syrophoenician worship of idols.

Catherine, on her mother's side, was descended from the family of the pagan priestess Mercuria, who had been converted by

Jesus at Salamis.[1] She had after her conversion emigrated to the holy land, received in baptism the name of Famula and, in the persecution that broke out after the stoning of Stephen, had gained the martyr's crown. There had long existed in her family the oft-told prediction that a great prophet would come from Judea to change all things, to overturn the idols, to announce the true God, and that he would come in contact with this family.

When Mercuria fled to Palestine with her two daughters, she left behind in Cyprus an illegitimate son whose father was then the Roman consul. He had been baptized as early as the time of Jesus and afterward left the island with Paul and Barnabas. This son married his mother's youngest sister, from which union was born Catherine's mother.

Catherine was Costa's only daughter. Like her mother, she had yellow hair, was very sprightly and fearless, and had always to suffer and to struggle. She had a nurse and, at an early age, was provided with male preceptors. I saw her making toys out of the inner bark of trees and giving them to poor children. As she grew older she wrote a great deal upon tablets and parchment, which she gave to other maidens to copy. She was well acquainted with the nurse of St. Barbara, who was a Christian in secret. She possessed in a high degree the prophetic spirit of her maternal ancestors, and the prediction of the great prophet was shown her in vision when she was scarcely six years old. At the midday repast she related it to her parents, to whom Mercuria's history was not unknown. But her father, a very cold, stern man, shut her up, as a punishment, in a dark vault. There I saw her, a bright light shining around her and the mice and other little creatures playing tamely by her.

Catherine sighed earnestly after that promised Redeemer of humankind; she begged him to come to her, and she had numerous lights and visions. From that time she conceived deep hatred toward the idols. She broke, she hid, she buried all she could lay her hands on. For this reason, as also for her singular and deeply significant words against the gods, she was often imprisoned by her father. She was instructed in all knowledge, and I saw her dur-

---

[1] See "Lady Mercuria, Pagan Priestess of Cyprus" in *People of the New Testament V.*

ing her walks scribbling in the sand and on the walls of the castle, her playmates copying what she wrote. When she was about eight years old, her father took her to Alexandria, where she became acquainted with him who was one day to aspire to her hand. After some time she returned with her father to Cyprus. There were no longer any Jews on the island, only here and there a few in slavery, and only a small number of Christians, who practiced their faith in secret.

Catherine was instructed by God Himself; she prayed and sighed for holy baptism, which was given her in her tenth year. The bishop of Diospolis sent three priests secretly to Cyprus to encourage and strengthen the Christians, and on an interior admonition he also allowed the child to be baptized. She was at the time again in prison, her jailer being a Christian in secret. He took her by night to the secret meeting place of the Christians outside the city in a subterranean cave, whither she often went for instructions to the priests by whom she was finally baptized. She received with the sacrament of baptism the gift of extraordinary wisdom. The priest, in performing the ceremony, poured water over the neophytes out of a bowl.

Catherine gave utterance to many wonderful things, though like all the other Christians she still kept her religion secret. But her father, though fondly attached to his beautiful and intelligent little girl, was unable any longer to endure her persistent aversion to idolatry, her discourses, and her prophecies. He took her to Paphos[1] and left her there in confinement, hoping thus to cut off all communication between her and her co-religionists. Her servants, both male and female, were by his orders frequently changed, as many among them were found to be Christians in secret.

Catherine had already had at this time an apparition of Jesus as her heavenly affianced. He was always present to her, and she would hear of no other spouse. She returned home from Paphos. Her father now wanted to marry her to a youth of Alexandria, named Maximin, a descendant of an ancient royal house and

---

[1] A coastal city in the southwest of Cyprus.

nephew to the governor of Alexandria who, being childless, had adopted him as his heir. But Catherine would not listen to such a thing. She smilingly but fearlessly repelled all their advances, warded off every temptation. So great were her wisdom and learning that few could be found who were not forced to acknowledge her superiority.

Before these marriage proposals she had, at the age of twelve years, seen her mother die in her arms. Catherine told her mother that she was a Christian, instructed her, and prevailed upon her to receive baptism. I saw her with a little green sprig, sprinkling water from a golden bowl on her mother's head, forehead, mouth, and breast.

There was always frequent intercourse between Cyprus and Alexandria. Catherine's father took her to a relative in that city, hoping she would at last yield to his wishes concerning her marriage. She was then thirteen. Her suitor went out in a vessel to meet her, and again I heard her uttering admirable, profound, and Christian sentiments. She inveighed against the idols, whereupon the suitor playfully struck her several times on the mouth. Catherine laughed and spoke more enthusiastically than before. On disembarking, he took her to his father's house, in which everything breathed of the world and its delights. All hoped that Catherine's feelings would soon change, but here too she showed herself fearless and dignified, though affable as before. Her suitor, who lived in another wing of the house, was as if mad from love and disappointment, for Catherine spoke incessantly of her other affianced. Every means was taken to change her; learned men were sent to argue with her and turn her from the Christian faith; but she confounded them all, put them all to shame.

At this time the patriarch Theonas was in Alexandria. He had obtained by his great sweetness that the poor Christians should not be persecuted by the pagans; but still they were greatly oppressed—they had to keep very quiet, and carefully repress every word against idolatry. From this state of affairs resulted very dangerous communications with the pagans and great luke-warmness among the Christians, for which reason God ordained that Catherine, by her superior intelligence and burning zeal, should rouse them to renewed fervor in His service. I saw Theonas give her the holy eucharist, which she carried home on her breast in a golden pyx; but she did not receive the precious blood.

I saw at that time in Alexandria many poor men, apparently hermits, who were now prisoners. They were frightfully treated, forced to labor at buildings, draw heavy stones, and carry great burdens. I think they were converted Jews who had established themselves on Mount Sinai, but who had been forcibly dragged into the city. They wore brown robes woven of cords almost as thick as one's finger, and a cowl of the same color, which fell on the shoulders. I saw that the blessed sacrament was also secretly administered to them.

Catherine's suitor now set out on a journey to Persia and she herself returned to Cyprus, hoping to be left in peace, but her father was greatly displeased at not seeing her married. Again he sent her to Alexandria, and again she was the victim of new attacks. Later on she joined her father at Salamis, where she was triumphantly received by the young pagan girls, who loaded her with attentions and prepared all sorts of diversions for her—but all to no purpose. Then she was taken back to Alexandria to be the object of redoubled importunities. Here I saw a great pagan festival at which Catherine was compelled by her relatives to assist. But though forced to appear in the temple, nothing could induce her to offer sacrifice; yet more, as the idolatrous ceremony was being performed with great pomp, Catherine, inflamed with zeal, stepped up to the priests, overthrew the altar of incense with the vessels, and exclaimed aloud against the abominations of idolatry. A tumult arose. Catherine was seized as mad and examined in the courtyard, but she only spoke more vehemently than before, whereupon she was led away to prison. On the way thither, she adjured the followers of Jesus Christ to join her and give their blood for him who had given his for their redemption.

She was imprisoned, beaten with scorpions, and exposed to the beasts. Here the thought struck me: "It is not lawful thus to provoke martyrdom!"—but there are exceptions to every rule, and God has His own instruments. Violence had always been employed to force Catherine into idolatry and a marriage abhorrent to her. Immediately after her mother's death, her father frequently took her to the abominable festivals of Venus in Salamis, at which however she constantly kept her eyes closed.

At Alexandria, Christian faith lay dormant. The pagans were well pleased that Theonas should console their ill-treated Christian slaves and exhort them to serve their barbarous masters faithfully. They were so friendly toward him that many weak Christians thought paganism not so bad, perhaps, after all; therefore did God raise up this fearless, intrepid, enlightened virgin to convert by word and example—above all by her admirable martyrdom—many who would not otherwise have been saved. She made so little concealment of her faith that she went among the Christian slaves and laborers in the public squares, consoling and exhorting them to remain firm in their religion—for she knew that many of them had grown tepid and fallen off, owing to the general toleration. She had seen some of these apostates in the temple taking part in the sacrifices, and hence her holy indignation.

The beasts to which Catherine was exposed after her scourging licked her wounds, which were miraculously healed when she was taken back to prison. Here her suitor attempted to offer her violence, but he was put to shame and withdrew utterly powerless.

Her father returned from Salamis. Once more was Catherine taken from her prison to the house of her lover, and all possible means employed to make her apostatize; but the young pagan girls sent to persuade her were converted by her to Christ, and even the philosophers who came to dispute with her were won over. Her father was mad with rage; he called the whole affair sorcery and had Catherine beaten and imprisoned again. The wife of the tyrant visited her in prison and she too was converted, as also one of her officers. As she approached Catherine, I saw an angel holding a crown over her and another presenting her with a palm branch; but I cannot say whether the lady saw it or not.

Catherine was next taken to the circus and seated on a high platform between two broad wheels, stuck full of sharp iron points like a plowshare. When the executioners attempted to turn the wheels, they were shivered by a thunderbolt and hurled among the pagan crowd, about thirty of whom were wounded or killed. A terrible hail storm followed, but Catherine remained quietly seated with outstretched arms amid the shattered wheels. She was reconducted to her prison, where she remained for several days. More than one pagan tried to offer her violence, but she drove them back with her hand, and they stood spellbound, motionless as statues. When others attempted similar violence, she pointed to those victims of her power and thus averted further attacks.

All this was regarded as sorcery, and Catherine was again led to the place of execution. She knelt before the block, laid her head on it sideways, and was beheaded with a piece of the iron from the broken wheels. An extraordinary quantity of blood flowed from the wound, spouting up into the air in one continuous jet, until at last the flow became colorless as water. The head had been completely severed. The body was thrown upon a burning pile, but the flames turned against the executioners, leaving the holy remains enveloped in a cloud of smoke. It was then taken from the pile and thrown to the ravenous beasts which, however, would not touch it. Next day it was cast into a filthy ditch and covered over with elder branches. But that night I saw two angels, in priestly vestments, wrapping the luminous body in bark and flying away with it.

Catherine was sixteen years old at the time of her martyrdom in AD 299. Of the crowd of maidens who had followed her in tears to the place of execution, some fell away; but the tyrant's wife and the officer bravely suffered martyrdom. The two angels bore the virgin's body to an inaccessible peak on Mount Sinai, on which was a level space sufficiently large for a small house. The peak was a mass of colored stone that bore the imprint of entire plants. Here they placed the remains face downward. The stone seemed to be soft like wax, for the body left its impress on it as if in a mold. I could see the distinct imprint of the backs of the hands. Then they placed a shining cover over the whole. It arose a little above the surface of the rock. Here the saint's body lay concealed for hundreds of years, until God showed it in a vision to a hermit of Mount Horeb, who lived with many others on the mountain under the conduct of an abbot. The hermit related the vision, which he had seen several times, to his superior and found that another of the brethren had had a similar one. The abbot ordered them in obedience to remove the holy body. This was an undertaking not to be accomplished by natural means, for the peak was absolutely inaccessible, overhanging and craggy on all sides. But I saw the hermits set out and in one night make a journey which, under ordinary circumstances, would have required many days—they were, however, in a supernatural state.

The night was cloudy and dark, but brightness shone around them. An angel carried each in his arms up the steep peak. The angels opened the tomb and one of the hermits took the head, the other the light shrunken body with its winding-sheet in his arms, and both were borne down again by the angels. At the foot of Mount Sinai I saw the chapel, supported by twelve columns, wherein rests the holy body. The monks seemed to be Greeks; they wore coarse habits made by themselves. I saw Catherine's bones in a small coffin, the snow-white skull and one entire arm, but nothing more. All things around this spot have fallen to decay.

Near the sacristy is a little vault hollowed in the rock; in it are excavations containing holy bones, most of them wrapped in wool or silk and well preserved. There are among them some bones of the prophets who once lived on the mountain. They were venerated even by the Essenes in their caves. I saw the bones of Jacob, and those of Joseph and his family, which the Israelites brought with them from Egypt. These sacred objects seemed to be unknown, venerated only by the devout monks. The chapel is built on the side of the mountain facing Arabia.

Cecilia and Valerian

I SAW St. Cecilia sitting in a very plain four-cornered room, on her knees a flat triangular box, about an inch high, over which were stretched strings that she touched with both hands. Her face was upturned and over her hovered bright, shining spirits like angels or blessed children. Cecilia seemed conscious of their presence. I often beheld her in this posture. There was also a youth standing by her, of singularly pure and delicate appearance. He was taller than she, and full of deference for her. He seemed to obey her orders. I think it was Valerian, for I afterward saw him bound with another to a stake, struck with rods, and then beheaded. But this did not happen in the great circular martyr-place; it was in a more remote, a more solitary spot.

Cecilia's house was square with a roof almost flat, around which one could walk. On the four corners were stone globes, and in the center there was something like a figure. Before the house lay a circular courtyard, the scene of Cecilia's own execution. Here burned a fire under an immense cauldron in which sat Cecilia, full of joy, clothed in a shining white robe, her arms outstretched. One angel, surrounded by a rosy light, held out to her his hand, while another held a crown of flowers above her head. I have an indistinct remembrance of having seen a horned animal—like a wild cow, though not such as we have—led in by the gate and through the court to a dark recess. Cecilia was then removed from the cauldron and struck three times on the neck with a short, broad sword. I did not witness this scene, but I saw the sword. I also saw Cecilia wounded, but still alive, conversing with an old priest whom I had formerly seen in her house. I afterward saw that same house changed into a church and divine service celebrated in it. Many relics were there preserved, among them Cecilia's body, from the side of which some portions had been removed.

Cecilia's paternal home stood on one side of Rome, and like Agnes's house it had courts, colonnades, and fountains. I rarely saw her parents. Cecilia was very beautiful, gentle though active, with rosy cheeks and a countenance almost as lovely as Mary's. I saw her playing in the court with other children and almost always by her side an angel under the form of a lovely boy. He conversed with her and she saw him, although he was invisible to others, to whom he forbade her to speak of him. I often saw him withdraw when the other children gathered around her. Cecilia was then about seven years old. I saw her again sitting alone in her chamber, and the angel standing by her teaching her how to play on a musical instrument. He laid her fingers on the right strings and held a sheet of music before her. At times she rested on her knees something like a box over which strings were stretched, while the angel floated

before her with a paper to which she occasionally raised her eyes; or again, she supported against her neck an instrument like a violin, the chords of which she touched with her right hand, while at the same time she sang into the mouthpiece, which was covered with skin. It produced a very sweet sound.

I often saw a little boy (Valerian) by Cecilia, along with his elder brother and a man in a long white mantle who lived not far off and seemed to be their preceptor. Valerian played with her; it seemed as if they were being reared together, as if destined for each other. Cecilia had a Christian servant through whom she became acquainted with Pope Urban. I often saw her and her playmates filling their dresses with fruit and all kinds of provisions. Then, hooking them up at the sides like pockets and wrapping their mantles around them, they slipped stealthily with their loads to a gate of the city. The angel was always at Cecilia's side. It was a charming sight!

I saw the children hurrying along the high road to a building made up of heavy towers, walls, and fortifications. Poor people dwelt in the walls. In the underground caves and vaults were Christians—whether imprisoned or only concealed there, I do not know—but the poor creatures nearest the entrance seemed always to be on their guard against discovery. Here it was that the children secretly distributed their alms.

Cecilia used to fasten her robe around her feet with a cord and then roll down a steep bank. She passed into the vaults, and thence through a round opening into a cave where a man led her to St. Urban, who instructed her from rolls of parchment. Some of these rolls she brought to him concealed in her garments. She took others back home with her. I have an indistinct remembrance of her being baptized there. Once I saw the youth Valerian and his preceptor with the little girls as they were at play. Valerian tried to throw his arms around Cecilia, but she pushed him off. He complained of it to his preceptor, who reported the affair to her parents. I do not know what they said to Cecilia, but she was punished by being confined to her own room. There I saw the angel always with her teaching her to sing and play. Valerian was often allowed to visit and remain with her; at such times she invariably began to play and sing. Whenever he wanted to press her in a loving embrace, the angel instantly flung around her a glittering, white garment of light. This had the effect of gaining Valerian over to Cecilia's way of thinking. After that he often remained in her room alone, while she went to St. Urban; her parents, meanwhile, imagining them together.

Lastly, I had a vision of their betrothal. I saw the parents of both and a numerous company of people young and old in a hall magnificently adorned with statues; in the center stood a table laden with dainties. Cecilia and Valerian wore festive suits of many colors, and crowns and garlands of flowers. They were led to each other by their parents, who presented them—one after the other—with a glass of thick red wine, or something of the kind. Some words were pronounced, some passages read from manuscripts, something was written, and then all partook of the refreshments standing. I saw the angel ever at his post between Cecilia and her bridegroom. Then they went in festal procession to the back of the house where, in an open court, stood a round building supported by columns; high up in the center were two figures embracing each other. In the procession, little girls, two by two, carried a long chain of flowers suspended on white drapery.

As the betrothed stood before the statues in the temple, I saw the figure of a boy that seemed to be inflated with air, flying down, moved by some kind of machinery, first to Valerian's lips, then to Cecilia's, to receive from each a kiss. But when it flew to Cecilia the angel laid his hand over her lips. Then Cecilia and Valerian were entwined in the flower-chain by the little girls, so that the two ends should meet around and enclose both. But the angel still stood between them, thus preventing Valerian's reaching Cecilia, or the chain's being closed. Cecilia said some words to Valerian like these: Did he see nothing? She had another friend and he, Valerian, should not touch her. Then Valerian grew very grave, and asked if she loved any other of the youths present. To this Cecilia only answered that, if he touched her, her friend would strike him with leprosy. Valerian replied that, if she loved another, he would kill them both. All this passed between them in a low tone, one would have thought it only modesty on Cecilia's part. She told Valerian that she would explain herself later.

Then I saw them alone together in an apartment. Cecilia told him that she had an angel by her. Valerian insisted on seeing him too. She replied that he could not do so until he was baptized, and she sent him to St. Urban. At this time Valerian and Cecilia were married and in their own home.

During the Investigation
of Anne Catherine's Stigmata

ON the feast of St. Cecilia, my cowardice again forced itself upon me and I felt remorse for not having been more patient during the investigation. I invoked Cecilia for consolation, and she came to me instantly through the air. O heart-rending sight! Her head half-severed from her body, lay on her left shoulder! She was short, slight and delicate, black hair and eyes, and a fair complexion. She wore a yellowish white robe with large heavy golden flowers, the same in which she had been martyred. She spoke as follows:

Be patient! God will forgive your fault if you repent. Be not so troubled for having spoken the truth to your persecutors. When one is innocent, he may speak boldly to his enemy. I too reproached my enemies. When they spoke to me of blooming youth and the golden flowers on my robe, I replied that I esteemed them as little as the clay of which their gods were formed and that I expected gold in exchange for them. Look! with this wound I lived three days and tasted the consolation of Jesus Christ's servants. I have brought you patience, this child in green. Love him, he will help you!

She disappeared and I wept with joy. The child sat down by me on the bed and stayed with me. He sat uncomfortably on the edge, kept his little hands in his sleeves, and hung his head with a mournful but kind air, asking for nothing, complaining of nothing. His demeanor touched and consoled me more than I can say. I remember having had the patience-child by me once before. When the people from Holland tormented me almost to death, the Mother of God brought him to me. He said: "See, I allow myself to be taken on either arm, nursed or put on the floor, I am always satisfied—do you the same!" Since that time, even in my waking state, I see that child seated near me, and I have really acquired patience and peace.

She endured in vision torments equivalent to exterior persecution to satisfy the justice of God.

Clare

I HAD Clare's relic by me and I saw her life. Her pious mother, when devoutly praying before the blessed sacrament for a happy delivery, was interiorly warned that she would give birth to a daughter brighter than the sun; hence, the child was named Clare. Before the event the mother went on a pilgrimage to Rome, Jerusalem, and the other holy places. The parents were noble and very pious.

From her earliest infancy Clare was wonderfully attracted by whatever was holy. If she were taken into a church, she stretched out her tiny hands to the blessed sacrament; but other objects, no matter how highly colored, such as pictures, etc., made no impression upon her. I saw the mother teaching the child to pray and the little one zealously practicing self-renunciation. The devotion of the rosary must have been in use at the time, for I saw Clare's parents reciting every evening with their whole household a certain number of *Our Fathers* and *Hail Marys*. I also saw the child seeking little smooth stones of various sizes that she then carried around her in a leathern pouch with two pockets into which she dropped the stones alternately as she prayed. Sometimes she laid them in a row or circle as she prayed; and she always observed a certain number in her meditation or contemplation. If she feared having prayed inattentively, she imposed a penance on herself. She wove very beautiful little crosses out of straw. I saw her make a garden, in which she planted the little crosses. She had a little house in the garden. She was about six years old when I saw her in the yard in which the servants were slaughtering hogs. She took the bristles, cut them small, and put them around her neck, thus occasioning herself great suffering.

Later on her extraordinary piety began to be noised abroad, and St. Francis, divinely inspired, came to visit her parents. Clare was called to see him and was deeply impressed by the earnest words the saint spoke to her. After this a youth sued for Clare's hand. Her parents did not flatly discourage him, although they had not yet consulted their child. But she, interiorly warned of what was pending, ran to her chamber, and kneeling before her oratory vowed her virginity to God, which vow she solemnly made known when her parents introduced her suitor. They were truly amazed; but they ceased to urge her. She now engaged in all kinds of good works, exercising great charity toward the poor, to whom she gave her own meals whenever she could abstain from them unnoticed. I saw her visiting Francis at Portiuncula and becoming more and more firm in her determination to serve God alone.

On Palm Sunday she went to church in her best attire. She remained standing in the lower part of the church while the bishop distributed the palms at the altar. Suddenly he saw a beam of light shining over her head; he went down himself to where she stood and gave her a branch. Then I saw the light spreading over many others around her.

I saw her leave her parent's house by night for the church of Portiuncula, where Francis and his brethren received her with lighted candles, chanting the *Veni Creator*. I saw her in the church, receiving a penitential habit and cutting off her hair, after which Francis took her to a convent in the city. She already wore a horse-hair girdle with thirteen knots, which she now changed for one of boar skin, the bristles turned next to her person.

In vision I once beheld how, not wishing to wed, she went by night to Francis, and how she clung to the altar when others tried to carry her away. I saw also how at a time when she was very ill the devil lingered outside the city, and she had herself borne by some sister nuns to the city gate along with in a small box containing the sacrament, upon which was a crucifix. A cloth covered the sacrament and I saw that the cloth was laid over her hands while she was given the sacrament to hold, which she held out against the devil as he blessed, as she prayed. And I saw much else besides. Clare was small, brownish in color, quick and lively.

Working in the Vineyard

YESTERDAY I worked my way through a whole row in the vineyard, and all the while the holy Clare was there beside me, holding the sacrament; and when I collapsed quite exhausted at the end of the row, she refreshed me with the sacrament, and gave me also to drink.

I saw a nun in her convent who had conceived bitter hatred for her and who would not be reconciled to her. This religious had been sick for some time when Clare lay on her deathbed. The dying saint sent to be reconciled to the sister, but the latter refused. Then Clare prayed fervently and bade some of the nuns bring the sick sister to her. They went to her, raised her up, and lo! she was cured! She was so deeply affected by this that she hastened to Clare and begged her pardon. The saint responded by begging hers in return. I saw the Mother of God present at her death with a troop of holy virgins.

Clare of Montefalco

I KNELT alone with my guide in a large church before the blessed sacrament, which was surrounded by indescribable glory. In it I saw the resplendent figure of the infant Jesus, before whom since my childhood I have always opened my heart and poured out my prayers. As I presented my petitions, I received an answer to each one from the blessed sacrament in the form of a ray that pierced my soul and filled me with consolation. I was, also, gently reproved for my faults. I passed almost the whole night before the tabernacle, my angel at my side.

Anne Catherine's humility would not allow her to give the details of this vision. It was immediately followed by apparitions of Augustine and two holy Augustinians—Rita of Cascia and Clare of Montefalco— who prepared her to undergo sufferings such as they themselves had formerly endured for the blessed sacrament. She fell into ecstasy, and to the amazement of her confessor and the pilgrim, who were conversing together in the antechamber, suddenly stood up on her bed (a thing she had not done for four years), her countenance radiant with joy, her hands raised to heaven, and recited slowly and devoutly in a sweet, clear

voice, the whole of the Te Deum. Her face was emaciated and slightly
sallow, but her cheeks were flushed and a look of enthusiasm beamed
from her dark eyes. She stood upright, firm and secure in her position.
At certain parts she joined her hands and inclined her head suppliantly,
her voice betraying a tender, caressing accent like a child reciting verses
in its father's honor. Her ample robe fell below the ankles, giving her a
most imposing appearance, and her prayer, repeated in a loud voice,
excited in the hearer a feeling of mingled piety and awe.

The next day, after reciting a vision of St. Augustine, Anne Catherine
continued: After this my guide led me on my own road to the
heavenly Jerusalem, and I saw that I was now far beyond the
place where I had seen the little notes of warning in a previous
vision. I had left the straight way in favor of a side path, then
climbed a mountain and reached a circular garden of which the
stigmatic Clare of Montefalco had charge. In her hands I saw
luminous wounds and around her brow a shining crown of
thorns—for although she had not had the exterior marks of the
wounds, she had felt their pain. She had had various kinds of spiritual experiences, but I can no long remember anything about
them.

Clare told me that this was her garden and that, as I loved gar-
dening, she would show me how it should be carried on, as it was
to be mine now. There was a wall around it, but it was only symbolical, for one could both see and pass through it—it was built
of round, variegated, shining stones. The garden was laid out in
eight beautiful beds all verging toward the center. There were
some handsome large trees in full bloom and a fountain that
could be made to water the whole place. A vine was trained all
around the wall.

I stayed almost all night in the garden with Clare. She taught
me the virtue and signification of every plant and how to use it.
We passed from one flower bed to another, but I do not now
remember where she got the roots. It seemed to be supernaturally in the air, or from an apparition. I worked with her near a fig
tree, though I do not now recollect at what. I only remember that
there were beds of bittercress and chervil. Clare told me that, if
my taste were too sweet, I must take a mouthful of cress, and if
too bitter, a mouthful of chervil. I have always been very fond of

these herbs. I used to chew them when I was a child; indeed I could have lived on them.

The hardest thing for me to understand was Clare's management of the vine, how she trained it, divided it, and pruned it. I could not succeed. It was the last thing she taught me in the garden. During our work the birds flocked around us, perched on my shoulders, and were just as familiar with me as they had been in the convent cloister.

On another occasion Clare told me that she had the instruments of the passion engraved on her heart, and that after her death three stones had been found in her gall. She spoke also of the graces she had received on the feast of the Holy Trinity, bidding me prepare for a new labor on the coming feast. She looked very thin, pale, and exhausted.

Clement

IT is now a year since the wonderful journey to Clement's grave, and the discovery of his reliquary. Yesterday evening I forgot to take the relic of Clement with me, but after the vision of Cecilia it came again to mind, and so I took it out to venerate it. Thus did I come to see Clement in the time shortly before his persecution. He was indescribably wan and careworn—in truth, he looked nearly as destitute as Our Lord with his cross. His cheeks were hollow and his mouth tightly creased from his grief over the blindness and perfidy of the world.

He was seated on a stool, teaching in a great hall. His auditors were of many minds: some were sad and much affected; some had come more out of a kind of surreptitious pleasure in the knowledge of Clement's imminent sufferings; while others vacillated in their opinion of him.

At this point Roman soldiers entered and took him captive, after which they dragged him out of the hall and placed him on a wagon. The wagon was very different than those we are accustomed to. It was a long, low cart or barrow, with astonishingly thick wheels, like great discs sawn from a tree, through which four holes had been bored. They were something like the wheels on our toy wagons for children. The cart had several open seats at the front, and toward the back a covered one where Clement was placed, along with six Roman soldiers. Other soldiers accompanied the wagon on foot. The horses were smaller and shorter than those of our day and harnessed very differently as well, with much less tack.

For many days and nights Clement journeyed patiently but in great sadness. When the company arrived at the seashore, he was brought aboard a ship, and the cart and horses commenced their return journey.

A little later I saw in vision the region where he was taken. It was a destitute, waste, infertile land, punctuated with many deep pits, such as we find on our peat fens. All was melancholy and grim. Here and there were widely dispersed buildings, some of them inhabited. There was deprivation and hunger, and many cavities in the earth that I took to be graves. Clement was brought to a house with two wings, one intersecting the middle of the other. They were separated by surrounding arcades.

Referring to the drawing, Clement was brought in through the open arcade (a), moved thence to the wing occupied by the superintendant of the place (b), and then on to the room where prisoners were held (c):

The ceiling of this room (c) was perforated with openings for light and ventilation along the side contiguous with arcade (a), whose columns were ornamented in various places with all sorts of simply-executed pictures. I frequently saw people at prayer in this arcade. The images on the columns were not in any way provoking or offensive, and yet there seemed to be something sinister about them. Some depicted an arm extended over a head, or two arms so extended, or a hand holding a spherical object like an apple; other figures wore a kind of cap surmounted with a tuft or crest. They had a natural feel, not at all stiff.

Arcades (d), (e), and (f) were plastered shut and seemed to con-

tain bones and debris. The whole building was set low to the ground, close by a waste area.

The sea was at some distance. Then I saw Clement's grave at a great, solitary rock from which water had drained away. It lay some little distance from the bank of the sea. Through the entrance was a room with a stone sarcophagus. I could not tell whether it contained remains. When the sea rose to full flood, nearly the entire rock was submerged below the waves—but perhaps this part of the vision stems from a more recent time. In any case, things were more or less as I had seen them in earlier visions. I had the sense also that on the other side of the rocky island lay another saint at rest (Pope Martin).

On another occasion, regarding Clement's relations with others, Anne Catherine said she did not think she had ever seen him actually in the company of Paul, but much together with Barnabas in the region from which Cosmas came. She did see him with Timothy and Luke, as well as Peter. He was a Roman, but also Jewish through his grandparents, who were from a place near the borders of Egypt.

Then Anne Catherine described Clement's capture, poverty, and arduous labors breaking stones in a quarry, as is generally known. She saw him thrown into the sea, and how at the place where his body came to rest, a cavity formed on the rocky sea-bottom. Later, through land and water changes, this resting-place rose up as part of an island, and Christians hewed out from the stone a small chapel, which however would often still be covered by the waves.[1]

On the reverse side of the page upon which the above notes were written is the following:

"Anne Catherine said she thought Clement was to be married, but that at the nuptials he was told through an illumination that he was to demur, while his betrothed received the same message. She believed both were later martyred. She saw Clement as having been the third pope, with Anaclet the fourth pope, after him.

---

[1] According to one tradition, Clement was martyred by being tied to an anchor and thrown from a boat into the Black Sea. The legend recounts that every year a miraculous ebbing of the sea revealed a divinely built shrine containing his bones.

According to Anne Catherine, already at the time of Peter she saw Clement sometimes in ecclesial attire, sometimes in lay clothing. He had been baptized in company with many others."

Cunegundes

I HAD another singular vision. St. Cunegundes[1] brought me a crown and a little piece of pure gold in which I could see myself. She said: "I have made you this crown, but the right side [where Anne Catherine's great pain was] is not quite finished. You must complete it with this gold. I made you this crown because you placed a precious stone in my crown even before you were born"—and then she pointed to a stone or pearl in one side of her crown so dazzlingly bright that one could scarcely look at it. And this I had put there! I thought that really laughable, and so I said right out: "How can this be? It would indeed be strange had I done that before my birth!"

To this the saint replied that all my labors and sufferings, as well as those of all humankind, were already portioned out and divided among my ancestors; and she showed me pictures of Jesus working in the person of David, our own fall in Adam, of the good we do already existing in our ancestors, though obscurely, etc. She showed me my origin on my mother's side up through several generations to her own ancestors, where a thread appeared connecting them. She explained to me how I had put the jewel in the crown. I understood it all in vision, but now I cannot explain it. It was as if the property of patient suffering that sprang from the thread of life connected with my existence, had

---

[1] Saint Cunegundes of Luxembourg, OSB (c. 975–1040), was empress of the Holy Roman Empire by marriage to Holy Roman Emperor Saint Henry II. She served as interim regent after the death of her spouse in 1024. She is a Roman Catholic saint and the patroness of Luxembourg and Lithuania. She was a seventh-generation descendant of Charlemagne. She married St. King Henry in 999. It is said that she had long wanted to be a nun, and that her marriage to St. Henry II was a spiritual one (also called a "white marriage"); that is, they married for companionship alone, and by mutual agreement did not consummate their relationship.

been communicated to her; and thus I—or something of mine in her—had gained a victory that was represented by the jewel in her crown.

In the beginning of the vision I saw Cunegundes in a heavenly sphere or garden in company with kings and princes. I saw the emperor Henry, her holy spouse, in a sphere. He appeared fresh and younger than she, as if she had existed there a longer time in the persons of her ancestors. But this I cannot explain—indeed I did not understand it at the time, and so I let it alone. There was, above all, in this vision something unspeakably disengaged from the conditions of time; for although wondering to find that I had even before my birth labored at a pearl in Cunegundes's crown, yet it seemed very natural. I felt that I had lived in her time—yes, that I was even anterior to her, and I felt myself present to myself even in my earliest origin.

Cunegundes showed me on her left her extraction according to the flesh, and on the right her descendants according to the spirit—for she had had no children. Her spiritual posterity was very rich, very fruitful. I saw her ancestors as well as my own far, far back to people who were not Christians. Among them I saw some who had received a merciful judgment. This astonished me, since it is written: "Whoever believes not and is not baptized shall not enter into the kingdom of heaven." But Cunegundes explained it thus: "They loved God as far as they knew Him, and their neighbor as themselves. They knew nothing of Christianity, they were as if in a dark pit into which light never penetrated. But they were such as would have been perfect Christians had they known Christ; consequently, they found mercy in his sight."

I had then a vision of my being before my birth, or that of my forefathers, not like one genealogical tree, but like numerous branches spread over all the earth and in all sorts of places. I saw rays extending from one to another which, after uniting in multiplied beams, branched out again in different directions.

I saw many pious members among my ancestors, some high, some low. I saw a whole branch of them on an island; they were wealthy and owned large ships, but I know not where it was. I saw very many things in this vision. I received many clear lights upon the importance of transmitting to the world a pure posterity and of maintaining pure, or of purifying in ourselves, that which our ancestors have handed down to us. I understood it to refer both to spiritual and to natural posterity.

I saw, too, my father's parents. His mother was named Rensing. She was the daughter of a rich farmer. She was avaricious and during the Seven Years' War buried her money near our house. I knew almost the exact spot. It will be found long after my death when the house will have passed into other hands. I knew this long ago, even when a child.

Cunegundes was with me a long time last night. During the last few days I have learned an infinity of things from her, chiefly concerning our origin and our participation in another life. I have seen innumerable histories and details of our ancestors. Today she told me that, like myself, she had been freed from her youth from all temptations of the flesh and had early vowed herself to God. She did not dare to tell her mother; but she informed her husband, who made with her the vow of chastity. And yet she was afterward subjected to frightful calumnies and sharp trials.

I did not see last night the cause of her subjection to the fiery ordeal, but I had already seen it. She was too good to one of her servants, who also had endured much from false accusations. I saw her death and that of her husband. The latter was interred in a church he had built and dedicated to St. Peter (at Bamberg). I do not know whether it was in this church or in another that Cunegundes, in magnificent imperial robes, assisted at a service for her husband. After it was over, in the presence of five bishops, she laid aside her crown and royal attire for the humble habit of a religious, like that of Sister Walburga, and covered her head with a veil. The people who had witnessed her pompous entrance, were moved to tears on seeing her leave the church in her lowly garb.

A few days before her death, her angel told her that her husband would come for her at the last moment. I beheld him doing so with crowds of souls—the poor whom they had fed, and others to whom they had done good. I understood that they were their spiritual children. Her husband presented them to her as the fruit of their union.

Cunegundes is connected with me by a secret tie existing

between those that from infancy have been freed from the concupiscence of the flesh. It is impossible to explain this to the impure world. It is a secret of an unknown nature. I am, moreover, related to the saint through our ancestors.

Dionysius the Areopagite

I SAW this saint in his boyhood. He was the child of pagan parents and of an inquiring turn of mind.[1] He always recommended himself to the Supreme God, who enlightened him by visions in sleep. I saw his parents reproving him for his neglect of the gods and placing him under the charge of a stern preceptor; but an apparition came to him by night and bade him flee while his preceptor slept. He obeyed, and I saw him traversing Palestine and listening eagerly to whatever he could hear concerning Jesus. Again I saw him in Egypt, where he studied astronomy in the place in which the holy family had sojourned. Here I saw him standing with several others before the school, observing the sun's eclipse at the death of Jesus. He said: "This is not in accordance with nature's laws. Either a god is dying, or the world is coming to an end!"

I saw the preceptor himself, a man of upright intentions, warned to seek his scholar. He did so, found him, and went with him to Heliopolis. At one time Dionysius returned to his home, with great honor, but he was not yet a Christian, as it was long before he could reconcile himself to the idea of a crucified god.

After his conversion he often traveled with Paul. He journeyed with him to Ephesus to see Mary (Anne Catherine did not see him present at her death and assumption). Pope Clement sent him to Paris, where I saw him martyred at an advanced age, as is also told in the histories. He took his head in his hands, crossed them on his breast, and walked around the mountain (Montmartre), a great light shining forth from him. The executioners fled at the sight, and a woman gave him sepulture. He was then very old.

---

[1] Brentano remarks that what Anne Catherine saw of the life of Dionysus conformed in general with extant legends regarding him.

He had had many celestial visions, besides which Paul had revealed to him what he himself had seen.[1] He wrote magnificent works of which many are still extant, though some have been falsified. His book on the sacraments was not finished by himself but by another, who incorporated therein some errors. In his books on the *Divine Names*, the *Celestial Hierarchies*, and the *Mysteries*, much is incorrect; nonetheless they still contain much of great value.[2] Perhaps, with God's help, I will be told in the night how to correct them.

Dionysius and Anne Catherine in a Heavenly Garden

DIONYSIUS had many visions of heavenly gardens, such as I have had, and some of his visions I was able to see also. When in vision he came to me, I was in a garden with beautiful apples, of which I had just picked a large number. Many priests were there, and they were meant to be rejuvenated with the apples. But there was one who would not take one of the lovely fruits, but instead accepted from a distinguished looking man a plate full of pastries in many figures, which pastries he commenced to eat. These figures appeared to me then like living, creeping, crawling things: toads, snakes, beetles, worms, and lizards. I horrified that he had consumed these creatures. Then someone I did not know came and took the fruits.

So much needed doing, and the apples were so heavy that they kept falling from of my apron. In this vision Dionysius came to me and led me along an arduous path to another garden. Along the way the soul of the woman who taught me to sew appeared to me. She was active and nimble and helped me in all sorts of ways, including gathering up the apples that fell from my apron. She was lively and helpful.

---

[1] Anne Catherine saw Carpus (who traveled with Paul, John, and Luke) together also with Dionysius Areopagite. See "Carpus" in *People of the New Testament II*.

[2] Though Anne Catherine was unaware of it, an old Latin edition of the works of Dionysius was just then lying on the table by her bed. CB

Dionysius led me then to a wide and rushing river. I had to cross it, but knew not how. Then he said I was to cross over upon my apples. And so I set the apples upon the waters, whereupon the river ceased flowing. I stepped out upon the apples, reaching back to the hintermost ever and again and setting it again to the front, in this way merrily passing over the water as though upon a bridge, with an apron full of apples still left over.

On the river's further shore was a garden still more beautiful than the one I had just quit. Here the fruits were very large and completely transparent, and upon these flawless fruits did I pass into a church comprised in truth of three churches, one above another. And so I progressed, making my way still upon the apples, to the middle church, which had windows, or transparent places, that were covered in something like gauze. It was as though here and there the very walls were transparent, so that I could on all sides see through them to a starry heaven. Each star was a garden, and when I looked into these gardens I saw the most wonderful pictures. Many of these pictures were of Dionysius. I saw choirs of spirits, and great tables laden with a heavenly banquet. For instance, I saw John seated in one garden, writing with his reed pen just as I have seen him writing upon the earth, so that I chuckled to myself: "Ah! Now he's sitting in a star! Are then all holy things set in stars and gardens?!"

Above me in the third and highest church I saw the feast of St. Dionysius. I saw therein pure, mobile, hovering spirits, but could not myself enter. Heaven opened above, ascending up and up into a most inexpressible Light.

Then from the second church I looked down into the first, the lowest, and felt great longing for the pilgrim, whom I saw below with another man in a woman's room. I would have liked so very much to be able to show him the pictures I had seen, and the fruits also, and to have given him some of the latter. But Dionysius said this was not possible—that the pilgrim was too heavy and would fall through. Nevertheless, I had the feeling that he did in fact come to me, but had first to make a detour of some kind—however, what followed next I can no longer recall. The season seemed like May, and yet there were so many apples.

The Fulfillment of the
Vision of the Feast of St. Dionysius

SOME *months later Anne Catherine beheld in vision the same events described above. She made the great journey across the river upon some of the many apples she bore. Dionysius appeared to her as before, though on this occasion she described how she took hold of his surplice in order not to sink into the waters. She was led into the threefold church and from the vantage-point of the second of the three beheld angels, gardens, and the hierarchies of heaven. Again she encountered the soul of her deceased former sewing mistress (who had a special devotion for St. Dionysius, of whom she had often spoken in life).*

At the time of this second vision of the same events, Anne Catherine had been very sick for several days and was unaware that only two months before she had already beheld the events she once more described.

It was when she was at the worst stage of her illness that Dionysius bid Anne Catherine take hold of the crucifix upon his surplice so that he could carry her over the waters to the church of his feast. Again she saw below in the first or lowest church her former sewing mistress, the pilgrim, and a certain brother of the holy cross. The first, Anne Catherine could not at all understand; the brother of the holy cross unwillingly turned away from both Anne Catherine and the pilgrim, after which he was seen making his way down a dark and dangerous footpath. Anne Catherine could not understand why he would take this route when the place they were presently in was so bright and clear. To the pilgrim she was unable to speak. The fact that the brother of the holy cross appeared in the vision of Dionysius had to do with the fact that he had a part in the convoluted history of a relic of Dionysius that had been a factor in the occasion of the original vision.

Dorothea

AGAIN I recognized this saint's relic and saw a large city in a hill country. Playing in the garden of a house built in the Roman style were three little girls between five and eight years old. They took hold of hands, danced in a ring, stood still, sang, and gathered flowers. After a while the two eldest ran away from the youngest, tearing up their flowers as they went, and leaving the little one deeply hurt at their treatment of her. I saw her standing there all alone with a sharp pain in her heart, a pain I also felt. Her face grew pale, her clothing became white as snow, and she fell to the ground as if dead.

Then I heard an interior voice saying: "That is Dorothea!" and I saw the apparition of a resplendent boy approaching her with a bouquet of flowers in his hand. He raised her, led her to another part of the garden, gave her the bouquet, and disappeared. The little thing was delighted; she ran to the other two, showed them her flowers, and told them who had given them to her. Her companions were amazed; they pressed the child to their heart, appeared sorry for the pain they had caused her, and peace was restored. At this sight I felt an eager desire for some such flowers to strengthen me. All at once, Dorothea stood before me as a young maiden and made me a beautiful discourse in preparation for communion. "Why do you sigh after flowers?" she asked, "you who so often receive the Flower of all flowers!"

Then she explained the vision I had just had of the children, the desertion and return of the two elder ones, and I had another vision referring to her martyrdom. I saw her imprisoned with her elder sisters, a contest going on among them. The two elder wished not to die for Jesus, and so they were set free. Dorothea was sent by the judge to the two apostates in the hope that she would follow their example and advice. But the contrary was the case—she brought her sisters back to the faith. Then Dorothea was fastened to a stake, torn with hooks, burned with torches and, finally, beheaded. While she was being tortured I saw a youth, who had mocked at her on her way to martyrdom and to whom she had addressed a few words, suddenly converted. A resplendent boy appeared to him with roses and fruits. He entered into himself, confessed the faith, and suffered martyrdom by decapitation. With Dorothea suffered many others; some by fire, some by being fastened to animals and quartered.

Engelbert of Cologne

THE *pilgrim handed Anne Catherine a relic and next day she said*: I recognized that relic. It belongs to Engelbert of Cologne. Last night I saw many incidents of his life. He was very influential at court, where he was occupied with important diplomatic affairs. He led an upright, fervent life, but on account of his position was not so much given to interior things as other saints. His devotion to Mary was very great. I saw him busy in the cathedral, arranging in caskets precious relics no longer known, and burying them altogether under the altars. But that was not proper.

I saw his death. He was attacked while on a journey and horribly maltreated by a relative whom he had once been obliged to punish. I counted over seventy wounds on his body. He was sanctified by his earnest preparation for death, for he had shortly before made a fervent general confession. The unspeakable patience with which he endured his slow murder also contributed thereto, for he never ceased praying for his assassins. The Mother of God was with him visibly consoling and encouraging him to suffer and die patiently; he was indebted to her for his holy death.

Ermelinda

LAST night I saw the holy maiden Ermelinda, a most innocent child, who in her twelfth year was introduced to a youth whom her parents intended she should marry. She was noble and rich, and resided in an elegant mansion. One day as she ran to the door to meet the youth, Jesus appeared to her, saying; "Dost thou not love me more than him, Ermelinda!" In transports of joy, she exclaimed: "Yes, my Lord Jesus!" Then Jesus led her back into her room and gave her a ring, with which he espoused her. Ermelinda at once cut off her beautiful hair and informed her parents and the youth that she had pledged her troth to God. I begged Ermelinda to take me to the dying and to the poor souls, and I think I traveled with her through Holland—a most tiresome journey, over water, marshes, bogs, and ditches. I went to poor people who could get no priest, so far over the water did they live. I con-

soled them, prayed for them, assisted them in various ways, and
went on further toward the north.

Eulalia

AMONG *Anne Catherine's relics were two teeth marked Eulalia.*[1] *After
some time, she said*: Only one of these teeth belongs to the holy vir-
gin-martyr Eu-lalia of Barcelona. The other belongs to a priest
who received holy orders at an advanced age, and whom I have
seen journeying around helping widows and orphans. Eulalia's
tooth was drawn about six months before her martyrdom. I saw
the whole operation. The tooth caused her much suffering, and
she had it extracted at a young friend's house because her
mother, through excessive tenderness, could not endure that it
should be done at home. The old man who drew the tooth was a
Christian. He sat on a low stool, Eulalia before him on the floor,
her back to him. She rested her back against him and he quickly
drew the tooth with an instrument that fitted closely around it.
The instrument had a transverse piece to the haft. When the
tooth came out, he held it up in the pincers before the two girls,
who both began to laugh. Eulalia's friend begged her to make her
a present of it, which she readily did.

All Eulalia's companions loved her, and after her martyrdom
the tooth became a more precious object, a sacred relic to the pos-
sessor. It passed successively into the hands of two other women.
Later on I saw it in a church, enclosed in a silver box shaped like a
little censer. It hung before a picture of St. Apollonia. In this picture Apollonia was represented not as old, but young, with pincers in her hand and a pointed cap on her head. Then I saw that
when this church had been despoiled of its silver, the tooth fell
into the possession of a pious maiden far away from Eulalia's
native land. A little piece of one of the roots had been broken off,
which I also saw preserved as a relic, but I cannot name the place.

---

[1] Anne Catherine had frequently felt and referred to the presence of this
relic, saying: "There must be a St. Culalia in my church! She belongs to Barcelona." She had seen the name in vision in small Roman letters and had mis-
taken C for E.

The tooth shines, but not with the glory of martyred bones. It shines by reason of Eulalia's innocence and the ardent desire to die for Jesus that even then animated her; and also on account of the intense pain she endured so patiently from it.

I do not see the bones that the saints lost before martyrdom shining with the colors of the glory that distinguishes their other relics. To the light of this tooth was wanting the martyrdom of the whole person.

Eulalia's parents were very distinguished people. They lived in a large house surrounded by olive trees and others with yellow fruits. They were Christians, but not very zealous ones; they allowed nothing of their faith to be remarked in them. Eulalia was intimate with a female older than herself, a zealous Christian who lived not far from Eulalia's home, in which she was often employed to do great pieces of embroidery. I saw her and Eulalia making church vestments secretly by night, fastening in round-stitch figures on cloth. They used a lamp with a transparent shade, which gave a very clear light. I used to see Eulalia retired in her own chamber, praying before a simple cross that she had cut out of box wood. She was consumed with a desire to confess Jesus openly, for he often showed her in vision the martyr's crown. I saw her walking with other maidens and expressing to them the longings she dared not utter in her father's house.

Francis of Assisi

ON *the feast of St. Francis of Assisi, Anne Catherine had the following vision:* I saw the saint two years prior to his death among some bushes on a wild mountain in which were scattered grottoes like little cells. Francis had opened the gospel several times. Each time it chanced to be at the history of the passion, and so he begged to feel his Lord's sufferings. He used to fast on this mountain, eating only a little bread and roots in order not to die of hunger. He knelt, his bare knees on two sharp stones, and supported two others on his shoulders.

It was after midnight and he was praying with arms extended, half-kneeling, half sitting, his back resting against the side of the mountain. I saw his guardian angel near him holding his hands, his countenance all on fire with love. Francis was a slight, gaunt man. He wore a brown mantle open in front with a hood like those worn at the time by shepherds, and a cord bound his waist. At the moment in which I saw him he was as if paralyzed.

A bright light shot from heaven and descended straight down upon him, and in this glory was an angel with six wings, two above his head, two over his feet, and two with which he seemed to fly. In his right hand he held a cross, about half the usual size, on which was a living body glowing with light, the feet nailed crossed, the five wounds resplendent as so many suns. From each wound proceeded three rays of rosy light converging to a point. They shot first from the hands toward the palms of the saint's hands; then from the wound in the right side toward the saint's right side (these rays were larger than the others); and lastly, from the feet toward the soles of the saint's feet.

In his left hand the angel held a blood-red tulip in whose center was a golden heart, which I think he gave to the saint.[1] When Francis returned from ecstasy he could only with difficulty stand, and I saw him going back to his monastery suffering cruelly, and supported by his guardian angel. He hid his wounds as well as he could. There were large crusts of brownish blood on the back of his hands, for they did not bleed regularly every Friday; but his side often bled so profusely that the blood flowed down on the ground. I saw him praying in the form of a cross, the blood streaming down his arms.

I saw many other incidents of his life. Once, even before he knew him, the pope beheld him in vision supporting the Lateran on his shoulders when it was ready to fall.

---

[1] Anne Catherine often saw things in emblematic forms, and so this gift may have been such a representation of some inner grace then bestowed. CB

During the Forced
Investigation of Her Stigmata

I BEHELD crowds of children who came from Münster with some grown people to see the impostor;[1] but they were all kind to me; they loved the impostor very much. It seemed as if I taught them something. Several saints were around me in this vision and—what pleased me greatly—St. Francis, dressed in a long, coarse robe was among them, his forehead very broad, his jaws hollow, his chin large. He consoled me, and told me not to complain, that he too had been persecuted. He had kept his wounds very secret, but the blood from his side often streamed down to his feet. Although some had seen his wounds, they did not in consequence believe. It is better to believe and not to see, for seeing does not make them believe who have not the gift of faith. He (Francis) was tall, thin, vigorous, his hollow cheeks ruddy as of one interiorly inflamed, and he had black eyes. I saw no beard. He was not infirm, but very winning and sprightly.

When Anne Catherine was informed then of her superior's desire that she should appeal to a higher court, she suddenly closed her eyes and fell into ecstasy, her countenance becoming very grave. She afterward said:

I invoked God the Father. I begged Him to look upon His Son who satisfies for sinners at every moment, who every moment offers himself in sacrifice, that He might not be too severe toward that poor, blind Landrath, but to assist and enlighten him for the love of His Son. At the same instant I saw a vision of Good Friday, the Lord sacrificing himself upon the cross, Mary and the disciples at its foot. This picture I saw over the altar at which priests say mass. I see first the church here, then the churches and parishes all around, even as one sees a nearby fruit tree lit up by the sun, and in the distance others grouped together like a wood. I see mass celebrated at all hours of the day and night throughout the world, and in some far-off regions with the same ceremonies as in the times of the apostles. Above the altar, I see a heavenly

---

[1] That is, the alleged impostor, Anne Catherine herself. See *The Life of Anne Catherine Emmerich* for more details on this difficult episode in her life.

worship in which an angel supplies all that the priest neglects. I offer my own heart for the want of piety among the faithful and I beg the Lord for mercy. I see many priests performing this duty pitiably. Some, mere formalists, are so attentive to the outward ceremonies as to neglect interior recollection; they think only of how they appear to the congregation, and not at all of God. The scrupulous ever long to feel their own piety.

I have had these impressions since childhood. Often during the day I am absorbed in this far-off gazing on the holy sacrifice. Jesus loves us so much that he constantly renews his work of redemption. The mass is the hidden history of redemption, redemption become a sacrament. I saw all this in my earliest youth and I used to think everyone did the same.

Francis Borgia

I SAW many things in the life of St. Francis Borgia, both as a man of the world and as a religious. I remember his having scruples about daily communion and his praying before a picture of the Mother of God, where he received a stream of blood from the child Jesus and another of milk from Mary. He was told not to deprive himself of that on which he lived, daily communion. This reception of milk from Mary I have often seen represented in the pictures of saints, where they are painted in the act of suckling at her breast, like children, or the milk flowing from her breast to them; but all that is wrong and absurd! I saw it in an entirely different way: from Mary's breasts, or from the region of the breasts, something like a little white vapor streamed out to them and was breathed in by them. It was like a stream of manna from her, while from the side of Jesus shone upon them a ray of rosy light. It is like wheat and wine, like flesh and blood—but quite unspeakable!

Francis de Sales • Jane de Chantal

THE *pilgrim saw the mistake he had made in marking some relics, and Anne Catherine promised to look in "her church" for those of St. Francis de Sales and St. Jane de Chantal. He records in his diary:*

"This afternoon I found Anne Catherine in ecstasy. I offered her the box of relics, which she took and pressed to the bosom, her features, drawn by pain, immediately becoming serene. I asked if Francis de Sales were not in 'the church'? She answered with an effort, as if speaking from a great height: 'There they are!' pointing meanwhile to the shelf before her closet. Surprised, I hunted for the relic, but in vain; when she, tearing, so to speak, her right hand from its ecstatic rigidity, removed quickly and in the greatest order the books from the shelf. With anxious curiosity I glanced at the empty shelf while that wonderfully endowed hand went groping between the shelf and the panel, until it grasped the missing treasure: a particle of bone wrapped in green silk. She pressed it reverently to her lips and handed it to me as the relic of Francis de Sales.

"I must not neglect to state that during this search she, with the exception of the right hand and arm, remained perfectly rigid, her head immovable, her eyes closed, her left hand firmly pressing the box of relics to her breast. While I wrapped and labeled the relic, she replaced in the same mechanical way all she had removed from the shelf and then, opening her eyes, glanced into the box of relics and allowed her hand to rest some moments on a tiny parcel that she afterward presented to me as the relic of St. Jane de Chantal. I asked her how it was that these relics had got mixed up with those of the early Roman martyrs. She answered: 'Long ago, repairs were made in the church of Überwasser, Münster, when all the relics of the different altars and shrines were thrown together indiscriminately.'"

She afterward saw at various times the following symbolical figures of Francis de Sales's apostolic ministry:

I saw a young ecclesiastic of high rank, zealously laboring in a mountainous country between France and Italy, and I accompanied him in his numerous journeys. I saw him in his youth an earnest student. One day with a firebrand he put a shameless woman to flight. Then I saw him going from village to village with a burning torch enkindling a fire everywhere; the flames leaped from one to the other and finally reached a large city on a lake. When the fire ceased to burn, there fell a gentle rain that lay on the ground like pearls and sparkling stones. The people gathered them up and took them into their houses. Wherever they were carried, prosperity followed, all became bright.

I was amazed to see Francis so indescribably gentle and at the same time so zealous in his undertakings, so vigorous in pushing things forward. He went everywhere himself, climbing over snow and ice. I saw him with the king in France, with the pope, and then at another court between the two. Day and night did he journey on foot from place to place, teaching and doing good, often passing the nights in a wood.

Through him I was introduced to a noble lady, Frances de Chantal, who took me over all his journeys, showing me all he did. I traveled with her here and there, and spoke much with her. She was a widow and had children—once I saw them with her. I received an account of something concerning her and all the sorrow it caused her, and I saw many scenes of the same.

A little frivolous lady of distinction, seemingly penitent, was introduced by her to the bishop; but she constantly relapsed into her evil ways. Frances said that this lady had caused her much trouble; indeed, she thought she had been bewitched by her. Later on the bishop founded a convent in concert with Frances, and the bad person, who seemed to have corrected, did penance in a small house nearby. I remember Frances's showing me the present state of this person in a dark place.

I saw the bishop saying mass in a place in which many of the inhabitants doubted the real change wrought in the blessed sacrament. During his mass he saw in vision a woman who had come to the church merely to please her husband; she believed not in transubstantiation and had a piece of bread in her pocket. In his sermon the bishop remarked that the Lord could as truly change the bread of the holy sacrifice into his body as he could change bread in the pocket of an unbeliever into stone. On leaving the church, the woman found the bread in her pocket turned into stone.

The holy bishop was always neatly and properly dressed. I saw him surrounded by enemies, and I also saw him concealed in a hut to which about twenty persons came by night for instruction. His life was sought and snares were laid for him in the forest to which he had fled.

I went with the lady (St. Frances) to a large city where, as she told me, the bishop had disputed with a heretic, who in his arguments never kept to the points under discussion. The saint, without losing sight of the truth, had followed him in all his windings in order to bring him back to the right road; but the man would not be saved.

The lady and I had to cross a large square in this city. It was crowded with citizens and peasants who were being drilled in separate troops. I was dreadfully afraid of their attacking us and, besides, the good lady said she could not possibly remain longer without food; she would faint from hunger. I looked around and saw a man eating bread and meat from a paper. I begged him for just one mouthful, and he gave me some bread and a piece of chicken. When the lady had eaten it, she was able to proceed to her convent.

With regard to those visions in which I exercise some act of charity toward the apparition of a saint, I have from my childhood been interiorly instructed that they are works the saints demand of us with the design of turning them over to others; they are good works which they cause to be performed for themselves, but which are in reality for the benefit of others. "We do for the Lord what we do for the neighbor," is here reversed; for here we do for the neighbor what we do for the saints.

I went to the convent which the lady had founded in concert with the bishop. It was a singular old building; I saw every nook of it. In many of the rooms were large stores of various kinds of fruits and grains, quantities of clothing, and odd-looking caps. The religious must have given away much to the poor. I put everything in order. A saucy young nun continually followed me, reproaching me and accusing me of trying to steal. She said I was avaricious; for, though declaring money to be mire, yet I turned over every penny; that I mixed myself up unnecessarily in worldly affairs; that I wanted to accomplish so many things and yet never finished any, etc. She kept at my back, not having the courage to face me. I told her to stand out before me, if she could. But she was in fact the tempter, who tormented me greatly during those days.

Away off in a remote corner of the convent I found a nun with a pair of scales. She had been placed there by the foundress. On a plate by her side were heaps of mixed peas, little yellow seeds, of what kind I know not, pearls, and dust—all which she was to pick out and clean. Then she was to carry half the good seed to the front of the convent for seed-corn. But she would not do it; she refused to obey. Then came another in her place, but she was no better than the first; and at last I undertook to sort and separate the mixture. It signified that from the spiritual harvest of this monastery clean, fresh seed-corn would be taken to the front of the house; that is, that the end and blessing of the saint's institution were to be renewed by the merits proceeding from the good discipline of former times; that what was injured by the faults of the last superioresses was to be repaired.

At a later period Anne Catherine was given to see the entire life of Francis de Sales from his infancy to his death, but she had neither the strength nor opportunity to relate even a few of its details.

St. Jane Frances again appeared to her at different times, claiming her prayers and sufferings for the renewal of her order. On one occasion she related the following:

Last night I was at Annecy, in the convent of the daughters of the Holy Lady de Chantal. I lay very sick in bed and saw all the preparations for the feast of the Visitation. I seemed to be in a choir from which I could look down on the altar that was being dressed for the feast. I was very sick and about to swoon when St. Francis de Sales came to me quickly with something that relieved me. He wore a long, yellow festal robe corded. St. Chantal also was by me.

Gertrude of Nivelles

I SAW that Gertrude's mother had a prophetic dream before her child's birth. It appeared to her that she brought forth a little daughter who held in her hand the crosier of an abbess, from which sprang a vine. The mother dwelt in an old castle, and once she and all her neighbors were greatly annoyed by mice that destroyed the crops and provisions. She had a great horror of these pests. Once I saw her in tears, recounting to her little Gertrude the ravages they had made. Gertrude instantly knelt down and fervently begged God for deliverance from the plague.

Instantly, I saw all the mice scampering out of the castle and drowning in the waters of the moat. Gertrude, by her childlike faith, obtained great power against these and other noxious animals. She had some pet mice that she fed and that obeyed her call; she had also birds and hares. She was asked in marriage, but she rejected the proposal, and exhorted her suitor to choose the Church for his spouse, that is, to become a priest. He did so, but only after having seen the other maidens whom he sought die suddenly. I saw Gertrude as a religious, her mother as abbess; later on she herself held that office. At the instant the crosier was presented her, there sprang from its top a vine-branch with a bunch on which were nineteen grapes, which she gave to her mother and her eighteen religious. Two mice ran around the crosier, as if paying homage to her authority. Thus was the mother's prophetic dream realized.

Gregory

I HAD visions of Ambrose, Liborius, and of St. Gregory's pontificate. They referred chiefly to the communications of these saints with holy women, which had given rise to many calumnies. Gregory established numerous convents of nuns. On the ancient pagan festivals, public prayers were offered and penances performed by hundreds of their members clothed as penitents, to repair the scandals then committed. A great deal of good was thus effected and the number of festivals consecrated to the demon and sin was thereby diminished; but St. Gregory had much to suffer from it.

Hermann Joseph

I HAD visions of the childhood years of Hermann Joseph.[1] He had a tiny picture of Mary on parchment. He made a case for it, attached a plain string, and hung it around his neck. This he did with the utmost faith and simplicity, and he never forgot to

---

[1] Saint Hermann Joseph, O.Praem., (ca. 1150–1241) was a German Premonstratensian canon regular and mystic. Never formally canonized, in 1958 his status as a saint of the Roman Catholic Church was formally recognized by

honor it. When Hermann played alone in his garden, two other boys always joined him. They were not the children of men, but this the child suspected not. He played with them quite simply and oftentimes sought, but never found them, among the other children of the city. Even when he left his other companions to seek them, they came not; they came only when he was all alone.

Once I saw him playing in a meadow near Cologne, by a brook that flows through St. Ursula's martyr-field. He fell into the stream, but, with childlike trust, held his little picture of the Mother of God above the water that it might not get wet. The Blessed Virgin appeared, caught him by the shoulder, and drew him out. I saw many other incidents in his childhood indicative of his great familiarity with Mary and the infant Jesus: for instance, once I saw him in church, reaching an apple to Mary, which she graciously accepted; and, again, I saw him when he found the money under a stone (which had been pointed out by her) with which to buy himself a pair of shoes. I saw Mary helping him also in his studies.

Hubert

AS I took up his relics, I saw the holy bishop. He said: "That is my bone. I am Hubert!" Then I had visions of his life, and I saw him as a boy in a solitary old castle surrounded by a moat. He wore a close-fitting suit and roamed with his crossbow in forest and field shooting birds, which he afterward gave to the sick around the castle. I often saw him cautiously crossing the moat on a floating plank to distribute his alms. Then I saw him a young married

---

Pope Pius XII. He was born in Cologne. According to the biography by Razo Bonvisinus, a contemporary and prior of Steinfeld Abbey (*Acta Sanctorum*, 7 April, I, 679), Hermann was the son of noble but poor parents. At the age of seven he attended school and very early he was known for devotion to the Blessed Virgin. At every available moment he could be found at the church of St. Mary on the Capitol, where he would kneel wrapt in prayer to Mary. Bonvisinus claims that the boy once presented an apple, saved from his own lunch, to a statue of Jesus, who accepted it. According to still another legend, on another occasion, when on a cold day he made his appearance with bare feet, Mary procured him the means of getting shoes.

man in a distant country, joining with many others in a great hunt. He wore a leathern cap; on his breast hung a bent tube, over his shoulder a crossbow, and in his hand he carried a light spear. The huntsmen all had little tawny dogs. I saw a large one at Hubert's side; he had also a sort of barrow between two asses on which to take home the game.

The hunters crossed a vast, wild district to the scene of action, a broad plain near a running stream. Hubert and his dogs followed a small yellow stag for a long time; but when the dogs had nearly overtaken it they ran back to their master whining as if to tell him something. The stag paused, looked at Hubert, started on again pursued by the dogs until the latter, as before, ran back to their master. This they repeated several times. At last Hubert set the hounds of his fellow-sportsmen on it, but they too came running back whining.

Hubert's eagerness increased, and he noticed now that the stag grew larger and larger. He renewed the chase more ardently than before until he was far ahead of his companions, following the stag, which still seemed to increase in size. He pursued it to a dense thicket. Here he thought it would entangle its horns and be unable to proceed, but to his surprise the animal pressed through without difficulty, while he himself—accustomed to clear all sorts of hedges—followed only with effort. And now the stag paused. There he stood large and beautiful, in color like a yellow horse, with long silken hair on his neck. Hubert stood on his right, his spear raised to strike, when suddenly the animal cast upon him a glance full of gentleness, and behold, right between its antlers shone a dazzling crucifix! Hubert sank on his knees and sounded his horn. When his companions came up, they found him unconscious. The apparition was still visible; but soon the crucifix vanished, the stag resumed its original size and disappeared. Then I saw Hubert borne back to the house on the barrow between the asses.

Hubert was a Christian. His father seemed to be a rather impoverished duke, for his castle was greatly out of repair. When a boy, Hubert had had in a wilderness an apparition of a youth who invited him to follow him alone; but the happy impression then produced had been dispelled by his love for the chase. On another occasion he pursued a lamb until the little creature took shelter in a thorn bush. Hubert built a fire around it; but the flames and smoke turned upon himself, leaving the lamb unharmed. Hubert was taken back so ill that it was thought he would die. He was deeply contrite and promised, if God would prolong his life, he would hereafter serve Him faithfully. He recovered, his wife died, and I saw him clothed in a hermit's garb.

He was favored with a vision in which he received as a reward for his self-victory that all the ardor and energy of his baneful passions should be changed into the gift of healing. By the imposition of hands he cured both soul and body of all maladies engendered by wrath, fury, or thirst for blood; he even cured brute animals. He laid his girdle in the jaws of mad dogs, and they were instantly cured. I saw him baking and blessing little loaves, round for men, oblong for brutes, with which he cured madness. I saw, as a certain fact, that whoever confidently invokes this saint will be protected by his merits and healing power against the attacks of rage and madness. I saw Hubert also in Rome, and the pope, in consequence of a vision, consecrating him bishop.

Ignatius of Loyola
(Xavier, Aloysius, and Others of His Order)

Ignatius of Loyola

DURING my last great sufferings, I had by me the relic that Dean Overberg sent me. All at once it became brilliant and—as I prayed to know what relic it was—I saw a resplendent figure surrounded by a white aureola descending toward me from on high. The light issuing from the relic united, as usual, with that from the apparition, and I heard interiorly these words: "That is one of my bones. I am Ignatius!" After that I had a long night of torture, of expiatory sufferings. It was as if a knife were being slowly buried in my breast and then turned round and round on all sides, and my wounds pained me so intensely that I could not repress my groans and complaints. I cried to our Lord for mercy. I begged him not to let me suffer beyond my strength, for I feared I should yield to impatience. I gained by my prayers an apparition of our

Lord, under the form of a youth, my divine spouse, and I was inexpressibly consoled. In a few words—which I cannot repeat precisely—he said, "I have placed thee on my nuptial couch of pain. I have lavished upon thee the graces of suffering, the treasures of atonement, and the jewels of good works. Thou must suffer, but I shall not abandon thee. Thou art bound to the vine, thou wilt not be lost." In such words as these the Savior consoled me, and I suffered patiently and quietly the rest of the night.

Toward morning I had another vision of St. Ignatius. I saw his relic shining. I invoked the dear saint—whom I now knew—and clasped his relic lovingly and reverently. I called to him through the sweet heart of Jesus. He immediately came as before, the two lights uniting, and again I heard the words: "That is my bone!" He consoled me, telling me that he had received everything from Jesus. He promised to stand my friend, to assist me in my labors, to relieve me in my pains, and he bade me make the usual devotions in his honor during the following month. Then he arose in the air and vanished, after which I saw some scenes of his life.

I thought that I lay on a little bed at the entrance of a church whose choir was shut off by a grating. There were some people in the church, but not many. In the choir were about twelve of Ignatius's companions, among whom I recognized Francis Xavier and Favre. It seemed as if they were about to start on a journey. They were not all priests. They wore a habit something like that of Ignatius, but not exactly like it. It was very early, and still quite dark; the candles were burning on the altar. Ignatius, not entirely vested for mass, a stole around his neck, and attended by another who carried the holy water, passed down the church among his companions and gave the blessing with the asperges. I too prepared to receive it. He came, indeed, to my little bed and sprinkled me abundantly. At the same instant I experienced a sensation of sweet relief throughout my whole being. Returning to the sacristy, he came forth again in full vestments and went to the altar for mass, during which a flame suddenly appeared over his head. One of the twelve ran with outstretched arms to his assistance, but when he saw his countenance all on fire he respectfully retired. Then, when mass was over, I saw the saint led from the altar by his companions. He was bathed in tears and so agitated as to be unable to walk. His mass usually lasted an hour, much longer than our ordinary masses.

After that I saw men whom I had before seen in a maritime city introduced to the pope. He was in a large hall seated on a magnificent chair before a table covered with papers and writing materials. The pope wore a short cloak; I think it was red. I know for certain that he wore a red skull-cap. At the door were standing several ecclesiastics. The companions of Ignatius entered. They knelt before the pope and one spoke in the name of all. I do not remember distinctly whether Ignatius was there or not. The pope blessed them and gave them some papers.

Then I saw some other pictures of the saint's life:

I saw him make so earnest a confession of his past life to a bad priest that the latter burst into tears, quite converted. Again, I saw him while on a journey suddenly leave his companions and go to a house in which dwelt a bad man, a slave to his passions. I saw the latter trying to elude the saint who, however, caught him. Falling on his knees before him, he embraced him and implored him to think of his salvation. The man was converted and followed him. I saw the saint in a beggar's garb, journeying alone through a gloomy, mountainous district, and the devil lying in wait for him under the form of a dragon with a thin body and a great, crispy head. Ignatius drove his stick into its neck, from which there immediately issued fire. He then pinned him down firmly with a stake, took up his stick, and coolly went on his way.

That evening the pilgrim found Anne Catherine reciting in a low voice and without a book the Office of St. Ignatius in Latin. When finished, she related what follows:

I received from Ignatius such comfort and kindness, I saw him so penetrated with ardent love for Jesus that I turned earnestly and reverently toward him, and his apparition descended from on high in a beam of light, the most holy Name of Jesus shining in his heart like a sun. Then I wanted to make some devotions in his honor, when lo! words and antiphons streamed toward me from him, and I found great sweetness in this gift of prayer.

She concluded her devotions then with the prayer Oratio recitanda ante imaginem Sancti Ignatii, *a prayer to be recited before the image of St. Ignatius. The following night Ignatius again appeared to her and strengthened her to endure her pains. Next day she related the following vision to the pilgrim:*

I saw Ignatius and Xavier and their intimate union of heart in Jesus Christ. I saw them shedding around consolation and relief while they instructed and served the sick and incurable. As I contemplated their powerful and efficacious action among the people, my heart turned to them with the words: "If during your life as frail creatures you so loved and served in the strength God gave you, O how much more efficacious must be your influence now that you revel in light and love! See, here are your sacred relics that once labored so much for your fellow-men! O help us still! Work, pour around grace, O ye perfect vessels of the fountain of grace!" Then all things earthly vanished and I saw the two saints in heaven standing together in a sphere of light. Ignatius's aureola was perfectly white; Xavier's of a rosy tinge, something like the glory of a martyr. And while I gazed upon them, while life and light streamed down upon me from them, my soul rose up and gave back as it were in heartfelt, earnest prayer the light and love God shed upon me through them.

Just as I received yesterday the prayer to Ignatius, so today words of love and joy flowed into my soul, and I called all creatures to praise and to invoke; my heart swelled and poured itself out in jubilation.

I praised and prayed through all the choirs of the blessed, and the whole heavenly court was set in motion. My prayer went up to God through our Lord Jesus Christ, to Christ through his Holy Mother, to the Holy Mother through all the saints, and to all the saints through Ignatius and Xavier. It seemed as if I knew exactly what flowers and fruits, what perfumes, what colors, what precious stones and pearls, were the purest, the most agreeable to my God; as if from the inexhaustible abundance of these treasures I had lovingly made and presented to him a crown, a pyramid, a throne; and as if all precious things streamed down to me in the light from the two saints.[1]

---

[1] That afternoon, the pilgrim having read to her an old canticle of Sts. Ignatius and Xavier in which all creatures are invited to praise the heavenly choirs, she exclaimed: "That's it! That is just the way I prayed to them!"

In this jubilee of prayer and praise and supplication, the vision continued to unfold before my soul; but with this change—I went with the two saints into the heavenly Jerusalem. What words can describe the joy, the bliss, the splendor that I there beheld!

It was not as when I saw it before with its walls and gates—a city seated on the summit of the mountain of Life—but it was an immense world of light and splendor, the streets stretching far and wide in all directions, and all in perfect regularity, order, harmony, and unending love. High up, over the center of the city, in light incomprehensible, I see the Most Holy Trinity and the twenty-four Ancients, and below in a world of glory the angelic host. I see the saints in their different ranks, bands, and hierarchies, all in their own palaces, on their own thrones, and in their various relations. They with whom I am more particularly connected, whom I honor most frequently, whose relics I have, are more distinct to me—or rather I am nearer to them—and they introduce me to the others. I have seen, also, their wonderful influence.

When I invoked them, they turned to the Most Holy Trinity, from whom streamed rays of light upon them; then they went to some marvelous trees and bushes that stood between the palaces and gathered fruit, dew, and honey, which they sent down upon the earth. I saw the part the angels play. They are swift as lightning, passing quickly to and fro, carrying blessings down to earth and, as it were, multiplying them. I saw Ignatius and Xavier scattering graces over my own land, chiefly on those for whom I had prayed, and sending quantities of dew and honey into far-off countries. I saw in separate pictures sufferers relieved and becoming fervent; people suddenly converted and changing their life; in dark, distant countries light shining out and increasing in brilliancy, and holy souls praying in its brightness. I saw that the saints do indeed dispense graces everywhere, but more especially where their relics repose and where they are invoked. These relics shine with the same light and color as the saints themselves; they always appear as a part of themselves.

I saw many holy men around Ignatius: Francis Borgia, Charles Borromeo, Aloysius, Stanislaus Kostka, Francis Regis, and numerous others. I saw *him* also.[1] I saw him not with Ignatius but in a choir of bishops. I saw multitudes whom I knew, and I drew near many of them by prayer. At first I dared look only at Ignatius, the others I saw from a distance; but all were so kind and good that after a while I ventured to go around among them.

The streets were paved with pearls in all shapes and figures, and some of them also with stars. I thought in my simplicity (for it was dull nature thinking: "Look! there are the stars that we see above the earth!") that I saw, too, Augustine and his whole order, and Bishop Ludger with a church in his hand as he is usually represented, and many others with their various insignia, some of whom I recognized, among them St. Joachim and St. Anne. I was quite sure about the last-named, as this is Tuesday, the day on which I always honor holy mother Anne. Both held a green branch and, as I knew not what it signified, I was given to understand that it was a sign of their ardent desire for the advent of the messiah who was to spring from them according to the flesh. Then I had visions of their ardent desires, their prayer, mortification, and penance.

The whole night I was consoled in the midst of my pains by these contemplations. I cannot repeat all the magnificent things I saw, nor their truth and clearness. The figures were not thrown together at random but formed one grand whole—one explained another, lived and loved in the other. During this vision my heart beat with joy, my lips sang canticles of praise.

[1] Anne Catherine said this while pointing to someone who seemed to appear at the moment. The pilgrim thought, at first, that she meant St. Francis of Assisi, but it was St. Francis de Sales whom she beheld before her, attracted by his relic lying near. She was in ecstasy, her eyes wide open, and—forgetful of our blindness to the spirit world—spoke to us as if we could see what she herself saw. CB

Aloysius

I WAS at a grand spiritual festival, a great solemnity with numerous processions: maidens in white with lilies in their hands carried the Mother of God on a throne, and then came Aloysius borne by youths also in white. The saint wore over his black habit a white surplice with golden fringe, and like his companions bore a lily in his hand. There were a great many white banners with gold fringe. Aloysius sat on a throne above the altar, and above him again was enthroned the Mother of God, to whom he was espoused. The upper part of the church was filled with the heavenly choirs, and around Aloysius were Ignatius, Xavier, Borgia, Borromeo, Stanislaus, Regis, and numbers of other holy Jesuits. Higher up were crowds of other holy religious, and there were countless souls of youths, maidens, and children who by following the example of Aloysius had found favor with the Lord. Only the Blessed were in the church.

When Aloysius had been honored with garlands, crowns, etc., he in his turn honored those who had paid him homage; for such is the custom at these feasts—the honored one becomes the servant. I cannot describe the splendor of the scene; it was the feast of chastity and innocence, of humility and love.

Then I saw the saint's life. I saw him still a little boy alone in a large hall whose walls were hung with all kinds of armor, among which was a knapsack. The child seemed to be attracted by it. He unbuckled it, took out a large box that appeared to contain firearms, and carried it away with him. But soon he was seized with remorse. He returned weeping bitterly and replaced it in the knapsack. He was full of repentance for the theft. Then I saw a tall female enter the hall, go to the child—who was leaning against the wall under the knapsack—and try to comfort him. She led him still weeping to his parents, who were in a beautiful room, and he confessed his fault with many tears. I saw him afterward entrusted to a man who was always with him.

I saw him while still a child sick in bed for a long time, but so patient that all the servants loved him. I saw them carrying him around in their arms and, in spite of his fever and sufferings, he always smiled on them sweetly. I saw him in another very grand house. He was always a gentle, earnest boy. Again, I saw him sitting in the midst of ecclesiastics, speaking to them gravely while they listened in deep attention, highly edified at his words. They seemed to be preparing him for holy communion but, enlightened by God, the pupil taught his masters. He was filled with wonderful devotion and intense desire for the holy eucharist. Wherever he was, wherever he went, he always turned toward the blessed sacrament in some church. He often drew on the wall of his room a chalice with a host or a monstrance, before which he prayed with inexpressible devotion, quickly effacing it on the approach of anyone. It reminded me of St. Barbara, whom I had seen doing the same in her prison.

I saw him afterward in a church receiving holy communion, the sacred host shining before him and, as it were, flying into his mouth. Then I saw him in the convent, his cell so small as to admit of no furniture but a bed. I often beheld him radiant with light when he disciplined himself and prayed. It was told me that his greatest sin had been a distraction for the space of an *Ave Maria* at the end of a prayer that had lasted all day.

Aloysius's companions loved him very much. They used to follow him to the door of his cell, which however he would never allow them to enter for fear of their praising his poverty.

Anne Catherine wept when the pilgrim told her that St. Aloysius's father had tried to prevent his entrance into religion.

Isidore

I SAW many scenes of the saintly peasant in Isidore's[1] domestic life. His costume was quite gay: a short brown jacket with buttons before and behind, a scalloped trimming on the shoulders, and scalloped cuffs; his small-clothes short and wide trimmed with ribands, his feet laced. His low cap was of four pieces, turned up and caught together by a button on the crown; it looked a little like a biretta.

---

[1] Isidore the Farm Laborer, also known as Isidore the Farmer (c. 1070–May 15, 1130), was a Spanish farm worker known for his piety toward the poor and animals. He is the Catholic patron saint of farmers and of Madrid. His real

Isidore was a tall, handsome man, with nothing of the peasant in his appearance; his features and his whole demeanor were very distinguished. His wife too was tall, beautiful and, like himself, holy. They had one son, whom I saw with them, once as a very young child, and again when about twelve years old. Their house stood near an open field about half a league from the city, which they could distinctly see. In it reigned order and neatness. I saw that it had other occupants beside Isidore and his family, but they were not his servants.

Isidore and his wife accompanied all their actions with prayer; they blessed each particular kind of food. Isidore never knelt long in prayer before he was rapt in contemplation. I saw him, as he passed along the fields before beginning his work, blessing the earth, and he always received supernatural assistance in his husbandry. I often saw several ploughs with white oxen and driven by shining apparitions breaking up the ground before him. His work was always finished before he had hardly thought of it; which circumstance, however, he appeared not to notice, as his mind was ever fixed on God. When he heard the bells in the city, he used to leave everything standing just as it was in the fields and run to holy mass or other devotions, at which he assisted, ravished in spirit. When the service was over he would return joyously to find his work finished.

Once I saw his little boy driving the plough to the field. The oxen appeared rather unmanageable. Suddenly the bells rang for mass and off ran Isidore to the church. The restive animals became calm and, guided by the weak child, went on quietly with the work until their master's return. On another occasion, as Isidore was

---

name was Isidro de Merlo y Quintana. He was born in Madrid of poor but very devout parents and christened Isidore from the name of their patron, St. Isidore of Seville. Isidore spent his life as a hired hand in the service of the wealthy Madrilenian landowner on a farm in the city's vicinity. He shared what he had, even his meals, with the poor. It was said that he stood two meters (6.5 feet) tall. Isidore and his wife Maria had one son. On one occasion their son fell into a deep well and, at the prayers of his parents, the water of the well is said to have risen miraculously to the level of the ground, bringing the child with it. In thanksgiving Isidore and Maria then vowed sexual abstinence and lived in separate houses.

praying before the blessed sacrament, a messenger hurried in to tell him that a wolf was tearing his horse to pieces. But Isidore stirred not; he recommended the affair to God and, when he returned to the field he found the wolf stretched dead before the horse. I often saw his wife in the fields with him, at morning and noon, hoeing the ground, invisible workmen laboring by them. Their task was soon accomplished. Isidore's field was more luxuriant, more productive than any others; its fruits appeared to be of superior quality. He and his wife gave all they had to the poor, and sometimes, when they had nothing at all in the house, they recurred to God with great confidence. Then they sought again and found abundant provisions. I often saw Isidore's enemies trying to injure his cattle when he left them to go to mass, but they were always hindered and put to flight. I had many other pictures of his holy life, and then I saw him among the saints; once in his odd-looking peasant costume, and again, as a blessed, shining soul.

Justina and Cyprian

I SAW Justina, a child in the courtyard of her father's residence, which was only a square from the pagan temple of which he was a priest. She was with her nurse. She went down into a cistern, where she stood on a stone in the middle of the water. Underneath were numerous holes in which different kinds of serpents and horrible-looking creatures lurked. They were kept and fed there. I saw Justina coolly take up a large serpent in one hand and several smaller ones in the other. She held them by the tail and amused herself watching them straightening themselves up like tapers, their heads moving from side to side. They did not hurt her; they were quite at home with her. Among them were some about a foot long, like those we call chubs (salamanders); they were used in the worship of the idols.

Justina once heard in a Christian church a sermon on the fall of humankind and the redemption. She was so impressed by it that she received baptism and converted her mother. The latter informed her husband who, having been very much troubled by an apparition, was baptized also with his wife, and they afterward lived most piously and happily.

One scene struck me especially. Justina had a lovely round face and the most beautiful yellow hair that shone like gold. It was wound round her head in exquisite silken braids, or fell on her shoulders in luxuriant curls. I saw her standing at table by her father and mother, eating little loaves. The father, glancing with admiration at her hair, said: "I fear, my child, you will not be able to pass through the world. Like Absalom, you will remain hanging in it by your hair." Justina had never thought of her hair, and these words made her very grave. She withdrew, and I know not what she did to her beautiful hair, but she completely disfigured it as well as her eyebrows. They looked as if she had singed them. In this trim she went through the city to her father, who scarcely recognized her.

I saw a youth in love with her. He was about to carry her off by force, as he could not hope to win her. He waited for her with armed companions in a lonely road between walls; but when he seized her, she repulsed him with both hands, commanding him to remain standing where he was. And there he stood until she was out of danger. Then I saw the same youth engaging the assistance of the magician Cyprian, who confidently promised him success.

This Cyprian, though he was naturally noble and generous, was entirely given up to necromancy. In his youth he had been instructed in sorcery. He had journeyed afar in pursuit of knowledge and had finally settled with great renown in Antioch, where Justina and her parents had been converted. He was a bitter pagan. He had gone so far as often to revile Jesus in the Christian churches and to chase the people out by his sorcery. I used to see him calling to the demon. He had in his house a semi-subterranean vaulted cellar that was lighted from above. Around the walls stood hideous idols in the form of animals and serpents. In one corner was a hollow statue the size of a man, the open jaws resting on the edge of a round altar on which was a pan of live coals. When Cyprian invoked the demon he put on a particular costume, lighted the fire on the altar, read certain names from a roll of parchment mounted upon the altar, and pronounced the same into the jaws of the idol. Instantly the spirit stood in human form beside him, under the appearance of a servant. There was something sinister and frightful, like a bad conscience, in the features of these apparitions. The spirit twice attempted to seduce Justina under the form of a youth, waylaying her in the courtyard; but she put him to flight by the sign of the cross and escaped his influence by the crosses she erected in the corners of her room.

Then I saw her in a secret vault of her house, kneeling in prayer before a niche in which were a cross and a little white infant. The latter seemed to be in a case, the upper part of the body free, its tiny hands crossed. While Justina thus knelt, a youth approached her from behind with evil intentions; when suddenly I saw the apparition of a lady, as if coming out of the wall, and the youth sank to the earth even before Justina had perceived his presence. She turned and fled.

Another time I saw her completely destroy her beauty with ointment. I saw Cyprian gliding around and sprinkling Justina's house at an unguarded moment for her, when she was not in prayer. She became violently agitated, ran around the house, and at last fled to her chamber, where before the crosses she had herself set up, she knelt in prayer until the charm was broken. When Cyprian made his third attempt, the enemy appeared under the form of a pious young girl who conversed with Justina on the subject of chastity. The latter was at first very much pleased; but when her companion began to speak of Adam, Eve, and marriage, Justina recognized the tempter and fled to her crosses.

Cyprian saw all this in spirit and became a Christian. I saw him lying prostrate in a church, even allowing himself to be trodden under foot as a fool. He was deeply penitent and he burned all his books on magic. He afterward became a bishop and placed Justina among the deaconesses. She dwelt next to the church. She made and embroidered grand church vestments. Later I saw both Cyprian and Justina martyred. They were hung by one hand to a tree and torn with hooks.

Louis of France

IT was shown me how St. Louis of France at the age of seven prepared by a rigorous fast for his First Communion. He told this to his mother. She had accompanied him to the church to implore the Mother of God for light as to whether her son should receive holy communion or not. Mary appeared to her and said that her son must prepare for seven days and then communicate, that she should receive at the same time and offer her boy to her (Mary) and she would ever be his protectress. I saw that all took place as was directed, and I learned that religious instruction at that period was both given and received in a different and more earnest manner than in our day. In all his expeditions, Louis had the blessed sacrament with him, and wherever he encamped the holy sacrifice was offered.

I saw Louis on the crusade. Once during a violent tempest the crew of his own vessel and those of the other ships cried to him for help, begging him to intercede with God for their delivery from danger. As the blessed sacrament was not on board, the saintly king took up a newborn, baptized infant, went on deck, and held it up in the storm, begging God to show pity for its sake. Then, turning slowly around, he gave benediction with the child, and the storm instantly ceased. He afterward exhorted his grateful people to an increase of devotion toward the blessed sacrament, telling them that if God had wrought so great a miracle for the sake of an innocent baptized child, what would He not do for the sake of His only Son?

Madeline of Hadamar and Colomba Schanold of Bamberg
(Two Stigmatics)

THE *pilgrim presented Anne Catherine a scrap of cloth stained with blood from the wounded side of Madeline of Hadamar. She was in ecstasy at the time, but she instantly exclaimed:*

What shall I do with this long garment? I cannot go to the nun; it is too far away! They tormented her so that she could not finish her task; she died before it was fully accomplished.

These words were incomprehensible to the pilgrim; but the following more extended vision she had later on explained all:

I have seen little Madeline, to whom the garment once belonged. But I saw her only at a distance; she could not come to me. I saw her in the cemetery of her convent. In one corner stands a little ossuary with the station of our Savior carrying the cross. Nearby on the churchyard wall there is another station of the *Via Crucis.* An elder tree and a nut hedge make it a shady, retired spot. All around lay piles of unfinished work, sewing, etc., which I was to arrange and finish. I fell earnestly to work, making, mending, and at the same time saying my breviary until I began to perspire profusely and feel violent pains in my hair. Every hair seemed to have its own peculiar pain. The good little Madeline had indulged her devotion too much in this pleasant nook, so well suited to prayer, and so had neglected much work begun for the poor.

When at last I had leveled the mountain, I found myself standing before a cupboard in a small house. Madeline came forward joyously thanking me as if she had not seen anyone for a long time. She opened the cupboard, and there I saw stowed away all the morsels of which she had deprived herself for the poor. As she thanked me for arranging and finishing her work, she said: "In life we can do in one hour what we can, by no means, make amends for in the other world, if left undone here!"—and she promised me some pieces for my poor children. She told me that through kindheartedness she had undertaken more than she could accomplish; and that order and discretion are essential in time of suffering, else confusion arises.

Madeline was not tall; she was very thin, though her face was full and rosy. She showed me her parents' house and even the door through which she had left it on going to the convent. I saw then many scenes of her cloistered life.

She was exceedingly kind and obliging, doing the work of others whenever she could. I saw her also sick in bed, suddenly attacked by different maladies, and just as suddenly cured. I saw her wounds bleeding, and I saw the supernatural relief she received in her sufferings. When the prioress or any other nun stood by her, I beheld on the opposite side of the bed the forms of angels or deceased religious, floating down to her, consoling her, supporting her, or giving her a drink.

She was well treated by her fellow-sisters, but her state became too public and she had to endure much from visits and false veneration. Her case was imprudently exaggerated, and this caused her great vexation, as she told me herself. Her confessor published an account of her state, rather expressive of his own admiration than a faithful record of facts.

After the suppression of her convent, she was subjected to an inquiry in which both ecclesiastics and surgeons took part; but the former were indifferent and left everything to the physicians. I saw nothing improper, but these men were very rude and coarse, though far less false and crafty than those with whom I had to deal. They tormented her exceedingly, trying above all to make her eat. Such attempts always brought on vomiting.

Even as a child, Madeline had been accustomed to privation, her parents being very poor, though very good people. Her mother particularly used often to say to her child at meals: "Now, one bite less, one mouthful less for the poor, for the suffering souls!" There were many wonderful things about Madeline, but she had become too public. She died before her time. She fretted and kept her sorrows to herself, consequently her life was shortened. I saw her death, not the ceremonies nor the obsequies, but the soul departing from her body.

When the pilgrim again approached Anne Catherine with the stained linen, she cried out: Why, there you are, little darling! O, she is so active and kind, so obliging and charitable!

Then, after a long silence, she asked in a quick, animated tone: Why did Jesus say to Magdalene, "Woman, why weepest thou?" I know, my affianced told me why he thus spoke! Magdalene had sought him so eagerly and impetuously that, when she did meet him, she took him for a gardener. Then said he: "Woman, why weepest thou?" But when she exclaimed: "Master!" and recognized him, he said to her: "Mary! As we seek, so we find!"

I saw all this by little Madeline. I saw her lying in a small, dark room into which many persons entered; they were going to examine her case. They were rough, but not wicked like those who examined into mine. They spoke of an enema, at which Madeline showed too great unwillingness. She began to complain, but when she resigned herself to their treatment her vexation vanished. It was at this moment that I had the vision of the garden before her window. Perhaps she had had the same herself, since she despaired of finding her affianced, although he was at her side. Madeline still owes me the pieces she promised me.

I saw also the Dominican nun Colomba Schanold of Bamberg. She was inexpressibly humble, simple-hearted, and unaffected; and notwithstanding her stigmata she was ever active and laborious. I saw her in her cell, praying prostrate on the ground as if dead. Again, I saw her in bed, her hands bleeding and blood flowing down from under her veil. I saw her receiving the holy eucharist, the form of a little luminous child escaping to her from the hand of the priest; and I saw also the visions she had had. They passed before her in pictures as she lay in her bed, or knelt in prayer. They were scenes from the life of our Lord, or others, for her own direction and consolation. She wore a haircloth, and around her waist a chain, until forbidden to do so.

Colomba was very well off in her convent, much less importuned than Madeline. She was consequently further advanced in the interior life, more simple, more recollected. I saw her also occupying a higher rank in the other world. But the way in which one sees such things cannot be explained. The clearest manner of expressing it is, that she traveled farther.

Marcella

FATHER *Limberg presented Anne Catherine a little package marked "St. Clement," asking if it really was a relic of Pope St. Clement. She laid it by her and next day answered, no, it was not St. Clement's, but one of St. Marcella, a widow. The confessor asked for more precise details. After some days, she gave the following:*

I have again seen the life of Marcella. I saw her as a widow living very retired in a beautiful large house built in Roman style, like St. Cecilia's; around it were gardens, courtyards, and fountains. I often saw St. Jerome with her opening rolls of writings. Marcella gave all she had to the poor and to prisoners, whom she used to visit by night—the prison doors opening of themselves to admit her. She was so deeply impressed on reading the life of St. Antony that she put on a veil and the monastic dress, and influenced young maidens to do the same.

I saw a strange people enter and pillage Rome. They tried to extort money from Marcella by blows, but she had given all to the poor. This is all I remember. The first time I saw her, she encouraged me respecting my visions on the holy scriptures and told me something for my confessor. But I have entirely forgotten it.

Marcellus and Lucina

ANOTHER *relic Anne Catherine recognized as belonging to St. Marcellus, of whom she related the following*: I had a vision of the saint. He used to go with his companions by night to hunt up the bodies of the martyrs and give them Christian burial, inscribing their names over their resting places. I often saw him going around by night with bones in his mantle. He carried also many holy bodies into the catacombs, laid rolls of writings by them—principally the acts of their martyrdom—and marked them. I think it was he who brought many of the things into the great vault in which I once saw so many relics preserved. I remarked again that we have many precious relics here, for many belong to bodies that Marcellus labeled.

I have seen the holy widow Lucina. She begged Marcellus to bury two martyrs who had long before perished of hunger in prison. During the night he and Lucina bore the remains of a man and a woman to the place where St. Lawrence lay buried; but as they attempted to lay them by him, the bones of Lawrence recoiled, as if unwilling to have them near him, and so they buried them elsewhere.

Later, I saw Marcellus led before the emperor. On his refusal to offer sacrifice, he was scourged to blood and sent to take charge of a large stable. The stable was circular, built around a court, and there were in it not only beasts of burden but also cages for the beasts intended to be let loose upon the martyrs. These Marcellus had to feed, but they were tame and gentle with him. Here, too, he found means to assist his brethren in secret.

Through the intervention of Lucina, who bribed the jailers, Marcellus often left the prison by night to bury the dead and encourage the faithful. I saw, also, that he received the blessed sacrament from other priests and distributed it by night. He was at last liberated, again imprisoned, and again liberated for having cured the wife of a great personage. After this he lived retired in the house of Lucina, which he secretly converted into a church, and wherein he practiced, as usual, his works of mercy. But his enemies again attacked him, turned the house into a stable, and condemned him to serve in it. As he still persevered in his spiritual labors for souls, they had him horribly scourged with the whips used for the beasts of burden. He died in a corner of the stable, on the ground, and the Christians gave him burial.

Margaret of Antioch

I SAW the life of St. Margaret of Antioch. Her father was a very distinguished pagan, a priest of Antioch, who resided in a splendid mansion almost like that of St. Agnes. There was a benediction attached to Margaret's birth, for she came into the world radiant with light. Her mother must have had some connection with Christianity, for I saw her die happily soon after the birth of her babe. She died with a great desire of baptism and requesting that Margaret might be reared a Christian. The father gave the infant over to a nurse who lived in the country, an unmarried woman, who had had a child and lost it, and who was now a Christian in secret. So impressed was she by the wonderful wisdom of her charge that she became most pious and virtuous and reared the child in a truly Christian manner. I often saw her mother and the angels bending over Margaret's crib.

On one occasion when the nurse took the child into the city to see its father, he wanted to present the little thing before his idols; but she struggled so violently that he had to desist, which circumstance very much provoked him. In her sixth year, I saw her placed by him at a school over which a pagan teacher presided. There were many children in it, boys and girls, with their mistresses. I often saw angelic apparitions and divine direction vouchsafed to Margaret. She learned all kinds of embroidery and how to make stuffed dolls. After a time her master sent her on a visit to her father, who tried to make her sacrifice to his idols. She absolutely refused and was severely punished. Her young companions all loved her and aimed at being with her. I often saw her punished, yes, even flogged on account of her Christian tendencies.

In her twelfth year I saw her shut up with youths charged to corrupt her, but she was always divinely protected. Once she was called upon to sacrifice in the temple. She refused, and was again severely punished by her father, who sent her with some others to guard sheep.

A distinguished judge of Antioch, happening to pass, noticed the maiden and asked her of her father in marriage. She was then taken back to the city and, as she declared herself a Christian, was submitted to trial and torture. Once I saw her in prison all bruised and mangled. As she knelt in prayer, her mother and an angel appeared and healed her, after which she had a vision of a fountain out of which arose a cross. By it she understood that her martyrdom was nigh. The fountain was emblematic of her baptism.

When her persecutors found her perfectly healed, they attributed the miracle to their gods; but Margaret cursed their idols. I saw her led to execution, burned with torches, and cast into a ditch. She was tied to stakes with several others and sunk so deep that the water rose above her head. Margaret had plunged into the water with an ardent desire of its being to her a baptism—at which a luminous cloud in the form of a cross descended upon her and an angel appeared bearing a crown. The miracle was witnessed by many of those around; they immediately confessed Christ, were imprisoned, and martyred.

But now a mighty earthquake shook the place, the virgin's fetters were severed, and she came forth from the water safe and sound. Then arose a tumult, in the midst of which she was reconducted to her prison. As she stood in prayer I saw a huge dragon with the head of a lion dart upon her; but Margaret thrust her hand into his jaws, made the sign of the cross, and forced his head into the ground. At the same moment two men with evil intentions rushed into her prison, but the earth trembled and they fled.

I saw the maiden again led to a place where an immense multitude was assembled. Around her was stationed a troop of girls for the purpose of intimidating her; but she begged leave to speak and addressed them so feelingly that they confessed Christ aloud and were beheaded with her.

This saint is invoked by women in childbed because her own mother died happily while giving her birth and, also, because in cruel sufferings she had herself brought forth many daughters to the Lord.

I had afterward a horrible vision which, at first, I knew not how to connect with Margaret. I saw a huge, frightful hog making its way out of a deep marsh. The sight of it made me tremble with horror. It was the soul of a noble Parisian lady who came to tell me not to pray for her, as it could do her no good. She was condemned to wallow in the mire till the end of the world. She implored me to pray for the conversion of her daughter, that she might not be the occasion of as many sins as she herself had been.

My vision of Margaret took place in a little chapel at Paris, the last remains of a ruined abbey, in which a portion of the martyr's arm and skull is still preserved. As I venerated these relics I saw the soul of the unhappy lady and scenes from her life, for her tomb was near the chapel. She was of high rank and had caused much mischief during the Revolution; through her intervention many priests had been put to death. With all her wickedness, she had yet preserved her youthful veneration for Margaret and, through her influence, the saint's chapel had been spared; therefore was the favor accorded her of being permitted to ask prayers for her daughter and thereby cut off the consequences of her own sins. I saw the daughter leading a worldly life. She was connected with the worst and most dangerous political parties in the country.

Nicholas of Flüe

ANNE *Catherine in her humility was often occupied with this thought: "For what have I, poor sinner, deserved that my persecutors should render themselves so guilty on my account?"—and although God had given her the consolation of knowing that she was not responsible, she begged for special sufferings to expiate their offence. From the last week in October, she was a prey to interior abandonment, while her frame was consumed by fever, her tongue adhered to her palate, and she had not the strength to reach the water placed at her side. The pain in her wounds often drew tears, and sometimes made her swoon away. These were sufferings she had voluntarily embraced for the good of her neighbor. In her distress she was consoled by an apparition of Blessed Nicholas von der Flüe,*[1] *who said to her: "I shall be your very good friend, I shall help you a little," and he held out to her a little bunch of herbs the smell of which gave her strength. "You suffer," he said, "in every member of your body, because the faults for which you atone are so manifold."*

On the nineteenth Sunday after Pentecost is read the gospel of the wedding feast and the nuptial robe. That night Blessed Nicholas was her guide in the following vision:

I saw Blessed Nicholas as a great, tall man with hair like silver. He wore a low notched crown, sparkling with precious stones; his tunic, which descended to the ankles, was white as snow, and he held in his hand another crown higher than his own and set with jewels. I asked him why he held that resplendent crown instead of the bunch of herbs. He spoke earnestly and in few words of my death, of my destiny, and said that he would take me to a great wedding feast. He placed the crown on my head, and I flew with him into the palace that I saw in the air above me. I was to be a bride, but I was so timid and ashamed that I knew not what to do.

It was a wedding of wonderful magnificence. I beheld the manners and customs of all classes of society on the occasion of a marriage festival, and the action of deceased ancestors upon their descendants.

First of all was the banquet for the clergy. Here I saw the pope, and bishops with their croziers and episcopal robes, and many others of the clergy, high and low. Above each one, in an upper choir, were the saints of his race, his ancestors, his patrons, and the protectors of his charge, who acted through him, judging and deciding. At this table there were also spiritual affianced of the highest rank. With my crown on my head, I had to join them as their equal, which filled me with confusion. They were all still living, though as yet they had no crowns. Above me stood the one

---

[1] Nicholas of Flüe (1417–March 21, 1487) was a Swiss hermit and ascetic who is the patron saint of Switzerland. He is sometimes invoked as Brother Klaus. A farmer, military leader, member of the assembly, councilor, judge, and mystic, he was respected as a man of complete moral integrity. Brother Klaus's counsel to the Diet of Stans (1481) helped prevent war between the Swiss cantons.

who had invited me, and as I was so abashed, he managed everything for me. The dishes on the table looked like earthly food, but they were not such in reality. I saw through everything, I read all hearts.

Back of the banquet hall were many different rooms filled with people, and there were new arrivals at every moment. Many among the ecclesiastics seated at the banquet were ordered out as unworthy, for they had mixed with worldlings, had served them rather than the Church. The worldlings were punished first, then the ecclesiastics were banished to other apartments, more or less remote. The number of the just was very small. This was the first table and the first hour.

The clergy withdrew and another table was prepared, at which I did not sit. I stood among the spectators, Blessed Nicholas still above me to help me. Emperors, kings, and sovereign princes placed themselves at table, great lords served them, and above were the saints reckoned among the ancestors of each. To my great embarrassment some of the kings noticed me, but Nicholas came to my aid and always answered for me. They sat not long at table. They were all alike, their actions imperfect, weak and inconsistent; if one happened to be a little superior to his fellows, it was not through virtue. Some came not quite up to the table, and all were sent away in their turn.

I remember in particular the Croy family. They must have had among them a holy stigmatisee, for she said to me, "See, there are the Croys!" Then came the table of the distinguished nobility, and I saw among others the good Vehme lady hovering over her family.

Then came the table of the wealthy citizens, and I cannot describe the frightful state of this class. Most of them were sent away and cast with those of the nobility who were as bad as themselves into a hole like a sewer, where they splashed about in mud and filth. After these came a class of a little better standing, honest old citizens and peasants. There were many good people here, among them my own family. My father and mother stood above my other relatives. Then came the descendants of Brother Klaus (Blessed Nicholas), right good, strong tradesmen—but some of them were rejected. Then came the poor and the crippled, from among whom many pious people were excluded, as well as the bad. I had much to do with them. Above them I saw numbers of persons and tribunals. I cannot recount all.

When the six tables were over, the holy man brought me back again to my bed from which he had taken me. I was very weak, quite unconscious; I could neither speak nor make a sign. I seemed about to die. Klaus signified to me that my life would be short, without however specifying any particular time for its close.

Again I had a great vision of persecution and I beheld my miseries increase. I saw my enemies watching, that no one should help me, and gathering up all that was said and done against me. The devil, furious with me, was rushing with open jaws on certain persons to confuse them and chase them away. But what hurt me most was that my nearest friends reproached and tormented me with inconsiderate advice and accusations. They that were willing to help me were few and they could do nothing. My persecutors assailed me in my abandonment, and I was deprived of spiritual and corporal assistance. My enemies loaded me with trials hitherto unknown. "Where," they asked, "are your spiritual superiors? Where your spiritual directors? Have they ceased to interest themselves in you? Who among the clergy are your protectors?" Their words tortured me, drove me almost wild, and the desertion of my dearest friends afflicted me keenly.

When I was almost in despair, Nicholas von der Flüe appeared. He told me to thank God for showing me these things, to arm myself with patience, and especially to avoid anger in my replies, which should be reserved, that the trial would be shorter, if borne well; and, finally, that I still had much to suffer from my friends, who would injure me and exact things of me, though not with a bad intention. If I endured this patiently, I should profit by it. He promised that the trial would not last long and that he would help me. Then he gave me his own little prayer on paper which I was to say. I had made use of it from my youth. It ran thus: "Lord, detach me from myself," etc. He gave me also a picture about the size of my hand. On top was a sun, and underneath the word "justice," from which I understood that divine justice would end my persecution. At the bottom was a face full of benevolence with the word "mercy," and this gave me the assurance that I should soon receive help from the divine mercy. Under the face was a coffin with four lighted tapers.

Nicostratus

THE bone marked *N*, belongs to Nicostratus, a Greek who when a child was led captive to Rome along with his mother and other Christians. The mother, with many others, was martyred, and the child was reared in paganism. He was a sculptor. I saw him at work with three companions. The sculptors used to dwell in a certain quarter of the city where lay numerous blocks of marble, and they worked in upper halls into which the light entered from above. They wore hoods, apparently of brown leather, to protect the face from the scraps of stone and splinters flying around.

I saw Nicostratus and his companions getting marble from the quarries in which the Christians lived concealed. In this way they became acquainted with the old priest Cyril, who was full of cordiality and good humor. There was something about Cyril that reminded me of Dean Overberg—affable, kind toward everyone, even jocose, yet at the same time full of dignity. He converted numbers by his winning manners.

Nicostratus and his fellow workmen had heard from Cyril and other Christians the history of Jesus and Mary; so they made a most beautiful statue—a veiled lady in long robes who seemed to be sorrowfully seeking something. It was exquisitely lovely! Nicostratus and Symphorian put it upon a wagon drawn by an ass and took it to Cyril. "Here," said they, smiling, "here is the Mother of your God seeking her Son," and they set down the statue before him. Cyril was charmed with its beauty. He thanked them, adding words to the effect that he would pray that she would also seek and find them; then their joking would be changed to seriousness. This he said with his kindly smile, and the youths took it, as usual, in jest. But as they returned home a strange fear and emotion took possession of both, of which however they said nothing to each other.

Some time after, they set to work on a statue of Venus when, by a miracle which I do not now recollect, they made instead of a Venus an inconceivably beautiful and modest statue of a female martyr. In consequence of this, four of the young sculptors received instructions and baptism from Cyril. After this they made no more idols, though they still continued their occupation as sculptors. Actuated by faith and piety, they marked all the stone before using it with a cross, which wonderfully facilitated the success of their labors. I saw a statue of a holy youth bound to a column and pierced with arrows; a virgin kneeling before a block, her throat pierced by a sword; and a stone coffin in which lay the remains of a holy martyr who had been crushed to death under a marble slab. I saw a fifth sculptor, still a pagan, Simplicius by name, who said to them: "I adjure you by the sun, how is it that your work succeeds so well?" They told him of Jesus and how they always marked their stone with the sign of the cross, whereupon Simplicius also asked for instruction and baptism.

The emperor Diocletian highly prized the skill of these work-men, but when it became noised around that they were Christians, he ordered them to make an idol of Aesculapius. On their refusal to do so, he commanded their arrest. They were taken before the judge and martyred. Their bodies were enclosed in leaden cases and sunk in the river. But after some days they were miraculously found by a pious man and buried, an inscription with their names being interred with them.

These leaden cases did not sink near the shore, for fine holes were bored in them, that the water might enter only gradually. A clay mould, about the size of a man, was put into a hole and a thin layer of molten lead poured around it. The mould was then with-drawn and in its stead the holy martyrs were put into the hot case and covered up, the holes were pierced, and it was thrown into the water. I saw the feast of these martyrs today (November 8, 1821), but I think the seventh is the real anniversary of their martyrdom.

Odilia

ST. Odilia accompanied me on my last night's journey to Ratis-bon. On coming to a certain house, she said, "That's where Erhard lived; he gave me sight of soul and body." It seemed to me as if it had happened only yesterday. St. Walburga joined us. We entered the house, and I had to argue some points in it—I am worn out. Neither Walburga nor Odilia wanted me to dispute so long; the latter especially was anxious to proceed, for she said: "We must go! There is a place in Austria from which they are about to carry off a bride. You must arouse her brothers, otherwise her posterity will be utterly ruined." And she gave me no rest until we had set out.

We journeyed southward to a mountainous district in Austria, in which we saw beautiful spotted cows in magnificent meadows shut in by high rocks and large bodies of standing water full of reeds. The inhabitants are a simple-minded race, some of them apparently silly. They act like children. About two leagues from a large river stands a castle surrounded by other buildings. Here dwelt the bride. She had consented to elope with a stranger who was on the watch at the gate with a carriage and servants; she had packed up secretly and was all ready to start. Her own bridegroom was away; he was too rigid, too severe for her.

Urged by Odilia, I went to arouse the brothers, who were asleep in one of the neighboring houses—a difficult undertaking, for they were sound asleep. I shook them, I called them, and at last I held to their nose a little herb I had gathered on the way. This awoke them. I told them all and made them come with me. As the bride stepped out of the courtyard we seized her gently and bore her back. The seducer waited and waited and at last rode back home in a fury. He rushed into a beautiful apartment that was adorned with artificial flowers and hung with mirrors, all borrowed for the occasion. I saw some men bringing in still more. The man was fairly beside himself with rage; he would willingly have shattered everything in the room.

This labor cost me much. I found the roads all obstructed by rocks, stones, fallen trees, beams,[1] but I received the explanation of it. The bride is a distant parish in which a certain preacher has led a large number into heresy, and they have formed a project to separate from the Church; the sleeping brothers are two of their priests, good enough, but negligent; the lawful bridegroom living at some distance is the parish priest, somewhat stern and careless

---

[1] Symbols of difficulties to be overcome. CB

also; the seducer symbolizes vain boasting and frivolous joys. When this task was ended, Odilia went toward the east, Walburga to the west, for they still had others to perform.

Paschal and Cyprian

AS I took "my church" to arrange and venerate the holy relics, I recognized a splinter of an arm bone as belonging to the holy martyr Paschal.[1] He had been paralytic from childhood, though otherwise healthy. His father suffered in a persecution of the Christians, and young Paschal and his sister found a home with their elder brother, who had a son, a priest also named Cyprian. I used to see the latter saying mass underground, for the Christians all dwelt at that period in caves, ruined walls, and even in tombs.

Cyprian was full of love and compassion for the poor cripple, who had not the use of his limbs; he was so deformed that his knees and chin met. When sixteen years old, Paschal begged to be taken to the tomb of a martyr; and about twenty persons— among them Cyprian—bore him on a litter to a place of martyrdom. They proceeded silently along by the prisons to a spot on which a saint had either been martyred or buried, I do not now remember which, and here they prayed. Paschal was in a kind of litter that could be raised or lowered at pleasure, and he prayed most fervently. Suddenly he sprang up, cast away his crutches, and joyfully thanked God for his perfect cure, which he had confidently expected in this place. I saw his friends eagerly embracing him; he returned with them perfectly cured. Then I saw in a series of pictures how pious and charitable he was, and how zealously he aided Cyprian, his brother's son, in the care of the sick and poor, carrying on his shoulders those who could not walk. His elder brother died, and I saw them burying him secretly.

---

[1] Anne Catherine had this vision on February 26, 1821; consequently, she looked upon this day as the anniversary of the martyrdom, or the miraculous discovery of the sacred remains of these two saints. According to the *Acta Sanctorum*, they were presented February 26, 1646, by Cardinal Allier to the Jesuit College of Antwerp. St. Cyprian's body was given at a later period to the College of Mechelen.

And now there broke out a great persecution, I think under the emperor Nero. Multitudes of Christians—men, women, and maidens—were gathered together in a certain quarter of the city and, after a short examination, martyred in many different ways. Trees opposite one another were bent down, and the martyrs bound to them by a leg or an arm. When the trees were allowed to resume their upright position, the Christians were torn asunder. I saw maidens hung up by the feet, their head almost touching the ground, their hands tied behind their back. While they were in this posture, spotted animals that looked like great cats devoured the breasts of their still living body.

Paschal's sister fled with many other Christians; but Paschal and Cyprian courageously repaired to the place of execution to console and encourage their friends. They were at first driven off, but having declared themselves Christians, they too were interrogated and martyred. The Christians were sometimes condemned to be crushed between immense stone plates that covered the whole body, with the exception of the arms and feet, which projected beyond them. Sometimes two were laid, one upon another, face to face, and crushed together. Paschal and Cyprian thus suffered, but side by side.

Then my vision changed to a later period, one in which the Christians enjoyed more liberty, one in which they could visit and honor the tombs of the saints. I saw a father and mother carrying a lame boy about seven years old across a field in which many martyrs were interred. Monuments and little chapels stood here and there over the graves. At the end of the cemetery, which was named after Pope Calixtus, the parents halted with their afflicted child on a spot covered only with grass; for here, the boy said, lay two holy martyrs who would help him. They prayed. I think the child invoked them by name, and up he arose perfectly cured.

Then I saw the mother and child kneeling to thank God and the father running back to the city to proclaim the miracle. He returned with some men, among them priests, who carefully dug around until they came to the bodies of the two saints. They lay arm in arm, well-preserved, perfectly white and dry. The tomb was quadrangular, and at the spot in which the saints' arms locked there was a break in the low wall of partition between the bodies. They were not entirely disinterred at this time, but a festival was celebrated on the spot, the tomb was beautifully repaired, and a writing deposited in it. It was then closed, a roof supported by four or six columns raised over it, and the whole sodded. I saw various kinds of plants on it, one with very large leaves, a thick tuft like the house-leek. Under the roof was a stone before which was raised an altar with an opening on top that could be closed at pleasure. On the vertical stone was an inscription.

I saw the holy mass celebrated and holy communion given, the communicants holding under the chin a plate and white cloth. The sacred remains still lay buried there, though the little edifice over their grave was destroyed at a later period. Then I had a vision of many graves in this cemetery being opened and the holy remains removed, among them those of Paschal and Cyprian, now mere skeletons, but still lying in good condition. Then I saw them in two little four-cornered caskets, in possession of the Jesuits of Antwerp, who with many solemn ceremonies and in grand procession richly encased the relics and laid them in beautiful shrines.

Paula

FATHER *Limberg handed Anne Catherine a scrap of brown stuff from a package of relics, with the question: "What is this?" She looked at it attentively and then said in a decided tone:*

It belongs to the veil of the lady who went from Rome to Jerusalem and Bethlehem; it is a scrap of Paula's veil. I see the saint standing there in a long veil that falls over her face. She holds a gnarled stick in her hand.

Then she recognized another scrap of silk as part of the curtain that hung before the manger in Paula's little chapel:

The saint and her daughter often prayed behind this curtain. The infant Jesus frequently appeared to them there.

The pilgrim asked: "Was it the curtain of the true crib, the grotto?" She answered:

No! it hung before the little representation of the true crib which Paula's nuns had in their chapel. The monastery was so near the holy grotto that the chapel seemed to join it. It was right next to the spot in which Jesus was born. It was built only of wood and wickerwork, and the inside was hung with tapestry. From it ran four rows of cells lightly built, as the pilgrims' quarters always are in the holy land. Each had a little garden in front. Here it was that Paula and her daughter gathered together their first companions. In the chapel stood an altar with a tabernacle behind which, concealed by a red and white silk curtain, was the crib arranged by Paula. It was separated only by a wall from the true place of the birth of Jesus. The crib was a true representation of the holy crib, only smaller and of white stone; but so exact that even the straw was imitated. The little child lay closely wrapped in blue swathing-bands; and when Paula knelt before it, she used to take it up in her arms. Where the crib rested against the wall hung a curtain on which was wrought in colors the ass with his head turned toward the crib, its hair done in thread. Over the crib was fixed a star and before the curtain, on either side of the altar, hung lamps.

Perpetua and Felicity

LAST night, as I began to bemoan before God my pitiable state, I received this just reproach: "How can you complain, surrounded as you are by so rich a treasure of relics for which others had to journey so far. You have the privilege of living with these holy personages, of seeing all they did, of knowing all they were!" I felt then how wrong it was in me to repine, and I saw a whole troop of saints whose relics are here by me.

In the life of Perpetua I saw many scenes. Even as a child, she had visions of her future martyrdom. It reminded me of a dream I had had in my childhood in which I thought I was to have nothing but black bread and water. I thought this signified that I was to be a beggar; but now I think Walburga's black bread, which I received, explains the dream. I saw all the sufferings of Perpetua, Felicity, and others martyred with and after them in the same country. They were hunted by beasts and put to the sword.

At these words Anne Catherine took one of the relics, kissed it, laid it upon her heart, and said:

Perpetua is there by me!

Then, taking another little particle, she exclaimed:

This is very precious. It is the bone of a little boy who courageously suffered martyrdom with his father, mother, and two sisters. He was imprisoned with Perpetua and he suffered by fire.
There were little eminences in an enclosed place, and on them
stakes, or seats, on which the martyrs were placed, the fire being
lighted all around them. The bone shines with wonderful brilliancy, a glory of the finest blue with golden rays, such as surrounded the child-martyr. The light is so wonderfully invigor-
ating that no words can express it. I thought at first that Perpetua
and Felicity were martyred in Rome, because I saw them exe-
cuted in a building similar to the one in that city; but now I know
that it was in a place far distant.

As I have said, I had Perpetua's relic and saw many pictures of
her captivity and martyrdom; but all will be more clear on her
feast day. I saw the captive Christians in a round, subterranean
prison under an old building. They were separated from one
another by gratings through which they could talk, and even pass
the hand. It was very dark, excepting around the captives, where I
saw a faint light glimmering. The only egress was by a trapdoor in
the roof, besides which there were four gratings to admit air. I
saw four men imprisoned with Felicity and Perpetua, the latter of
whom was suckling her child. Felicity, who had not yet given
birth to hers, was in the adjoining cell.

Perpetua was tall, robust, well-proportioned, and very dignified in all her actions. Felicity was much shorter, more delicate,
more beautiful; both had black hair. Perpetua's confident, energetic words kept up the courage of all her companions. At some
distance were many other prisoners. The courageous little boy-
martyr was with his father in one cell, and the mother with her
two little girls in another. They were separated by a wall through
which their friends conversed with them.

Before the grating of Perpetua's cell I saw a disconsolate old
man tearing his hair and weeping bitterly. He was not a Christian. I think it was her father. There was a kind officer among the
guards who often brought bread or other things to Perpetua,
who divided the provisions among her companions. She kept
carefully hidden by her a roll of parchment. All wore the long,
narrow prison-costume; the women's of coarse white wool, the

men's brown. The prison of the latter was near the entrance, that of the women further back. I saw a young man die here and his body taken and buried by his friends.

One evening I saw Perpetua conversing with a man. That night as she lay on her side asleep she had a wonderful vision. The whole prison was lighted up, and I saw all its inmates either asleep or in prayer. In this light I beheld a marvelous ladder reaching up to the sky, leading as it were into the heavenly gardens; at the foot of it lay, right and left, two dragons, with outstretched heads. The ladder was only a pole, far too slender, one would say, considering its great height. I wondered it did not snap. The rungs stood out on either side, long and short alternately. Where a short one jutted out to the left, to the right was a long one bristling with hatchets, spears, and other sharp instruments of torture, and so on all the way up. How any one could mount it was perfectly incomprehensible; and yet, I saw a figure ascending on one side and descending on the other, as if to help some one up.

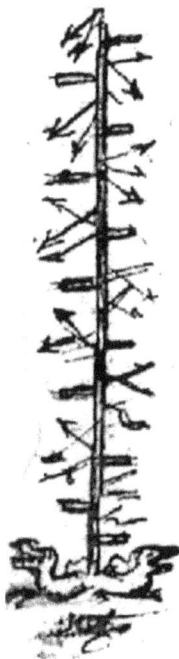

Then I saw Perpetua, who lay there asleep, stepping over the head of the dragon, which meekly bent its neck. She mounted the ladder, followed by others, and entered the garden where several blessed spirits awaited to encourage and strengthen them. Again, I saw by the sleeping Perpetua a vision of her little deceased brother. I saw a large, dark abode and in it a boy seemingly very miserable; he was parching with thirst. He stood by a vessel of water from which, however, he could not drink, as it was beyond his reach.

When Perpetua had the vision of the ladder I saw by the light that filled the prison that Felicity, her neighbor, had not yet been delivered. Suddenly I saw all the captives prostrating on the ground in prayer; and soon after, I saw a little child lying on Felicity's lap. A woman in tears, in great trouble, took the child, which the young mother joyfully resigned to her.

And now I saw the martyrs led to death. They left the prison between two files of soldiers who cruelly pushed them from side to side on their way to the place of execution. This place consisted of several communicating enclosures, not exactly like that of Rome. Twice on the way did persons approach the procession and hold up Perpetua's child for her to see: first at the gate, where a halt was made and a contest arose between the soldiers and their prisoners about something that the latter refused to do; and secondly at a crossroad where they ran to meet her. All the other Christian captives had been brought out merely to witness the martyrdom—for only Perpetua, Felicity, and three men suffered at this time.

I cannot say how unspeakably noble these martyrs appeared! The two women looked perfectly glorious, while the men boldly exhorted the spectators. They were forced to pass slowly between two files of executioners, who struck them on the back with whips. Then the two men were stationed opposite the cage of a wild beast that looked like an enormous spotted cat. It sprang forth furiously but did not harm them much; after this they were set upon by a bear. A wild boar was let loose upon the third; but it turned upon the executioner, whom I saw borne off covered with blood.

On another occasion Perpetua and Felicity came and gave me a drink, and then I had a vision of their youth. I saw them with other little girls playing in a circular garden enclosed by a wall. In it were numbers of slender trees higher than a man and so close together that their top branches interlaced. In the center stood a round summer house, on the roof of which was a walkway protected by a railing. In the center stood a white statue the size of a child, one hand raised, the other lowered, and holding something between the two. Nearby played a fountain that was surrounded by a railing stuck with sharp points to prevent the children from climbing it. By means of an opening, they could make the water flow into a shallow stone basin like a shell, in which they played. Here they amused themselves with puppets on wires and little wooden animals. I often saw the two saints withdrawing from the other children and tenderly embracing each other, by which I knew that their love began in childhood. I was told that they had promised never to separate. They had often played that they were Christians and were being martyred; but even then they would not be separated. St. Monica (of whom I had a relic) told me that the city is called Carthage.

Then again I was with Perpetua and Felicity, and I saw successive pictures of their youth up to the time of their imprisonment. They did not reside in the place in which they were imprisoned and martyred, but about half a league distant, in the suburbs where the houses stood far apart. It was connected with the city by a road running between two low walls and several high archways. Perpetua's home stood by itself. It was tolerably large, and her parents seemed to be people of distinction. It had an enclosed court and inner colonnade, though not exactly like that of Agnes's house in Rome, and there were statues in the walks. In front was an open space, and behind, though at some distance, the circular garden I lately saw. Perpetua's mother was a Christian, but in secret, and she knew that her children were the same. The father alone was a pagan. I saw some young men in the house.

Felicity was younger than Perpetua. She was the child of very poor people who lived in another part of the city, in a miserable little house built in the city wall. The mother was a stout, active, dark-complexioned woman; the father was already old at the time of the martyrdom. I saw them as they carried fruit and vegetables to the market in baskets, and I often saw Perpetua going to visit them. As a little girl she was very much attached to Felicity, with whom she and her brothers and other little boys used to play together most innocently. I often saw them in the garden. In their childish games, Perpetua and Felicity were always Christians and martyrs; the former was wonderfully courageous even from childhood, boldly promoting good and the Christian faith, on which account she often ran great risks. Felicity was pretty and delicate, and altogether more beautiful than Perpetua. The features of the latter were more strongly marked, her manners rather independent and masculine. Both were dark, like all the people of that country, and they had black hair. I saw Perpetua when a young girl often going to Felicity's home; and once I saw their future husbands, good, pious men, Christians in secret.

Perpetua had seen in vision that if she married she would attain martyrdom more speedily. In the same vision she had also seen her father's displeasure and the greater part of her own sufferings. After her own marriage she forwarded that of Felicity and assisted her in her poverty. Perpetua's husband seemed to me to be far beneath her in station; she accepted him only through respect for his virtue. When she left the house of her father—who was greatly dissatisfied with his daughter's marriage—her friends neglected her, and she lived a retired life with her husband.

Felicity's husband was also a pious Christian, but very poor. I used to see them going by night to a distant, retired place, like a large underground cave, supported on square pillars. It lay beyond the walls under a ruined building. Here about thirty Christians met quietly, closed all the entrances, lighted torches, and ranged in groups. I saw no divine service, but only instructions.

Another day, I saw two holy men approach my bed on one side, and three holy women on the other. They were the two husbands, and Perpetua, Felicity, and Perpetua's mother-in-law, a dark-complexioned old woman. Perpetua and Felicity took me up and laid me in a bed with blue curtains bound with red, and the mother-in-law moved a round table up to it, on which she laid all sorts of marvelous food. It seemed as if she did it in Perpetua's name. The table stood in the air near my bed without any support. Then the two holy women passed into another and larger apartment and, as I fancied that their silent departure betokened some trouble for me, I became sad. The mother-in-law followed them, and the two men likewise disappeared. Then I perceived that my hands and feet were bleeding. Suddenly several men rushed toward me, crying out: "Ah! Ah! She is eating!" and the alarm was soon spread. The saints returned. The mother-in-law told me that I should have had a cruel persecution to endure on account of the bleeding of my wounds, if the prayers of the saints had not averted or mitigated it; that the three children whom I had clothed for communion would by their prayers ward off many trials from me; and that, instead of a new persecution, I should endure a painful illness. It was in view of this that I had received the nourishment of fruits and flowers and fine bread on the golden plates with blue inscriptions.

The holy woman—the mother-in-law—stayed by me and told me many things. She was surrounded by a white aureola that dissolved into gray. She told me that she was the mother of Perpetua's husband and that she had lived near them. She had neither been imprisoned nor martyred with them, but she now enjoyed their companionship because, like so many others during the persecution, she had died of grief and want in her place of concealment. This circumstance God rewarded as martyrdom. Perpetua and Felicity could have escaped very easily, but the former longed for martyrdom. She had openly declared herself a Christian when the persecution broke out. She told me also that Perpetua had married in consequence of a vision she had had, and also in order that she might more easily leave her father's house.

I saw the father, a short, stout old man; he was seldom at home. When I saw him, he was standing in the second story of his house, in an apartment next his wife's. He could see all she did, for there was only a light wicker partition between the rooms, at the upper part of which was an opening with a slide. Although he busied himself but little with her, yet he seemed to regard her with suspicion, as she was a Christian. I often saw her in this room. She was rather stout, not very active, and she generally sat or reclined in her oratory, doing some kind of coarse knitting with wooden needles. The walls of the room, like those of the houses in Rome, were colored, but not so delicately. When the father was at home, the whole house was silent and restrained; but when he was away, the mother was bright and cheerful among her children.

Besides Perpetua, I saw two youths in the family. When the former was about seventeen, I saw her in a room nursing and bandaging a sick boy of seven years. He had a horrible ulcer in his face, and he was not very patient in his sickness. His parents came not near him. I saw him die in Perpetua's arms. She wrapped the body in linen and concealed it. The father and mother saw him no more.

Felicity was a servant in the same house as one of her fellow martyrs, but she often went to her parent's house to spend the night. Perpetua frequently carried thither at dusk something in a little basket or under her mantle, which they either used themselves, or took to the Christians in concealment. Many of the latter died of hunger. All these goings and comings went on before my eyes.

Perpetua was not beautiful in face. Her nose was rather short and flat; her cheek bones high; her lips a little too full, like those of the people of her country; her long black hair was braided around her head. Her dress was in the Roman style, though not quite so simple, being scalloped round the neck and skirt, the upper garment laced. Her figure was tall and imposing; her whole air fearless and confident.

I saw in Perpetua's house the two husbands taking leave of their wives before their flight from persecution. When they had gone, I saw Perpetua and Felicity tenderly embracing each other as if they were now right joyful. Perpetua's home was plainer than that of her parents. It was only one story high, the yard enclosed by a wooden paling. At daybreak next morning the house was attacked by a troop of soldiers who had already taken two young men into custody. Perpetua and Felicity were led away full of joy; the mother-in-law had the child, and no one molested her.

The four were now dragged with many cruel blows and much ill-usage, not by the ordinary way along the walls and under the arches, but by another route across the fields to a distant part of the city, where they entered a miserable old building that stood by itself, like a temporary fortress. Here they were to stay until taken to the ordinary prison. I saw a young man rapping at the prison gate. The soldiers let him in and put him with the other captives. Perpetua's father followed her here, praying, beseeching, conjuring her to renounce her faith; he even struck her in the face, but she answered in a few earnest words and bore all patiently.

Then I saw the prisoners conducted through a section of the city and along many walls to an underground prison where there were already many captives. Here I again saw Perpetua's vision of the ladder. She ascended to the top, received strength, and then descended, in doing which she glanced to one side, caught her dress below the waist on one of the spears, and tore it. It was exactly the same spot that was afterward torn when she was tossed by the cow. I saw her lying on the ground, and then suddenly rising to arrange her dress. This was what the torn dress of the vision signified.

I often saw her while in prison speaking undauntedly to the guards, defending her companions, and gaining for herself universal esteem. During her torture, when being tossed by the cow, she seemed to be in vision, utterly unconscious of pain. She was dragged horribly from side to side and hurled up into the air in a frightful manner; on falling she arranged her dress and seemed for an instant to have some consciousness of her position. As they were leading her across to another court, I heard her asking if she would soon be martyred now. She was in continual contemplation, conscious of nothing. In the middle of this second court were little seats to which the martyrs were dragged and their throats pierced. Perpetua's death was horrible to behold! She could not die! The executioner pierced her through the ribs and then through the right shoulder to the neck, she herself guiding his hand; and, when lying on the ground apparently dead, she still stretched forth one hand. She was the last to die and only after a long and hard agony. The two women had been stripped and put into a net and, owing to the tossing and scourging, their whole bodies were covered with blood. Their remains were taken away secretly and buried by the people of Carthage. I saw that many were converted by Perpetua's heroic behavior, and the prison was soon filled again.

Several days later I had the relics of Perpetua and Felicity by me all night, but to my great surprise I saw nothing of the two saints! I had hoped for some pictures of their life, but I got not even a glance; therefore I see that such visions are very special; one cannot have them at pleasure.

Placidus

I RECOGNIZED the bones of Placidus and Donatus, the former of whom was as elegant in appearance as St. Francis de Sales. He was martyred in Sicily with his brothers. I saw many scenes of his life, particularly of his infancy. He was the youngest of five children, three brothers and one sister older than himself. Even as a child he was looked upon as a saint. I saw him, an infant in his mother's arms, seize a roll of writings and joyously lay his tiny hands upon the names of Jesus and Mary. He was universally loved. Often whole families gathered round him on his mother's knee. Then I saw him as a boy in the garden with his pious tutor, where he amused himself tracing crosses in the sand, or weaving them of flowers and leaves, the birds hopping familiarly about him. When older he was taken to another place to make his studies, and afterward to the convent of St. Benedict, which still had a few scholars. He was slender, handsome, and rapidly developing into a most distinguished-looking youth. At the same time I had a vision of another saint of very low condition in life, reared as a herdsman, but who afterward became pope. I saw the life of each side by side. I spoke with Placidus and he again promised me help, telling me that I had only to invoke him when I wanted him and he would surely come.

Stephen, Lawrence, and Hippolytus

ANNE *Catherine said*: I feel that there is among my relics one of St. Lawrence. It is just a tiny splinter of bone.

The pilgrim hunted in the box of relics and found a small parcel containing two scraps of bone in a brown envelope tied with gold thread. He handed her both. Scarcely had she touched them when she exclaimed:

O one is Stephen's! O what a treasure! This belongs to Lawrence.

And, becoming more profoundly absorbed, she continued:

See, there they both stand, Lawrence behind Stephen! Stephen wears the white robe of a Jewish priest with lappets on the shoulders, and a broad girdle. He is a beautiful youth, taller than Lawrence. Lawrence wears the flowing robe of a deacon.

Anne Catherine's joy at having found this treasure was very great. The vision she beheld seemed so real that, all at once, she exclaimed:

But we have none of their bones; they are still alive! There they are! It is truly laughable! How could I think we had their relics when they are yet alive!

Later on she said: Besides the white priestly robe and broad cincture, Stephen wears on his shoulders a scalloped cape, woven in red and white, and carries a palm branch in his hand. Lawrence appeared in a long plaited robe of bluish white with a wide cincture; he wore a stole around his neck. He was not so tall as

Stephen—but he was young, beautiful, fearless like him. His relic must have been scorched by fire; it is wrapped in a scrap of black stuff.

The pilgrim here opened the cover, and found the relic just as described:

The gridiron had a rim around it like a pan, and in the middle of each side was a handle by which to lift it; it had six feet and four flat crossbars. When the saint was stretched on it, a bar was placed over him from right to left. When Lawrence appeared to me, the gridiron was near him.

On the feast of St. Lawrence, she related the following:

I saw that Lawrence was a Spaniard, a native of the city of Huesca. His parents were pious Christians, the mother's name Patience, the father's I have forgotten. All the inhabitants were not Christians, and the houses of the latter were marked with a cross cut in stone, of which some had a single, others a double transverse arm. Lawrence had a special devotion to the blessed sacrament. When about eleven years old he was endowed with a supernatural consciousness of its presence, so that he felt its approach even if it were carried concealed. Wherever it was borne he followed with liveliest veneration. His pious parents had not so great a devotion themselves, and they blamed his zeal as excessive.

I saw him give a touching proof of his love for the blessed sacrament. He once saw a priest carrying the blessed sacrament secretly to a leprous woman, a most disgusting object, who lived in a miserable hovel near the city wall. Impelled by devotion, Lawrence stealthily followed the priest and prayerfully watched all the ceremonies. Just as the priest laid the sacred host on the poor creature's tongue, she vomited, ejecting the sacred species at the same time. The priest, whose name I knew, was a holy man; he became a saint. But just at this moment, he was perfectly bewildered, not knowing how to withdraw the sacred host from the filth in which it lay. From his hiding place the boy Lawrence saw all. Unable to control the ardor of his love for Jesus in the blessed sacrament, he rushed into the room and, conquering every sentiment of disgust, threw himself on his knees and reverently took up the body of his Lord with his lips. For this heroic self-victory he received from God indomitable strength and fortitude of soul.

I saw, also, in an indescribable manner, that Lawrence was *not born of the blood nor of the will of man*, but of God. He was shown me as a newborn babe, and it was told me that he had been begotten in the spirit of renunciation, with sentiments of confusion and penitence. His parents were in the state of grace, having devoutly received holy communion; so that, in his very conception, Lawrence had been consecrated to God, thereby receiving as an inheritance his early veneration for the blessed sacrament and the consciousness of its presence. I was filled with joy on beholding a child begotten as I have always thought it should be in Christian marriage, a state that ought to be looked upon as one of humiliating penance.

Soon after his heroic act, Lawrence, with his parents' consent, went to Rome. There I saw him visiting the sick and prisoners in company with the holiest priests. He soon became especially dear to Pope Sixtus, who ordained him deacon. Lawrence always served the pope's mass. I saw the pope communicating him under both forms after his own communion, and then Lawrence distributing the sacrament to the Christians. There was no communion table such as we have; but to the right of the altar was a railing with a swinging ledge, behind which the communicants knelt. The deacons generally took turns in administering the sacrament, but Lawrence always discharged that duty for Sixtus. When the latter was led to prison, I saw Lawrence running and calling after him not to leave him behind. Sixtus, divinely inspired, predicted his deacon's approaching martyrdom and ordered him to distribute the treasures of the church to the poor.

Then I saw Lawrence hurrying with a large sum of money in his bosom to the widow Cyriaca, with whom were concealed numbers of Christians and sick people. He humbly washed the feet of all; relieved by the imposition of hands the widow, who had long suffered from violent headache; healed the lame, the sick, the blind; and distributed alms. Cyriaca aided him in every way, especially in converting the sacred vessels into money.

That night I saw him entering a vault, penetrating deep into the catacombs, giving alms and other relief, distributing the sacrament, and inspiring all with extraordinary courage. He was radiant with joy, full of supernatural fortitude and earnestness. Then I saw him with Cyriaca hastening to the pope's prison.[1] As the latter was led forth to death, Lawrence told him that he had distributed the treasure and he was now ready to follow him to death as his deacon. The pope again foretold his martyrdom, and Lawrence was arrested on the spot by the soldiers, who had heard him speaking of treasures.

Anne Catherine here saw every detail of Lawrence's imprisonment and martyrdom, just as related in the legend of the former and the Acts of the latter. She saw also the cures he wrought in prison, the conversion of Romain and Hippolytus, etc. She said:

Lawrence's tortures were long; they were continued all night with uncommon cruelty. Between two courtyards used as places of execution ran a colonnade in which were kept the instruments of torture, and in which all the preparations for the same were made. It was thrown open to spectators, and here Lawrence was stretched on the gridiron. Strengthened by his angel, he stepped lightly toward it with a gay remark, and laid himself upon it, refusing, however, to allow himself to be bound. I felt that, by divine assistance, he was insensible to the greater part of his torments; he lay as if upon roses. Other martyrs have had more terrible sufferings to endure. He wore the white robe of a deacon, a girdle, a stole, a scalloped cape, and a kind of upper garment like Stephen's. I saw him buried by Hippolytus and the priest Justin. Many wept over his grave and mass was said there.

Lawrence once appeared to me when I had scruples about receiving holy communion. He questioned me upon the state

---

[1] Elsewhere Anne Catherine speaks of a deacon of a similar name, Cyriacus, also associated with the catacombs: "I saw also a picture of a certain deacon Cyriacus, who suffered unspeakably. Once he lay hidden and almost starving in the catacombs not far from where St. Peter's now stands. He was, later on, martyred. I remember that the deacon Cyriacus received orders from Marcellus, and that, with two Christians, Largus and Smaragdus, he assisted the faithful condemned to labor at the public works. He was himself afterward condemned to do the same. He delivered the daughter of his persecutor from the power of the devil."

of my soul. When I had answered him, he said that I might communicate every other day.

✝ ✝ ✝ ✝ ✝

ON *recognizing a relic of St. Hippolytus, Anne Catherine spoke as follows:* I have had visions of his life. I saw him the child of indigent parents. His father died young; and his mother, a quarrelsome woman, was, although poor and mean herself, hard and proud toward others of her class. Several incidents of Hippolytus's youth were shown me which, as I was told, were the germs of future grace in store for him as a Christian, a martyr for Christ. I was then informed that graces are ever the reward of generous deeds, also those of pagans.

I saw his mother quarreling with another poor woman whom she treated shamefully, scornfully driving her out of the house. This greatly grieved the young Hippolytus, and he secretly took one of his undergarments and gave it to the poor woman, as if his mother had sent it to her in token of reconciliation. Hippolytus did not say this to the woman in express terms, but she naturally inferred it. She returned to his mother who, surprised at her bright, cordial manner after such treatment, now received her kindly. More than one of these charitable acts were shown me in the boy's life.

Hippolytus became a soldier. One of his companions was sentenced to severe chastisement for some fault, but Hippolytus presented himself before the judge instead of the guilty one. His generosity led to a mitigation of the punishment, which he suffered in the place of his friend. The latter was so deeply impressed by this act of charity that with Hippolytus he became a Christian, a martyr. I learned from this that kind acts and good works inspired by disinterested love are never overlooked by the Lord; they prepare the way for future graces.

Hippolytus was one of Lawrence's guards. He was greatly touched on seeing the saint present the poor to the emperor as the treasures of the Church. He was upright, a pagan in the same sense as Paul was a Jew. I saw him converted in the prison, and after Lawrence's martyrdom weeping and praying with the other Christians for three days and three nights over his grave. Justin celebrated holy mass on the tomb and gave holy communion. All did not receive, but over those who did not I saw shining the flames of desire. Justin sprinkled the Christians with water. The martyr's tomb stood by itself in a retired spot behind a hill.

Hippolytus was soon after arrested with many of his companions and dragged by horses in a deserted spot not far from the grave of St. Lawrence. The horses were unwilling to move; but the executioners struck them, pricked them, and goaded them on with lighted torches, so that Hippolytus was rather quartered than dragged. In many spots were prepared stones, holes, and thorns to tear the body. About twenty others suffered with him, among them his friend. He wore the white baptismal robe.

Susanna, Holy Martyr

I HAVE a relic of St. Susanna.[1] She kept me company all last night. I saw many scenes in her life, but I only remember some of them. I saw her in a large house with courtyard and colonnade in Rome. Her father was called Gabinus; he was a Christian and brother to the pope, who dwelt not far away. Susanna's mother must have been dead, for I never saw her. There were other Christians in the family of Gabinus. Like his daughter he was very charitable to the poor; he secretly shared his wealth with them.

I saw a messenger sent from the emperor Diocletian to Gabinus, who was his relative, proposing a marriage between Susanna and his own widowed son-in-law. Gabinus seemed at first well pleased with the offer, but Susanna met it with extreme repugnance. She said that, having espoused Christ, she could never marry a pagan. On receiving this answer, Diocletian caused her to

---

[1] Susanna, virgin and martyr, is said to have been the daughter of St. Gabinus of Rome. According to her Acts, she was beheaded about the year 295, at the command of Diocletian, in her father's house, which was turned into a church, together with the adjoining one belonging to her uncle, the prefect Caius or, according to other accounts, Pope Caius. The church became known as *Sancta Susanna ad duas domos* (cf. Kehr, "Italia pontificia," I, 61 seq.).

be removed from her father's house and brought to the court of his wife (Serena). He hoped by this to change her sentiments.

Now, the empress was a Christian in secret, and Susanna laid her case before her; they prayed together, and then she was reconducted to her father's house. And now came another messenger from the emperor, one Claudius, a relative of his own, who on saluting Susanna attempted to kiss her—not impertinently, but either through custom, or because they were relatives. But Susanna kept him off with her hand and, on his declaring his intention innocent, she replied that lips sullied with praises of the false gods should never touch hers. She then spoke to him earnestly, and pointed out his errors. Then I saw him, with his wife and children, instructed and baptized by the pope, Susanna's uncle.

As Claudius did not return with an answer, the emperor sent a brother of the same to see what detained him. On entering, he found Claudius and his family kneeling in prayer. Concealing his amazement, he asked his brother what was Susanna's reply to the marriage proposal. Claudius evaded a direct answer, but persuaded his brother to accompany him to Susanna and convince himself that such a person could never espouse an idolater. They went together to her presence, and lo! this second messenger was converted by Susanna and her uncle the pope!

The empress Serena had three Christians in her service, two men and one woman. I saw them all going together by night—Susanna along with them—into a subterranean apartment beneath the palace. In it stood an altar before which a lamp constantly burned. Here they prayed, and sometimes a priest came secretly to consecrate and administer to them the blessed sacrament. The emperor was furious when he heard of the two brothers' conversion. He ordered both to be imprisoned with their families; they were afterward martyred. Susanna's father also was imprisoned.

Then I had another vision in which I saw Susanna sitting alone in a large hall by a little round table ornamented with gilded figures; her hands were joined, her face raised in prayer. Round apertures in the roof admitted air, and in the corners of the apartment stood white statues as large as a child. Here and there were animals' heads, especially on the feet of the furniture. Some winged figures with long tails were sitting back on their hind legs; others held scrolls in their forepaws, etc.[1] As Susanna sat thus in prayer, I saw that the emperor sent his son himself to offer her violence. I saw the man leave his attendants outside and enter a door at Susanna's back, when lo! a figure stood before her and confronted the bold intruder! The latter instantly fell to the ground like one dead. Then only did the maiden turn. Seeing a man lying behind her, she cried out for assistance. The son's friends rushed in astounded, raised him up, and bore him from the room. The apparition still stood before Susanna, and when her enemy again approached her from behind—and when she was halfway between the two—the latter fell to the ground.

Then I had another vision. I saw a man with twenty others going to her, and two pagan priests who carried between them, on a platform furnished with handles, a gilded idol that must have been hollow, for it was very light. They placed it in a niche under the colonnade of the courtyard and stood before it a little round three-legged table which they had brought from the house. Then several went in for Susanna, who was still in the upper hall. They dragged her out to sacrifice to the idol. She prayed fervently to God, and even before she reached the spot, I saw a miracle. The idol, as if hurled by an invisible power, shot across the court and colonnade far out into the street, where it fell shattered into a thousand pieces! At the same time I saw a man running to spread the news.

Then they tore off Susanna's upper garment, leaving only a little covering on her breast. Her back and shoulders were bare. In this state she had to cross the crowded vestibule where the soldiers pricked and wounded her with their sharp spears, until she sank down apparently dead. They then dragged her into a side room and left her lying there on the floor. Again I saw them trying to force her to offer sacrifice in a temple, but the idol fell to the ground; lastly, she was dragged by the hair into the courtyard of her own house and beheaded.

The empress and Susanna's nurse came by night, washed the body, wrapped it in a winding-sheet, and buried it. The empress

---

[1] Probably sculptured ornaments, winged lions, griffins, etc.

had first cut off one of her fingers and some of her hair. I afterward saw the pope saying mass on the spot of her martyrdom. Susanna had a round face, a resolute expression, and black hair braided around her head. She was dressed in white with a veil that fastened under the chin and fell behind in two ends.

Thekla

THE *pilgrim inquired if she did not see Thekla, whose relic lay by her. Yes, was the answer.* I see her, now here, now there, in a vision, as if on the watch near the prison in which Paul is confined. Sometimes I see her gliding along by a wall, sometimes under an arch, like a person anxiously seeking something.

Anne Catherine beheld in its entirety the life of Paul's student Thekla, who—she was given to understand—as the first martyr of the Blessed Virgin, had been accorded a place alongside the Fathers of the Church:

At a time when she was engaged to be married, Thekla came to hear Paul's teaching, by which she was greatly stirred, particularly on the subject of virginity. (Indeed, Anne Catherine heard God praising her virginity.) Thekla was then living at her parent's house in Iconium. She was of medium height, with brown hair. Her countenance was both attractive and earnest. Her coloring was not rosy, but of a more brownish cast. Her forehead and nose were quite closely connected in a sort of line or crease. She gave an impression of uncommon piety and gravity. Her long wool-white garment had many folds and tucks and was cinched with a wide sash that narrowed toward the ends. The flaring sleeves were fastened with arm-bracelets ribbed in the middle and set along their edges with pearls. Her hair was parted in three and braided together with strips of a translucent, silvery-white fabric—or, better said, coiled or looped around her hair on both sides and behind, forming a chignon.

First I saw her alone with her father and mother, then with her betrothed—a large, handsome, virtuous man—who was received most congenially by all. The house was of the older kind, built with columns surrounding a forecourt. Before the house was a walled courtyard, beyond which opened a terrace surrounded with a balustrade. The balustrade was of varying height, with here and there openings through which one might see and hear. Tapestries were spread above to moderate the sunlight.

Paul was there with a disciple, but not Barnabas as far as I can recall. The place had a synagogue, but Paul preferred to teach in the open air at the homes of his friends. Just then he was teaching at a house opposite and at a somewhat higher elevation than Thekla's home. Many people, among them virgins, were in attendance. Paul was speaking on the subject of marriage. He said: "One who marries commits no sin; but one who abstains from marriage has done better," and so forth. Thekla sat on her terrace, listening to Paul's words from her side of the street, and was very moved by Paul's teaching. After this teaching, Paul was thrown in prison.

Somewhat later I saw Thekla alone in her room. She held a scroll, about a finger thick, from which she was reading. It was one of Paul's writings on the subject of marriage and virginity, and she was much affected by what she was reading. She folded her hands in prayer, then removed from her breast and laid aside a piece of jewelry her betrothed had given her. She then removed from her right shoulder—or perhaps her right ear—another piece of jewelry like a white stone with a small knob. This latter she lay in a small box that contained various other gems and treasures.

Toward evening I saw her with a dark-colored veil over her arm as she left the house for the city, where she sought out a man to whom she passed her valuables, after which she returned home. A short while later this man came to her home and presented her with a small, rectangular metal plate.

Now I saw how she dispossessed herself of all her jewels and finery, covered herself completely with cloth, and declared to her parents and betrothed alike that she had become a Christian and wished to remain a virgin.[1] Her mother took this news hard and

---

[1] Elsewhere Anne Catherine reports that as Thekla's wedding presents were being prepared, she saw an envoy from her betrothed arrive, whom she turned away. Then a servant she had commissioned to sell her jewelry accompanied her to the prison where Paul was being held.

was beside herself. Later the mother was taken to the house of a friend, who it was hoped might be able to alter her mind on the matter.

I saw Thekla slip into a dungeon under cover of darkness with a brown shawl over her head. She passed along stout walls and under arches. She came to a guard standing watch, but did not address him, continuing on till she encountered a man who seemed to be the head watchman, to whom she offered some gold. This man then took a lamp and led her further into the dungeon, till he drew to a halt before a door. It led to the cell where Paul was imprisoned.

Paul wore a long mantle. His cell was quite spacious, and he was not chained. Scrolls lay about him. I saw the two of them together. Thekla was most earnest and upright. She spoke with him about her situation and feelings, after which Paul explained many things to her. As she knelt before him, Paul baptized her with water from a flask he kept under his garments, by his heart, and a light shone down and around them both from above. The prison-master, who had listened also, later became a Christian. Thekla quit the prison then and returned home.

I saw Thekla's own mother denounce her before court as a Christian. She was cross-examined by a magistrate, whose questions she answered fearlessly, and sentenced. She was taken to a prison for gentrified inmates and then to a place of torture where she was stripped almost naked, left only with a strip of cloth covering her lower body, and then led in a circle before her tormentor, who with rods scourged her flesh until she collapsed upon the ground. She was then bound to a stake and lacerated with instruments like a grappling-iron. Her long hair hung in a tangle about her bloodied body. When she was unbound she leapt of her own volition upon a funeral pyre. But as she stood upon the pyre, her arms outspread, the flames were driven back and there came so mighty a downpour that everything washed away and the fire was extinguished.[1] She could easily have fled, but did not, and so was taken back to the prison. Many present were converted.

---

[1] On another occasion Anne Catherine says that after Thekla was sentenced, she was brought to a tall stone with a stairway that led to a great pile

That night, as she prayed in her prison cell, Paul, who at that time was no longer confined in the prison, came to her as an apparition and consoled her and healed her wounds. I understood that someone had written to Rome on Paul's account, and that is how he won his release.

Then she was led from the prison to be interrogated again, and afterward to a circular combat arena. Again her clothes were stripped away. At one end of the arena was chained a bear, and at the other a lioness. Chains were clamped also to her arms and scantily-draped hips, and then—four chains in all—secured at their further ends to the two beasts.

The beasts tugged at the chains, and Thekla fell on her back. The lioness then broke the chains, without injuring Thekla in the least. The animal did so by first setting its paws on a chain, holding them fast, and then—after lowering its head beneath the links of chain between its paws—raising its powerful head. For its part, the bear was sitting grim and fearful at some remove when the lioness fell upon and throttled it so suddenly that it dashed like a cringing dog to Thekla—who had in the meanwhile cast off her chains—and licked her feet. Thekla caressed the poor creature, taking its head and maw in her hands, at which a great cry of wonder broke forth from the spectators. The magistrate declared he would leave off any further punishment and was himself later converted.[1]

Others took hold of Thekla, however, and led her, covered only with a brown smock, to a watery place where was a brick cistern—the depth of three men—filled with slime and hideous

---

of wood intended as her funeral pyre. But when it was lit, and the flames were mounting, a sudden rainfall extinguished it and drove the onlookers away, after which she also was led away.

[1] Here again we have a further description on these events as follows: "Later, I saw Thekla stretched between four oxen, who were to tear her to pieces, but instead, the oxen turned around, tread on the ropes binding them to Thekla, and ripped them apart with their horns. Then again, I saw Thekla naked, but a cloud settled around her to protect her modesty. I saw a lioness lick her feet and then fall upon a bear that was threatening her, and how in the end the creatures killed each other. I saw how the acclaim of the people led to her release."

snakes. The culprits grabbed Thekla, intending to cast her head over heels into the odious pit. But before they could do so, she tore herself loose, made the sign of the cross over the pit, and leapt in herself, whereupon the snakes backed away from her on all sides. Undeterred, the young men opened a sluice and began filling the cistern from a nearby river, but as the water in the cistern rose, Thekla—standing upright with outstretched arms—rose with it, as also the snakes, which as before were pressing against the walls. At this point no more water could be let in, as otherwise the snakes would have come so near the top that they could have sprung upon the bystanders. The virgin Thekla, still unharmed, commenced to praise God. She was drawn out of the cistern, and many were converted. Then she was brought to the noblewoman Tryphena, who was converted also.

Many people, especially virgins, came flocking around Thekla, and on this account she was banished from the city. She made her way to a region of caves, where many women and virgins followed, remaining thereafter as a community. They wore brown, full-length habits that had hoods with extra folds of cloth to allow them to freely turn their heads. The caves where they resided were very well concealed.

At a later time I saw Thekla in Seleucia with Tryphena, where she wandered about begging for her worldly needs. She lived in a cave there as well. In this way she was able to teach without calling attention to herself, and I often saw her praying by the side of the sick, afterward healing them by a laying on of hands. All this she did without authority, or presumption, but merely as a pious woman with abundant gifts of grace.

Later I saw her in a hermitage with fifteen virgins. After that she journeyed once with Paul and preached. On one occasion he tried to dismiss her, but to no effect. On another occasion he came to visit her. I also saw how in his destitution she had appeared to the Emperor Zeno, presaging his return.

Thekla traveled extensively, teaching and converting wherever she went. Anne Catherine could not remember all the details pertaining to Thekla's journeys, because she was so preoccupied at the time with other visions.

✛ ✛ ✛ ✛ ✛

ONE *day Anne Catherine discovered fragments of the bones of Eugenia,*
Paula, Theodora, and Thekla in her collection of relics and presented
them to the pilgrim. In vision she beheld each of them among the heav-
enly choirs and was able to identify their relics, in her usual way. She
beheld many scenes from their lives, but much of this was lost:

When I took hold of Thekla's relic around noon yesterday, I
beheld the saint descending toward me from heaven. She was
clothed in light and held a branch bearing blossoms of whitish-
gold. She said to me: "That is a fragment of my bones." Thereafter, until the approach of evening, I beheld many more images
of Thekla. This morning, over the span of an hour, I beheld the
entire story of her martyrdom. (Unfortunately, owing to the usual disquiet in her surroundings, she could only relate small portions of what she had seen, and even this in a somewhat casual
way.)

Last night I saw Thekla living together with about seven wom-
en and virgins in a well-ordered hermitage in Seleucia. Arranged
next to each other in a half-circle of stone, several cells had been
hewn neatly from a rock face. At the middle of this half-circle
stood a six- or eight-sided column that supported a canopied roof,
covered with green sod, that extended from the cells over the surrounding area and was then supported upon some trees whose
branches has been interwoven with it.[1]

The side facing the front was closed off with trees and stones,
with narrow entries at either end. Light penetrated through the
canopy from above through openings made therein. The whole
structure was exceedingly elegant, stately, and charming. The
anchorites wove blankets and also wattling for their doors. The
cells were hewn cleanly from the stone, which was veined with
bright colors. In each cell was a stone bench covered with moss,
upon which the women slept, and also a niche, carved into a corner, where a wooden crucifix was kept.[2] On some of the crucifixes

---

[1] The drawing overleaf bears the caption "Thekla's hermitage."
[2] Here was drawn a small "forked cross" (*Gabelkreuz*).

I saw an image of Christ cut from parchment, on others a puppet-like piece of needlework to serve the same purpose.

The niches were closed with a hinged door which, when opened and let down, served as a small table. The anchorites kept switches and ropes woven of hair with which to mortify themselves. Their small brown bowls looked to have been carved directly from earth. I saw no hearth, so surmised they ate fruits and raw vegetables only. A spring stood before the hermitage. The angular middle column was surrounded at its base by a prominence, rather like an altar, that was hung on all sides with tapestries on which were simple figures, such as apostles and Mary, knit from colorful yarns. Just above this prominence was what appeared to be a cabinet built into the column, but I cannot remember what was kept in it. The women would gather around this central column to pray.

I saw Thekla, who was seventeen years old at the time she was tortured, now forty years of age as she lay near death in her cell. Her fellow anchorites knelt around her as a man who appeared to be a hermit gave her the holy sacrament. He kept the host in a long tin box that was now open halfway, so that I could see it within, wrapped in a piece of cloth. The priest was bearded and wore a long brown robe with a cord knotted around his waist. Thekla did not immediately pass away, but lay there for a long while quite calm and quiet, just as the Virgin Mary had done.

Later I saw some scenes from Thekla's funeral service. Her companions wrapped her body, as was the custom at that time, and she was then removed from the board on which she lay to another with pegs as handholds, so the body could be carried into a funereal cave and set down alongside the many other bodies interred there. I feel certain a chapel was later raised there.[1]

Theoctista

WHILE on my way to the holy land, I saw the life of this holy virgin, hitherto perfectly unknown to me. She belonged to the Isle of Lesbos. Before the city of her birth arose a chapel of the Mother of God in which was a statue of Mary without the infant Jesus. It had been chiseled from her portrait by Luke. The sculptor was a holy confessor of the faith belonging to Jerusalem, who afterward lost both his arms and legs in one of the persecutions. Around the chapel were cells in which dwelt pious women who followed a rule founded on the life of Mary and the holy women at Ephesus. They had erected on the mountain a way of the cross like that planned by Mary at Ephesus. They reared and instructed little girls and, as their rule ordained, examined their inclinations and dispositions in order to choose for them a state of life. Theoctista had been with them from childhood, and her only desire was to remain with them. Her parents were dead.

The chapel and convent being destroyed in war, Theoctista entered another community on the same island. The religious dwelt in caves on a mountain under the rule of a holy woman who, in consequence of a vision, recognized the chain of St. Peter—but I have forgotten her name. Here Theoctista remained

---

[1] This further reference to Thekla is found in Brentano's notes: "I recall once being present at her grave in a chapel, when the saint appeared and clothed me in a white garment with an especially beautiful white cowl of simple design that covered also my breast. Its delicate, finely-worked folds covered all but a small portion of my face. I don't remember why Thekla clothed me in this way, but I believe it was because I was to accomplish some task in the Nuptial House, and thus attired I would not be noticed. I came to the Nuptial House from Thekla's chapel through a rapid transposition, still wearing the garments in which Thekla had dressed me, and she herself—as it seemed to me—by my side. My task had to do with a new bishop. I don't recall of what we spoke, but he was quite shaken, scarcely believing what had befallen him. Neither do I remember what it was I did there in his regard."

until her twenty-fifth year, when she went to visit her sister, who lived at a distance. But the ship on which she was fell into the hands of Arab pirates when sailing from the Isle of Crete, and the whole crew was dragged into captivity.

The pirates landed on the Isle of Pares, which contained many marble quarries. While they were disputing over the ransom for their captives, Theoctista made her escape and hid in the quarries. Here she lived as a hermitess for fifteen years without human aid, until discovered one day by a hunter. She related to him her history and implored him to return with the holy eucharist in a pyx. This was permitted to lay people at that time, as the Christians were often scattered and priests were few. At the end of a year he returned with the blessed sacrament, which she received as viaticum. She died the same day. The hunter buried her, after first removing one of her hands and a piece of her clothing, which he carried away with him. Through that blessed hand he happily accomplished his voyage home in spite of the imminent risks he ran from pirates. When he related the affair to his bishop, the latter reproached him for not having brought away the whole body of the saint.

Ursula

URSULA and her companions were massacred by the Huns, about the year 450, near Cologne and in other places. Ursula was raised up by God to preserve the maidens and widows of her time from seduction and dishonor and to enroll them in the celestial army of crowned martyrs. She accomplished her mission with extraordinary energy and constancy. The archangel Raphael was given her as a guide. He announced to her her task, saying that the mercy of God willed not that at this frightful epoch of destruction so many virgins and widows—left defenceless and deprived of protectors by the bloody wars—should fall prey to the savage Huns. Rather should they die as innocent children than live to fall into sin.

Ursula was not exactly beautiful; she was tall and strong, resolute and energetic, of a very grave countenance and masculine bearing. She was, at the time of her martyrdom, thirty-three years old. I saw her as a little girl in the house of her parents, Deonotus and Geruma, in a city of England. The house stood on a broad street; it had steps before the door and a metal railing with yellow knobs. It looked like the paternal house of St. Benedict in Italy, which, too, had brass railings surmounting a low wall.

Ursula had ten playmates who joined her every morning and evening in an enclosed field where, divided into two bands, they exercised in running, wrestling, and even in the use of the lance. They were not all Christians, though Ursula and her parents were. Ursula was the instructress of her companions, and she exercised them thus by order of her angel. Her parents often watched their games, well pleased.

Maximian, a pagan, was then lord over England, and I am not now sure that he was not the husband of Ursula's eldest sister, Ottilia. Ursula had vowed herself to God. A warrior, powerful and renowned, requested of her father the privilege of witnessing the exercises of the maidens of whom he had heard so much. Though embarrassed by the request, Ursula's father dared not refuse. He tried at first to put him off, but the man insisted until he gained his purpose. He was charmed with Ursula's skill and beauty, and at once asked her in marriage, saying that her young companions should espouse his officers in a country beyond the sea not yet peopled. I thought of Bonaparte, who made matches for his officers. I saw the father's deep affliction and the daughter's fright when apprised of this offer, which could not be declined.

Ursula went by night to the practice yard and besought God in earnest prayer. The archangel Raphael appeared to her, consoled her, and instructed her to request that each of her companions might be allowed to choose ten other maidens, and to demand a delay of three years in which to practice all sorts of naval combats and manoeuvres. He exhorted her to confidence in God, who would not permit her vow of virginity to be violated. In these three years she was, with God's help, to convert her companions to Christianity. Ursula delivered these conditions to her father, who in turn proposed them to the suitor, who accepted them. Ursula and her ten companions then chose respectively ten other maidens, who became their pupils. The father had five small vessels fitted out for them, upon each of which were about twenty girls and also a few sailors to teach them how to manage the sails and engage at sea.

And now I saw them exercising daily, first in a river, then along the seashore. They sailed along quietly, gave one another chase, separated, leapt from ship to ship, etc. I often saw a crowd on the shore watching them, especially the father and suitor, the latter rejoicing in the prospect of soon having so valorous and skillful a wife; for he thought, with such a one by his side, he would be able to overcome every obstacle. After awhile I saw the maidens practicing alone without the sailors, Bertrand the confessor and two other ecclesiastics being upon the vessels.

Ursula had by this time converted all her maidens, among whom were some only twelve years old. They were baptized by the priests. Her courage and confidence in God increased every day. I saw them landing on small islands and practicing their naval tactics, all accompanied with prayer and the chanting of psalms, all performed with great freedom and boldness.

Ursula's wonderful earnestness and courage are quite indescribable. The maidens wore short dresses, descending a little below the knee; they were quite plain on the hips and had close-fitting bodies. Their feet were laced. Some had their hair uncovered and braided about the head, while others wore a sort of headdress with ends hanging behind. In their exercises they used light, blunt spears.

When the agreed-upon three years drew to a close, I saw that the maidens were of one heart and soul. When, having already taken leave of their parents, they were about to embark to go to their future husbands, I saw Ursula in prayer. A luminous figure stood before her bidding her trust all to God, the Lord, who would give them the martyr's crown as his own brides, pure virgins; that she herself should propagate Christianity wherever the Lord should lead her; and that many virgins would through her be saved from dishonor and enter heaven adorned with the crown of martyrdom. The angel ordered her also to proceed to Rome with some of her virgins. Ursula confided all this to her ten assistants, who were greatly encouraged thereby. But as many of the others murmured against her because, having started for their nuptials, as they thought, she now intended them to be brides of

Christ. And so, Ursula went from ship to ship, reminding them of Abraham, of the sacrifice of his son, and of the miraculous help he had received from God. She told them that they too should receive similar strength to offer Him a pure and perfect sacrifice. Then she ordered the cowardly to leave the vessels and return home; but in fact all were encouraged by her words to remain faithful.

As they sailed from England under pretence of joining their destined husbands, a great storm arose that separated their vessels from those of their attendants and drove them toward the Netherlands. They could make use of neither sail nor oar, and the sea miraculously arose as they neared the land. No sooner had they disembarked than their dangers began. A savage nation tried to oppose their progress; but at Ursula's words, the maidens were allowed to return unmolested to their ships. A city lay at the point at which they then quit the open sea to sail up the Rhine, and here they encountered great troubles; but Ursula spoke for all, answered all. When violent hands were about to be laid on the virgins, they boldly flew to arms and received supernatural assistance, which paralyzed their aggressors, rendering them powerless to harm them. Many maidens, as also widows and their children, joined them on their journey. Before reaching Cologne they were more than once challenged, interrogated, and threatened by the barbarous tribes along the shores. It was Ursula who always responded to such threats, and who urged her companions to ply their oars.

In due course they arrived safe at Cologne, where they found a Christian community and a little church. Here they sojourned for a time. The widows who had joined them on the journey, and many young girls also, remained behind when Ursula proceeded further on her way. Before setting out, however, she earnestly exhorted them to martyrdom as Christian matrons and virgins, rather than to allow themselves to suffer such violence from the pagan barbarians. They scattered throughout the surrounding district, spreading everywhere the teachings and heroic spirit of Ursula, who had departed with five vessels.

On reaching Basle, some of Ursula's little company remained there with the ships while she herself set out for Rome with about forty of her maidens, accompanied by priests and guides. They went processionally like pilgrims through wildernesses and mountainous districts, praying and chanting psalms. Wherever they halted, Ursula spoke of the espousals with Jesus and of the pure, immaculate death of virgins. Everywhere were they joined by recruits, while some of their number remained behind to diffuse their own spirit among the people.

At Rome they visited the tombs of the martyrs and the different places sanctified by their death. As they were informed that their short dresses and freedom of demeanor attracted attention, they procured mantles. The pope, Leo the Great, sent for Ursula, who disclosed to him the secret of her mission, related her visions, and received his advice with humility and submission. He gave her his benediction and presented her with some relics.

On their departure, they were joined by Bishop Cyriacus and two priests, one Peter of Egypt, and the other from St. Augustine's birthplace, a nephew of the one who had bestowed lands on the saint for his monastery. Reverence for the holy relics was their chief motive in following Ursula. She took with her to Cologne a relic of Peter that is still venerated as such, though none know whence it came; one of Paul; some hair of John the Evangelist, and a scrap of the garment he wore when cast into the boiling oil.

On the return of the pilgrims to Basle, they were joined by so many recruits that eleven vessels were necessary to convey them to Cologne. Meantime, the Huns had invaded the country, bringing with them misery and confusion. At some distance from the city, the angel Raphael appeared to Ursula in a vision, made known the approach of her martyr's crown, and told her all that she was to do—among other things, that she was to oppose resistance until her little army had been duly prepared and baptized. This vision Ursula communicated to her assistants, and all turned their thoughts to God.

As they approached Cologne they were saluted by the shouts and darts of the Huns, but they rowed vigorously and by-passed the city. They would not have disembarked at all in its vicinity, were it not that so many of their party were there awaiting their arrival. They landed therefore about a league and a half above Cologne and halted in a field between two thickets, where they pitched a sort of camp. Here I saw those that had remained behind hurrying to join them with their recruits. Ursula and the priests addressed the different bands and prepared them for the struggle.

The Huns approached and their leaders accosted Ursula; they insisted on being allowed to choose among the maidens. The latter however courageously prepared to defend themselves, while some of the inhabitants of the city and the country around who had suffered from the Huns—and others who had become acquainted with the virgins who had remained in Cologne—joined the pious little army equipped with poles, clubs, and whatever else they could find. This was what had been commanded Ursula by the angel, that time might be gained until all were prepared for martyrdom.

During the engagement I saw Ursula running hither and thither, zealously exhorting the bands in the rear, and ardently praying. The priests were everywhere busily baptizing, for numbers of pagan women and girls had come over to them. By the time all were prepared for death, the Huns had surrounded them on all sides. The virgins now ceased defending themselves and gave themselves up to martyrdom, singing the praises of God.

Then the Huns fell upon them and slew them with axe and spear. I saw a whole row of virgins fall at one time under a flight of the barbarians arrows; among them was one named Editha, of whom we have a relic. Ursula herself fell, pierced by a lance. Among the bodies that strewed the field of martyrdom there were, besides the British virgins, great numbers of those that had joined them at various places, also the priests from Rome, some other men, and some of their enemies. Many more were massacred onboard the ships.

Cordula was not among those who had accompanied Ursula to Rome. She had remained at Cologne, where many joined her. When the slaughter began, she hid at first through fear; but she afterward gave herself up with all her companions, requesting to be put to death. The Huns were eager to spare them, but they offered so sturdy a resistance that, after a long delay, they were placed in a line, bound together by the arms, and shot with arrows. They went joyfully singing and dancing to martyrdom as if to a marriage feast. Later on, many others gave themselves up and were similarly put to death in different parts of the country. Shortly after, the Huns withdrew from the district. The bodies of the virgins and other martyrs were soon interred in an enclosed field near Cologne. Deep pits were dug and walled in, and there the bodies were devoutly laid in rows.

The ships of the virgins were open, beautiful, and very light, with galleries around them from which floated little standards; they had masts and projecting sides. By the oars ran benches used both for seats and berths. I have never seen vessels so well ordered. About the time that Ursula left England, the saintly bishops Germain and Lupus were living in France; the former visited St. Genevieve, in Paris, who was then about twelve years old. When he crossed over to England with Lupus to combat the heretics, he consoled the parents of Ursula and those of the other maidens. The Huns mostly went bare-legged; they had leathern thongs hanging around the lower part of their body and wore wide jackets and long mantles. These last they often rolled up and carried on their shoulders.

Viliulphus and Chrysostomus

THERE *were two relics in Anne Catherine's possession that the preceding year she had identified as belonging to a particular saint, of whom she knew only that he had been bishop of Leiria in Spain [Portugal]. On this present occasion, unaware that the relics were near at hand, she said she was beholding Viliulphus, of whom she had hitherto known nothing. She saw in vision his whole life, but on account of the demands and distractions of her own domestic situation, forgot all but the few things that follow:*

I beheld Viliulphus as a student of St. Chrysostomus, whose feast is this very day. Viliulphus was a pagan, a Greek from a small place not far removed from Constantinople. (In trying to further describe this place, she said its name was something like Cussa, though she did not know for certain.) His father had died, and his mother lived still a pagan life. He was a young man.

When Chrysostomus was studying in Athens, I saw how he sent the young Viliulphus on all sorts of errands, all the while instructing him also in the teachings of Christianity. His mother, as I saw, was most dissatisfied with her son. Once, when Chrysostomus went on a journey, I saw Viliulphus hasten after him. He was baptized and thereafter served for five years as a deacon, then became a priest. As such, he later returned to his mother, whom he converted.

I beheld Viliulphus in many locales. In due course he was killed in Spain by some Saracens. His bones were miraculously discovered by a woman with the help of a cow, but I do not recall the particulars.

I saw in vision how Chrysostomus was granted many visions of Mary, and how—as she had done also with Anthony—she permitted Chrysostomus to embrace her child. She also instructed him in penitence. I saw a miracle regarding Chrysostomus. The unbelieving wife of a Christian had gone with her husband to the mass in order to make sport of it. She had brought along her maidservant and secretly offered her the host, while she herself ate a piece of bread she had with her. Chrysostomus beheld this in spirit, and prayed, after which the bread in the mouth of the wife turned to stone. Before all the people he then took the host from the mouth of the maidservant and the stone from that of the wife, who was then converted.

I saw Chrysostomus as a hermit, and also as Patriarch of Constantinople, and how the empress—a woman as wantonly godless as Semiramis had been—drove him away. But in punishment there came a great quaking of the earth, a conflagration, and a shower of stones. Yet was he driven forth again and again by this evil woman toward Armenia, to a place called Cocosa, where he died in great poverty.

Walburga

ANNE *Catherine took from "her church" a finger bone, looked at it in silence for a moment, and then exclaimed:*

What a sweet little nun! So clear, so beautiful, so transparent! She is altogether angelic! It is Walburga! I see her convent too.

Then followed visions of the saint and of the disinterring of her sacred remains, which Anne Catherine gives as follows:

Two blessed nuns took me into a church in which a grand festival was being celebrated, either the translation of a saint's relics, or a canonization. A bishop was superintending everything and assigning places to the assistants. It was not the church of the convent in which Walburga had lived; it was another and a larger one, and the crowd was far greater than I had ever seen around the crucifix at Coesfeld. Numbers were obliged to remain outside the doors. I stood near the altar, not far from the sacristy, the two nuns by me. On the steps of the altar was a plain white chest containing the holy body; the white linen cloth was raised and hung at either side. The body was white as snow, and one might have thought her alive, so rosy were her cheeks. Walburga always had the pure, fair complexion of a delicate little child.

The feast began with high mass. But I could not stand any longer. I must have fainted, for I found myself lying on the ground, my two companions at my head and feet. I saw an abbess of Walburga's convent in the sacristy preparing three kinds of dough for bread: two fine; the third coarser, of white flour indeed, but full of chaff, and I began to wonder for whom they were intended. Here I lost sight of the earthly festival and I entered a heavenly garden in which I was shown Walburga's reward in heaven.

I saw her with Benedict, Scholastica, Maurus, Placidus, and many holy virgins of Benedict's rule, at a table spread with marvelous dishes. At the head sat Walburga, completely surrounded by garlands and arches of flowers. When I returned to the church, the feast was over; but I received from the bishop and abbess a loaf of coarse bread, marked with the number IV. The fine bread was given to my companions.

The bishop told me that my loaf was for myself alone, that I must not give it away. Then he led me out before the church door where Walburga's nuns had their little oratory, and I had another vision of her.

She had, a short time before her blessed death, been found as if dead in her kneeling-place. Her brother Willibald was sent for, and to his surprise he saw her face and hands covered with white dew-drops like manna. He gathered it into a brown bowl and gave it to the nuns as a holy thing. They wrought numerous cures with it after Walburga's death. When she returned to herself, Willibald gave her holy communion. The dew prefigured Walburga's oil, which I saw had begun to flow on a Thursday, because the saint bore so great a devotion to the blessed sacrament and our Savior's agony in the Garden of Olives. As often as I take this oil, I feel strengthened as by a heavenly dew; it has helped me greatly in severe sicknesses.

Walburga was full of tenderest love for the poor. She used to see them in vision. She knew even before they came to her how she should distribute her bread among them. She gave to some whole loaves, to others half, and to others pieces that she cut herself. She gave them also a certain oil—thick poppy oil, I think—which she mixed with butter and spread on the bread; besides which she gave them some for their cooking. On account of her bounty and the soothing, consoling influence of her gentle, loving words, her relics have received the property of distilling oil. Walburga also protects against vicious dogs and wild beasts. I saw her going by night to the sick daughter of a gentleman in the neighborhood of her convent. She was assailed by his dogs, which, however, she put to flight.

Walburga wore a narrow brown habit, a broad girdle, and a black veil over a white one; it was more the dress of pious females of the time than a regular religious habit. I saw a miracle that took place at the time of the great pilgrimage to her tomb. Two assassins joined a pilgrim on his way thither, the latter kindly sharing with them his bread; but they, in return, killed him as he slept. Then one took up the corpse on his back to bury it out of sight; but he could not lay it down again, it stuck to him as if it had grown fast. I saw him wandering around in despair with the corpse on his back, until at last he plunged into the river to drown himself. But he could not sink, the waters would not have him—they cast him up on the opposite bank, the horrible load still clinging to him. Then I saw someone try to loosen the hands of the dead man with his sword; but, far from succeeding, he remained himself fastened to the corpse until he freed himself by prayer.

When the pilgrim objected to this narrative, saying that it was strange she should see as true so many singular things that even pious priests denied, she replied:

One cannot say how simple, natural, and connected all such things appear in the state of contemplation; and on the contrary how perverse, unreasonable, and even insane are the intentions and actions of the enlightened world compared with them! People who think themselves very intelligent and who are esteemed such by others, often appear to me insane enough to be confined in a madhouse.

Zephyrinus

I SAW the holy pope Zephyrinus[1] who, on account of his zeal for the dignity of the priesthood, suffered much from both Catholics and heretics. He was very strict in the admission of candidates, whom he closely examined and of whom he rejected many. Once, out of an immense number, he chose only five. I often saw him disputing with heretics who unrolled parchments, spoke angrily, and even snatched his writings from him.

Zephyrinus exacted obedience from priests, sending them here and there, and silencing them if they would not obey. I saw him send a man, not yet ordained, to Africa, I think, where he became a bishop and a great saint. He was a friend of Zephyrinus and a very celebrated man. I saw the pope exhorting the faithful to bring him their silverplate, when he replaced the wooden chalices of the churches by silver ones. The cruets were of clear glass. Zephyrinus retained the wooden vessels for his own use, but as some were scandalized at it, he had them partly gilded, and all the rest he gave to the poor. I saw him contracting debts for the relief of a poor family, whereupon one of his female relatives reproached him for running into debt for strangers rather than for his own poor relations. He replied that he had done it for Jesus Christ, at which she indignantly withdrew. Now, God had allowed him to see that, if he did anything for this woman, she would be perverted.

I saw that he caused candidates for the priesthood to be examined and ordained in presence of the faithful. He drew up strict

---

[1] Zephyrinus was bishop of Rome, or pope, from 199 till his death in 217.

rules for their observance when bishops celebrated, assigning to each his own rank. He also ordained that Christians of a certain age should receive the blessed sacrament at Easter in the Church. He no longer permitted them to carry it to their homes suspended from their necks in a box, since it was often taken into improper places where feasting and dancing were going on.

Zephyrinus bore deep veneration for the Mother of God, and he had many visions of her life and death. He arranged a bed for himself just like the couch on which she had died. He always kept it concealed by a curtain, and with fervent devotion he used to lie down to rest in the same position in which he had seen her die. He also wore secretly under his robe another of sky-blue in honor of Mary's sky-blue mantle.

I saw him receiving again, after their canonical penance, sinners who had been separated from the faithful for adultery and impurity. He had disputes on this point with a learned priest (Tertullian) who was too rigid and who afterward fell into heresy.

Relics and Blessed Objects

Anne Catherine's Gift of
Recognizing Relics and Blessed Objects

WITH *the gift of prophecy, Anne Catherine had also received the power of discerning holy objects, even by the senses. Blessed bells had for her a melody all their own, a sound essentially different from every other that struck her ear; her taste detected the blessing imparted to holy water as readily as others can distinguish water from wine; her sense of smell aided her sight and touch in recognizing the relics of saints; and she had as lively a perception of the sacerdotal benediction sent her from afar as when given in her actual vicinity. Whether in ecstasy or the state of consciousness, she would involuntarily follow the consecrated fingers of a priest as if deriving from their influence strength and benediction.*

This keen perception of all that was holy, of virtues, of spiritual properties, was not conveyed to her senses by previous knowledge received in vision. It was perfectly independent of the activity of the mind and as involuntary as is the transmission of ideas to it through the medium of the senses. This faculty of realizing what the senses could not perceive had, like the gift of prophecy, its very foundation in the grace of baptism and infused faith. Her angel once said to her: "You perceive the light from the bones of the saints by the same power you possess of realizing the communion of the faithful; but faith is the condition on which depends the power of receiving holy influences." Anne Catherine saw all that was holy radiant with light. She said once:

I sometimes see when lying fully awake, a resplendent form hovering in the air, toward which rise thousands of brilliant rays, until the two lights unite. If one of these rays should happen to break, it falls back, as it were, and darkness takes its place.

This is an image of the spiritual communion of the faithful by prayer and good works. She felt the influence of this light as of something that relieved and strengthened her, something that filled her with joy and

139

powerfully attracted her to itself; while on the contrary she turned suddenly and involuntarily, filled with horror and disgust, from whatever was unholy, from whatever was tainted with sin. She once said to the pilgrim:

It is very difficult to explain this clearly. I see the blessing and the blessed object endowed with a healing and helping power. I see them luminous and radiating light; evil, crime, and malediction appear before me as darkness radiating darkness and working destruction. I see light and darkness as living things enlightening or obscuring. For a long time I have had a perception of the authenticity of relics, and as I abhor the veneration of false ones, I have buried many such. My guide tells me that it is a great abuse to distribute as genuine relics objects that have only touched relics.

One day while I was baking hosts in the convent, I felt suddenly attracted toward a certain cupboard, indeed I was violently drawn to it. In it I found a round box containing relics, and I had no peace until I gave them a more honorable resting place.

On another occasion she spoke as follows:

I have been told that the gift of recognizing relics has never been bestowed upon any one in the same degree as God has given it to me, and this on account of their being so sadly neglected and because their veneration is to be revived.

These last words are fully explained by Anne Catherine's communications on the feast of the Holy Relics, 1819–1820. On the first Sunday of July, 1819, she related what follows:

I had to go with my guide into all parts of our country where lay buried the bones of the saints.[1] I saw entire bodies over which buildings had been erected and places upon which convents and churches had once stood. Here lay whole rows of bodies, among them those of some saints. In Dülmen I saw sacred relics reposing between the church and the school house, and the saints to

---

[1] "This vision appeared to me all the more remarkable," writes Brentano, "when I discovered that the feast of Holy Relics is celebrated at present in the diocese of Münster, a fact wholly unknown to Anne Catherine. Her obligation to satisfy for the negligence committed in the Church is indeed wonderful!"

whom they belonged appeared to me, saying: "That is one of my bones!" I saw that these neglected treasures confer blessings wherever they lie and ward off satan's influence. I have seen certain places preserved from serious calamities by them, while others of recent date suffered severely because possessing nothing of the kind. I cannot say in how many strange, out-of-the-way places, under walls, houses, and corners I have been where the richest treasures of relics lie unhonored, covered up by rubbish. I venerated them all and begged the dear saints not to withdraw their love from the poor people. I went also to the place of martyrdom in Rome and saw the multitudes of saints who there suffered death. My heavenly bridegroom there appeared to me under the form in which I am so accustomed to see him—that is, in his twelfth year. The saints seemed to me innumerable; they were divided into choirs headed respectively by him who had instructed and encouraged them. They wore long white mantles with crosses and caps, from either side of which hung long flaps down to the shoulders.

I went with them into underground caves full of passages, chambers, round apartments like chapels, into which several others opened, and in the center of which stood a pillar supporting the roof. Many of these pillars were ornamented with beautiful figures. In the walls were deep, quadrangular excavations in which reposed the bones of the dead. As we passed along, sometimes one of my guides, sometimes another, would say: "See, here we lived in time of persecution, here we taught and celebrated the mysteries of redemption!" They showed me long stone altars projecting from the wall, and others round and beautifully sculptured upon which the holy sacrifice had been offered. "See," they said, "we lived here for a time in poverty and obscurity, but the light and strength of faith were ours!"—and after those words the different leaders disappeared with their choir.

Sometimes we came to daylight, but only again to plunge into the caves. I saw gardens, walls, and palaces overhead and I could not understand how the people up there knew nothing of what was going on below, how all these things had been brought down into the caves, how it was all done! At last there remained with me of all the saints only one old man and a youth. We entered a spacious apartment whose form I could not determine, as I could not see its limits. It was supported by numerous pillars with sculptured capitals, and beautiful statues larger than life lay around on the ground. At one end the hall converged to a point where, standing out from the wall, was an altar, and behind it other statues. The walls were full of tombs in which rested bones, but they were not luminous. In the corners lay numberless rolls, some short and thick, others as long as one's arm, like rolls of linen. I thought they were writings. When I saw everything so well preserved, the hall so neat and cheerful, I thought it would be very nice to stay awhile, to examine and arrange things, and I wondered that the people overhead guessed not of its existence. Then I had an assurance that all would come to light someday through a great catastrophe. Were I present at the time, I should try to bring it about without injuring anything. Nothing was said to me in this place; I had but to gaze. Why? I know not. And now the old man disappeared. He wore a cap like the others with lappets on the shoulders, and a long beard. Then the youth took me back home.

Feast of Holy Relics, 1820

I AGAIN visited innumerable places where lie relics under buildings, buried and forgotten. I went through cellars in mud and dust, into old church crypts, sacristies, tombs, and I venerated the holy things lying there, scattered and unknown. I saw how they once shone with light, how they shed around a benediction, but their veneration ceased with the decline of the Church. The churches erected over them are dark and desolate, the saints under them are no longer honored. I saw that their veneration and that of their relics had decreased in the same measure as the adoration of the most blessed sacrament, and then I was shown how evil a thing it is to receive the holy eucharist through mere habit. Grievous sufferings were imposed upon me for this contempt. In the spiritual church I saw the value and efficacy of the holy relics now so little regarded on earth.

I saw an octangular church arising like a lily from a stalk and surrounded by a vine. It had no altar, but in the center, on a many-branched candlestick, reposed the richest treasures of the church like bunches of opening flowers. I saw the holy things collected and honorably placed by the saints on this candlestick, this ornamental stand, which seemed constantly to increase in size. While thus engaged, the saints very often saw their own relics brought in by those who lived after them. I saw the disciples of John the Baptist bringing in his head and other relics of him, and the Blessed Virgin with little crystal phials of the blood of Jesus. In one of them the blood was still clear and shining. All were in the costly reliquaries in which the church preserves them. I saw saintly men and women of Mary's time depositing in precious vases holy things that once belonged to her; they were given the place of honor on the right. There was a crystal vase shaped like a breast in which was some of her milk, also pieces of her clothing, and another vase with some of her hair.

I saw a tree before the church, and I was shown how it had fallen and been fashioned into the Savior's cross. I saw it now in the form in which I always see it, brought in by a woman wearing a crown. It hovered in the air over Mary's relics. The three nails were stuck in it, the little foot ledge was in its place, as also the inscription. And skillfully arranged around were the instruments of the passion—the ladder, the lance, the sponge, the rods, the whips, the crowbars, the pillar, the cords, the hammers, etc.— while the crown of thorns hung from the center.

As the sacred objects were brought in and arranged, I had successive visions of the places in which these relics of the passion were found, and I felt certain that of all I saw, some particles are still preserved and honored. There must be many relics of the crown of thorns in different places. I discovered that my particle of the lance is from the haft. I saw in all directions—on altars, in chambers, churches, vaults, in walls, in rubbish, under the earth and on the earth—portions of the relics and bones that were brought into the church. Many consecrated hosts in chalices and ciboriums were brought thither by bishops, and corporals stained with the precious blood. They were placed on high over the cross. Then came the relics of the apostles and the early martyrs, followed by those of whole bands of martyrs—popes, priests, confessors, hermits, virgins, religious, etc. They were deposited at the foot of the cross in costly vases, ornamented caskets, towers, and shrines wonderfully wrought in precious metal. A mountain of treasures arose under the cross which gradually ascended as the mound increased and, finally, rested upon what might be termed a transfigured Golgotha.

The relics were brought by those who had themselves honored them and exposed them to the veneration of the faithful; they were for the most part holy personages whose own relics are now held in benediction. All the saints whose relics were present ranged in choirs, according to their rank and profession. The church became more and more crowded, the heavens opened, and the splendor of glory gleamed around. It was like the heavenly Jerusalem! The relics were surrounded by the aureolas of the saints to whom they belonged, while the saints themselves sent forth rays of the same colors, thus establishing a visible and marvelous connection between them and their remains.

After this I saw multitudes of well-dressed people thronging around the church with marks of deep veneration. They wore the various costumes of their times; of the present day, I saw but few. They were people who honored the saints and their relics as they ought to be honored, as members of the body of Jesus Christ, as holy vessels of divine grace through Jesus, in Jesus. On them I saw falling like a celestial dew the beneficent influence of those saints; prosperity crowned all their undertakings. I rejoiced to see here and there, in these our days, some good souls (some of whom I know) still honoring relics in all simplicity. They belong chiefly to the peasantry. They salute simply and earnestly the relics in the church as they enter.[1]

The veneration paid the saints and their relics in the present day I see—yes, even thrown among filth and dirt—and yet they still shed light around, still draw down a blessing. The church itself was in as pitiable a state as the relics. The faithful still frequented it, but they looked like grim shadows; only occasionally was a simple, devout soul to be seen who was clear and luminous.

---

[1] "To my great joy I saw my brother among them. As he enters the church, he devoutly invokes the holy relics it contains, and I see that the saints give fertility to his fields."

The worst of all were the priests themselves, who seemed to be buried in mist, unable to take one step forward. They would not have been able to find the church door were it not that, in spite of their neglect, a few fine rays from the forgotten relics still reached them through the mist.

Then I had distinct visions of the origin of the veneration of relics. I saw altars erected over the remains of the saints which, by the Blessing of God, afterward became chapels and churches, but which were now in ruins owing to the neglect of their sacred treasures. I saw in the time in which all was misty and dark, the beautiful reliquaries broken up to make money and their contents scattered around, which latter desecration gave rise to greater evils than did even the selling of the caskets. The churches in which these sacrileges happened have fallen to decay, and many have even wholly disappeared. I have been to Rome, Cologne, and Aix-la-Chapelle, where I saw treasures of relics to which certain honors are paid.

In consequence of the dismantling of churches and the suppression of convents, innumerable sacred relics had been scattered and profaned and had finally fallen into irreverent hands. This was a source of deep sorrow to Anne Catherine, who sought every opportunity to revive veneration toward these holy objects. People soon discovered that they could not give the poor invalid greater pleasure than by bringing her something of the kind, or asking her advice on the subject. In this way she accumulated quite a treasure of holy things.[1] More than three hundred genuine relics, with whose whole history she was perfectly familiar, were in her possession at the time of her death. She had received them

---

[1] One day Clara Soentgen brought her friend Anne Catherine a little package of relics. She took it, saying: "O this is a great treasure! Here are relics of St. Peter, his stepdaughter Petronella, Lazarus, Martha, and Magdalene. It was brought from Rome long ago. This is the way the saints' bones lie around when they pass from the Church into private hands. This reliquary was first bequeathed as an inheritance, then given away among old worthless things, and at last it fell by chance into Clara Soentgen's possession. I must have the relics honored." On another occasion, a Jewess found among some old clothing she had purchased a reliquary that she forcibly opened; but, terrified at her own act, she hurried with the relics to Anne Catherine, who had witnessed the whole affair in vision. She could not help smiling at the woman's fright.

principally from Dean Overberg, Father Limberg, the pilgrim, and others, who knew of her ability to recognize such things. If she found any spurious among those presented to her, she had them buried in consecrated ground. The others constituted her spiritual treasure, upon which she had at various times lights more or less clear, as God ordained that the gift He had bestowed upon His servant should tend to the restoration of the honor due His saints. Anne Catherine's recognition of relics was a grace which, in accordance with the designs of God, was intimately connected with the mission of her life; and it was for this reason that her angelic guide guarded it so jealously against the caprice, vain curiosity, or love of the marvelous, which might actuate those who submitted it to the test of trial.

It was only at the close of those investigations which so closely scrutinized Anne Catherine's whole life, both interior and exterior, that God provided occasions for the manifestation of her extraordinary gifts. He willed the perfection of her virtue to prove the reality of her supernatural gifts, rather than that the latter should be made the touchstone of her holiness. The first trial made with false relics, and so condemned by her angel, is thus recorded by the pilgrim under date of August 30, 1820:

"The parish priest of N— had sent to Anne Catherine three small packages of bones by Christian Brentano, the pilgrim's brother. At the pilgrim's request one of them was laid by her. The next day she related the following":

I saw far away dark, desolate tombs full of black bones, and I did not feel that they were holy. I saw the Father take some of them, and then I found myself up high in a dark chapel around which all was cold and bleak and foggy. My guide left me, and I saw a stately figure approaching me with a most gracious air. At first I thought it was an angel, but soon I trembled with fright. I asked: "Who art thou?" The answer came in two unknown words. I thought of them all the morning, but now I cannot recall them. They signified: *Corruptor of Babylon, seducer of Judah.* Then the figure said: "I am the spirit that reared Semiramis of Babylon and built up her empire! I am he who brought about thy redemption, for I made Judas seize *him!*" (he named not Christ, and this he said with an important air, as if wishing to impress me with the greatness of his exploits).

I made the sign of the cross on my forehead, whereupon he

grew horrible to behold. He began to rage furiously against me for having once snatched a young girl from him, and then he disappeared, uttering fearful threats. As he pronounced the first of the unknown words, I saw Semiramis as a little girl under some beautiful trees, the same spirit standing before her and offering her all kinds of fruits. The child looked up at him unshrinkingly, and although she was very beautiful, there was something repulsive about her—she seemed to be full of thorns, full of talons. The spirit nourished her and gave her all sorts of trinkets.

The country around was lovely; it was covered with tents, green meadows, whole herds of elephants and other animals with their keepers. It was shown me also how Semiramis raged against God's people, how she drove Melchizedek from her realm and committed many other abominations; and yet, she was almost adored! At the second word the spirit pronounced, I had a vision of Christ on the Mount of Olives, the treason of Judas, and the whole of the bitter passion. I do not understand why this spirit appeared to me; perhaps these are pagan bones and, consequently, the enemy has power to approach me. My guide has strictly forbidden me ever to take such bones again. "I tell thee," he said, "in the name of Jesus, it is a dangerous experiment! There is treachery in it. Thou mightest be seriously injured by it. We must not cast pearls before swine; that is, before the unbelieving, for pearls should be set in gold. Attend to such relics only as come to thee by the direction of God!"

In September following, some relics were sent to Anne Catherine by a priest who had visited her in Dülmen. She remarked:

I have had no particular vision concerning these relics. But I saw that the priest who sent them is a good man, although there are in his parish certain souls inclining to pietism not in accordance with the spirit of the Church. He cannot detect them; he thinks them very devout; but I have seen them spreading darkness all around. They make little account of the ceremonies of our holy Church. They have not openly declared themselves as yet; the evil is, however, in them. Then I heard a voice repeating near me: "Thou forgettest me! Thou forgettest me!" It was a warning from the other relics, and I was again told not to accept any more unknown relics to recognize even if brought me by the holiest priest in the world, for serious harm might result to me from it. I must first arrange what I already have.

Very little notice, however, was paid to the prohibition so earnestly repeated by the poor invalid. Curiosity triumphed over other considerations. The pilgrim not long after presented her, while in ecstasy, a little package of relics from two Rhenish convents. They had been sent him by a friend. Anne Catherine took them unsuspectingly, thinking them her own, but the next day she said:

My guide has severely reprimanded me for taking those relics contrary to his orders, and in consequence I have quite forgotten all that I saw. He again repeated that it is not the time to recognize unknown relics, and my too ready acceptance of them might entirely mislead me. The gift of recognizing such things is not a privilege to be called into play at every moment. It is a special grace. The time will soon come for me to use it, but not now. My guide also bade me remember Curé N— and his package, the thoughtless remarks he had made somewhere about myself and my relics, and that such remarks might do much harm. I must for the future refuse such things and meddle with none but my own.

The same warning was again repeated, and she was told that the pilgrim's friend—an enthusiastic supporter of the theory of mesmerism—was merely trying experiments on her, which might have very serious consequences, as her gifts were not what he thought. They were not subject to her own good pleasure, not a natural faculty to be employed at the discretion of the curious. The pilgrim submitted—but not so his friend, who still found excuses for testing her wonderful powers. Some time later she again declared:

Your friend's judgment of me and of what he sees in me is false! Consequently, I have been expressly forbidden by my guide to receive even a saint's relic from him. He only wants to make experiments, which may prove very injurious to me; and besides, he speaks of them publicly and in a manner quite opposed to the real state of the case. My gifts, my means of knowing, are not what he imagines! I see the drift of his thoughts when he speaks with me. He is all wrong concerning me. I was long ago warned of it in vision.

Some further days later Anne Catherine said:

I have had a wonderfully clear vision on the subject of relics, which I saw all around me and in many churches on the banks of the Rhine. I saw a coach attacked by robbers, and a little box of relics thrown from it into a field on the roadside. The owner returned to seek it, but in vain; it was found by another person, who kept it for some time. In it I saw the bone, brought here by *the friend*, but I must not name it. *The friend* must wait until his heart is changed. He is still surpassingly high and broad in his views. Faith, also, is high and broad; but it must often pass through a key-hole! *The friend* is obstinate in his erroneous opinion of me and my mission, his ideas on this point are strange and unreasonable; therefore have I received positive commands to have nothing to do with relics coming from him. His views are false, he publishes them unnecessarily, and he may thereby bring trouble upon me. My time is not yet come.

On St. Thomas's Day (December 21st), the pilgrim, on entering to pay his accustomed visit, found Anne Catherine busily engaged with her box of relics—"her church," as she playfully called it. Among them she had discovered several very ancient ones. The pilgrim was surprised to see in what beautiful order she had arranged them during the previous night. Although in a state of contemplation, she had lined the box with silk as neatly as if she had been wide awake. The five relics of James the Less, Simon the Zealot, Joseph of Arimathea, Denis the Areopagite, and a disciple of John, whom she called Eliud,[1] she had folded separately:

I had a very bright night! I found out the names of all the bones by me and I saw all the journeys of Thomas, as also those of all the apostles and disciples whose relics I have. I had a vision of a great festival, and of how all these relics came to Münster. They were collected by a foreign bishop at a very remote period, and they afterward fell into the hands of a bishop of Münster. I saw all with the dates and names, and I trust in God it will not be lost! I received permission, also, to reveal to my confessor the name of the relic that the *friend* brought me that he may note it down; but I must not tell the *friend* himself.

---

[1] Presumably the Eliud described in "The Three Shepherd Youths: Eremenzear, Eliud, and Silas" in *People of the New Testament IV.*

The friend, however, would not understand these words so indicative of Anne Catherine's bond with the Church and the supernatural origin of her marvelous gift; and she, seeing his ideas still unchanged, felt a lively desire to make known to him the secret name. She says most ingenuously:

Ah! I thought, if I could only tell him the name of that relic! and I had the word on my tongue when all at once a shining white hand was stretched forth from the closet there and laid on my lips to prevent my uttering it. It came so suddenly, so unexpectedly, that I almost laughed out!

This scene was repeated under almost similar circumstances a few days later when she was again seized with desire to gratify the friend's curiosity on the score of the relic he had given her:

I was again tempted to name the saint whose relic had caused me so much annoyance; but just as I was about to pronounce it, I heard a rapping in the closet, which checked me, and I dared not, I could not say it. More than once I have had the word on my tongue, but I could not speak it, although I wanted to do so.

Her confessor and the friend had likewise heard the rapping in the closet and were unable to account for it. But when the former exclaimed: "The evil one shall play us no tricks"—Anne Catherine quietly took the relic from the closet, saying: "It is the saint the pilgrim's friend brought."

We here add some facts that clearly show the priest's power over this chosen soul. On January 18, 1821, Father Limberg placed by Anne Catherine a sealed package, saying to the pilgrim as he did so: "I do not know what it contains; but when she notices it, I shall tell her where I got it." Then, turning to the invalid he asked: "What is this? Is it good? Tell me what it is." Although interrupted in her vision, Anne Catherine answered after a short pause:

It belongs to a pious man in the seminary at Paris. He brought it from Jerusalem and Rome. It contains various things: some hair belonging to a pope; a particle of the body of a new saint who died in a convent in the holy land; a small stone from the holy sepulcher; some earth from the spot on which our Lord's body lay; and some hair belonging to another person.

The pilgrim remarked to Father Limberg: "You found these, I presume, among the Abbe Lambert's effects, for he received similar objects from Paris." "Yes," replied Father Limberg. "In arranging his papers, I found the little parcel," and *with these words he left the room. Then Anne Catherine exclaimed:*

Who is that miserable little nun! then exclaimed the invalid. The Father said nothing to me about her! He ought to go see her. She is much worse off than I; she is lying in the midst of thorns!

(Anne Catherine saw herself under this figure, because the sealed parcel contained some of her own hair, which the old abbé intended to send to his friend.)

One day she recognized a relic as belonging to a holy pope whose name, however, she failed to recall. The pilgrim begged the confessor to present it to her once more. He did so, and she held it but a few seconds when she exclaimed confidently:

It is a relic of Pope Boniface I.

On another occasion Anne Catherine said:

I was busy all last night with the sacred bones. I saw all the saints and I was told to say, for the souls of all resting here in our cemetery, as many *Our Fathers* as there are relics.

✝ ✝ ✝ ✝

THE *following fact will show in a most striking manner the powerful impression made upon Anne Catherine by profane, as well as by holy, objects. The pilgrim records under the date of May 9, 1820:*

"Dr. Wesener, while excavating a pagan tomb, found a vase of ashes with which were mingled some fragments of a human skull. The pilgrim placed one on Anne Catherine's couch as she lay absorbed in ecstatic prayer; but she who was so powerfully attracted by the relics of the saints as to move her head, her hands, her whole person trembling in every muscle after them, let this bone lie unnoticed on the coverlet near the fingers of her left hand.

"The pilgrim thought it an object of indifference to her, when she suddenly exclaimed: 'What does that old Rebecca want with me?' And when he moved the bone a little nearer, she hid her hands under the coverlet, crying out that a swarthy old savage woman was running around the room followed by children naked like frogs. She could not look at her, she was afraid; she had seen such dark, wild people in Egypt, but she knew not what this old woman wanted with her, etc. Then, catching up her box of relics, she pressed it to her bosom with both hands saying, though still in ecstasy: 'Now she cannot hurt me! and she slipped under the coverlet.'

"The pilgrim now put the bone in his pocket and stepped to the side of her bed toward which her face was turned; but instantly she changed her posture. He returned to the opposite side, and again she as quickly averted her head; at last, he removed the unholy object from her presence, when she exclaimed with a sigh of relief that the saints had preserved her.

"During this scene, her confessor held out to her his consecrated finger, toward which she moved her head so quickly as to seize it with her lips and press it eagerly. 'What is that?' he demanded. Instantly came the astonishing answer: 'It is more than thou dost comprehend!'

"He withdrew his finger and laid his hand on the foot of the bed where, then, she tried to follow. Rigid in ecstasy and still clasping her box, she arose to a sitting posture and endeavored to reach the consecrated fingers with her lips. Then the pilgrim laid near the hand that clasped the box of relics a fragment of the fossil remains of some animal that the doctor had found in the river Lippe. Anne Catherine willingly received it, saying: 'Ah! this is all right! There is nothing hurtful about this. It is a good animal; it never committed sin!'

"Then she exhorted the pilgrim not to meddle with heathen bones, not to bring them to her mixed up with the bones of the saints: 'Go, throw that old woman away! Take care, she might hurt you! she exclaimed earnestly at intervals.'

"Some days after, when the pilgrim alluded to the incidents just related, Anne Catherine severely represented to him how improper, how dangerous, it was for him to make such experiments upon her, to mingle thus the sacred with the profane, and to expose her to unbecoming impressions:

"'Pagan bones repel me, fill me with disgust and loathing! I cannot say that I actually felt that the woman is damned; but I perceived around her something sinister, something that turns away from God, that spreads around darkness, or rather, that is darkness itself—quite contrary to the luminous, attractive, beneficent bones of the saints. The old woman glanced around furtively, as if in connection with the powers of evil, as if she herself could harm. All round her, forest and heath, lay in darkness; not in the darkness of night, but in spiritual darkness, the darkness of wicked doctrines, in the darkness of separation from the light of the world, in the covenant of darkness. I saw only the woman and her children, but there were miserable huts of various forms scattered here and there, sunk in the earth, surmounted, some by round sod roofs, others by square reed ones, and some again by conical ones; between most of these huts were underground passages. The unholy, heathenish influence of such remains may produce much evil if made use of for unlawful, superstitious practices. They who so use them become thereby, though unknown to themselves, participators in their influence; they establish a communication with them, just as the veneration of holy relics imparts a share in the benediction, the sanctifying influence, of what is redeemed and regenerated.'"

It was not only in vision, but also in the natural state of consciousness that Anne Catherine felt the attractive influence of holy relics, saw them shining, and knew their names; a fact to which the pilgrim testifies in his journal of Dec. 30, 1818:

"Sister Neuhaus, Anne Catherine's former mistress of novices, came to see her, bringing with her a small package. As she entered the room, the invalid experienced, as she herself said, a thrill of joy and an interior conviction that the package contained relics: 'Ah! you bring the treasure from your room and you keep there the dust!' And when Sister Neuhaus laid the parcel on the table near her, so great was her emotion that she feared every moment she would be ravished in ecstasy. It was with the greatest effort that she could entertain her visitor, her attention being powerfully drawn to the relics.

"Sister Neuhaus asked if she were unusually sick. 'Not perfectly well,' was the answer, and then she spoke of indifferent subjects, hoping to divert her mind from its all-absorbing object. An interior voice seemed to be calling out to her: 'There is Ludger! There he is!'"

After the sister left, Anne Catherine said:

I saw the whole time over the relic a glimmering of light, white as milk and brighter than the day; and when a particle fell on the floor I saw, as it were, a bright spark drop under the box.[1] As the pilgrim looked over the relics, I was almost ravished, and I heard a voice, exclaiming: "There is Ludger! That is his bone!" and instantly I beheld the holy bishop with mitre and crosier in the assembly of the saints. Then others were shown me, one by one: first, Scholastica above a troop of nuns, and her relic on the table; then Afra[2] surrounded by nuns, and her relic on the table; Benedict over a crowd of monks, and his relic on the table; Walburga with her nuns, and her relic below by the pilgrim. Among the nuns one was pointed out as Emerentiana, and I heard these words: "That is Emerentiana, and there is her bone!" I was surprised, for I had never heard that name before. Then I saw a maiden with a crown of double roses round her brow, holding in one hand a lovely garland of roses, in the other a bouquet, and I heard these words: "That is Rosalie, who did so much for the poor. She now holds the flower garland as she once did her pious gifts, and there lies her relic!" Then I saw a nun in a shining troop, and I was told: "That is Ludovica, and there is her relic. See how she scatters her gifts!"—and I saw that she had her apron full of loaves which she distributed to the poor. Then I saw a bishop and heard the words: "He lived in Ludger's time. They knew each other; they labored together," and yet, I saw them far apart. And now, among other blessed maidens, I saw a very young secular clothed in a spiritual garment of the style of the Middle Ages. Her body had been found incorrupt and entire. Her sanctity had thus been recognized, and one of her bones was placed among other

---

[1] There I looked, poor blind man that I am, and found it! CB

[2] St. Afra died in AD 303. In the late third century, her pagan family journeyed from Cyprus to Augsburg, where Afra was dedicated to the service of the goddess Venus by her mother, Hilaria. According to one source, she was originally a prostitute in Augsburg, having gone there from Cyprus, maybe even as the daughter of the king of Cyprus. She is reputed either to have run a brothel in that town or worked as a hierodule in the Temple of Venus. As the persecution of Christians during the reign of Roman Emperor Diocletian began, Bishop Narcissus of Girona (in Spain) sought refuge in Augsburg and lodged with Afra and her mother. Through his teachings, Bishop Narcissus converted Afra and her family to Christianity.

relics. At the same time I saw her open tomb. Then I saw a delicate youth of the early ages and near him six others and a woman. The name Felicitas was pronounced, and immediately a round place enclosed by walls and arches was shown me, and I was told that in the dens on one side were the wild beasts, and in the prisons opposite the martyrs in chains waiting to be torn to pieces. I saw also people digging by night and carrying off bones, and it was said to me: "They do this secretly. They are the martyrs' friends. In this way their relics are carried to Rome and distributed." I saw Felicitas near seven youths.

A week later, the pilgrim presented Anne Catherine with the rest of the relics in Sister Neuhaus's package. He writes:

"I gave her seven parcels, all of which she recognized as belonging to Elizabeth of Thuringia: 'I see Elizabeth,' she exclaimed, 'a crown in one hand, in the other a little basket from which fall golden roses, large and small, on a poor beggar below.'

"Here she pointed to a relic, saying: 'That is Barbara! I see her with a crown on her head and in her hand a chalice with the blessed sacrament.' Then, turning to another little paper, she said: 'These are from the place of martyrdom in Rome.'

"With these words she fell into ecstasy and described the places she saw and the sufferings of the martyrs, while at the same time she named the relics and presented them to the pilgrim to fold and label."

Brentano was amazed at the rapidity of her speech and movements. He expressed his astonishment in these words:

"I must acknowledge, to my shame, that of such things I know almost nothing! Fancy to yourself this poor peasant girl gazing on ancient Rome, describing its manners and customs! She understands all that she sees, even the moral state of the martyrs; and yet her inexperience is such that, for the most part, she knows not how to name the objects, the localities, the instruments that fall under her eyes!"

At the close of her vision, Anne Catherine asked her guide how these relics had come where they were and why they had not received the honor due them. He answered that they had been exhumed long ago, had passed from place to place, and had at last reached Münster. Here they had been put aside to make way for other things:

I was in a strange, wonderful city. I stood on top of the round building enclosing the circular place. Over the entrance, right and left, ran an inside staircase to where I was. On one side were prisons opening into the enclosure; on the other, the cages of the wild beasts. Behind these were nooks into which the executioners slipped when they released the animals. Facing the entrance against the wall was a stone seat up to which steps led on either side. Here sat the wife of the wicked emperor with two tyrants. Just back of this seat, upon the platform, sat a man who appeared to superintend affairs, for he made gestures right and left as if commanding something.

And now the door of one of the cages was thrown open and out dashed a spotted animal like a huge cat. The executioners stood behind the door, slipped into the nook for safety, and then mounted the steps to the platform. Meanwhile two other executioners had dragged a maiden from the prison opposite and removed her white tunic. Like all the martyrs she shone with light. She stood calmly in the middle of the arena with raised eyes and hands crossed on her breast; she showed no sign of fear. The beast did her no harm but, crouching before her, sprang upon the slaves who were urging it on with spears and cries. As it would not attack her, they got it back into its cage, I know not how.

The maiden was then led to another place of execution around which there were only railings. She was fastened to a stone by a stake, her hands bound behind her, and beheaded. I saw her put her hands behind her back herself. Her hair was braided round her head; she was lovely, and she showed no fear. Then a man was led out into the arena; his mantle was removed, and only an undergarment left that reached to his knees. The beasts did him no harm, and he too was beheaded. He was, like the maiden, pushed from side to side and pricked with sharp iron rods. These grievous tortures were borne with such joy that the looker-on can but regret not sharing them. Sometimes the executioners themselves are so wonderfully affected by the sublime spectacle that they boldly join the martyrs, confess Jesus Christ, and suffer with them.

I see a martyr in the arena. A lioness pounces upon him, drags him from side to side, and tears him to pieces. I see others burned alive, and one from whom the flames turn away and seize upon the executioners, of whom numbers perish. A priest who secretly consoled the sufferers has his limbs cut off one by one and presented to him in the hope of making him abjure his faith; but the mutilated body, full of joy, praises God until the head is struck off.

I went also into the catacombs. I saw men and women kneeling in prayer before a table on which were lights. One priest recited prayers, and another burned incense in a vase. All seemed to offer something in a dish placed on the table. The prayers were like a preparation for martyrdom. Then I saw a noble lady with three daughters, from sixteen to twenty years of age, led into the arena. The judge seated on high was not the same that I had last seen. Several beasts were let loose upon the Christians, but they harmed them not; they even fawned upon the youngest. The martyrs were now led before the judge, and then to the other place of execution nearby. The eldest was first burned with black torches on the cheeks and breasts and under the arms, and pincers applied to her whole body; after which she was conducted back before the judge. She noticed him not, however, for she was intent upon her sister, whom they were now torturing. The same happened to all four, and then they were beheaded. The mother was reserved for the last, her sufferings intensified by the sight of her daughters' torments.

I saw a holy pope betrayed, dragged from the catacombs and martyred while one of the most furious of the Romans, suddenly touched with repentance, rushed among the martyrs and perished with them. I longed so for the same favor that I cried out; but a voice said to me: "Every one goes his own way! We suffered martyrdom but once, but thou art constantly martyred. We had one enemy, thou hast many!

On another occasion the pilgrim offered Anne Catherine some relics, which she took, pressed to her heart, arranged in order, again pressed to her heart, and regarded attentively. Then she gave them back separately, removing one from the lot as spurious and exclaiming:

They are grand! No words can describe their beauty!

To the question as to what she experienced from the sacred bones, she answered:

I see, I *feel* the light! It is like a ray that pierces me, ravishes me.

157

I *feel* its connection with the glorified spirit, with the whole world of light. I see pictures from the life of the saint, and his place in the Church Triumphant. There is a wonderful connection between body and soul, a connection that ceases not with death; consequently, the blessed soul can continue its influence over the faithful through particles of its earthly remains. It will be very easy for the angels to separate the good from the bad at the last day, for all will be either light or dark.

On another day, while rapt in contemplation, Anne Catherine took her little box of relics and, from among more than one hundred, chose out one particle that she said belonged to Ignatius of Loyola. On returning to wakefulness, she began again to hunt up fragments belonging to one another, and in about five minutes she had made up six separate piles. Of one of them she said:

I ought to have *ten* pieces.

She counted again, but found only nine.

There ought to be ten, she repeated.

At last, she found the tenth. She fell back exhausted, saying:

I can do no more. I can see no more!

After a pause, she exclaimed:

I felt irresistibly drawn to look for these relics. They attracted me, and I sighed for them! It is easy to recognize them at such times, for they shine with a different light. I see little pictures like the faces of the saints to whom they belong, toward which rays of light dart from the particles. I cannot express it! It was a wonderful state! It is as if one felt something confined in one's breast that strives to get free. The effort fatigues, exhausts.

Opening a paper, she remarked:

Here is a little stone.

And she picked it out from among many others precisely similar. She had no need of light for this occupation; indeed, she often performed it by night.

The Vicar Hilgenberg, having arranged some relics very elegantly, brought them to show Anne Catherine. She was delighted with them, saying:

I see some of them surrounded by an aureola of various colors. They shine with light, they are perfectly transparent. On looking more closely, I see a tiny figure that gradually increases in size until I behold the form, the clothing, demeanor, life, history, and name of the saint. The names are always under the feet for men, at the right side for women. Only the first syllable is written, the rest I perceive interiorly.[1] The letters are surrounded by an aureola of the same colors as the relics of the saints to whom they belong. It seems as if the names were something essential, something substantial; there is a mystery in them.

When I see the saints in a general way, without reference to my recognizing them, they appear to be in hierarchies and choirs, clothed according to their rank in the costume of the Church Triumphant, and not in that of the time in which they lived. Popes, bishops, kings, all the anointed; the martyrs, the virgins, etc., are in heavenly garments surrounded by glory. The sexes are not separated. The virgins have an entirely distinct, mystical rank. They were either voluntary virgins, or chaste married women, or martyrs to whom the executioners offered violence.

I see Magdalene in a high rank, but not among the virgins. She was tall, beautiful, and so attractive that, had she not been converted to Jesus, she would have become a female monster. She gained a great victory!

Sometimes I see only the saints' heads, sometimes the whole bust radiant with colored light. The glory of virgins and those who have led a tranquil life, whose combats have been only those of patience in daily trials, in domestic troubles, is white as snow, and it is the same for youths, whom I often see with lilies in their hands. They who were martyred by secret sufferings for the honor of Jesus shine with a pale red light. The martyrs have bright red aureolas and palms in their hands. The confessors and doctors are yellow and green, like a rainbow, and they bear green branches. The martyrs are in different colored glory, according to the various degrees of torments they endured. Among my relics I see some saints who became martyrs by the interior martyrdom of the soul without the shedding of blood.

---

[1] Whenever Anne Catherine, in compliance with Brentano's request, tried to trace the names of the relics as shown her in vision, she invariably wrote only the first syllable, and that in Roman characters.

I see the angels without aureolas. They appear to me, indeed, under a human form with faces and hair, but they are more delicate, more noble, more beautiful than men. They are immaterial, perfectly luminous and transparent, but in different degrees.

I see blessed souls surrounded by a material light, rather white than resplendent, and around them a many-colored glory, an aureola whose tints correspond to their kind of purification. I see neither angels nor saints moving their feet, excepting in the historic scenes of their life upon earth, as men among men. I never see these apparitions in their real state speaking to one another with the mouth; they turn to one another, interpenetrate one another.

Among Anne Catherine's relics were two of Hildegarde, one small, the other larger, a piece of the hip bone. One day she looked up with an air of surprise, as if someone were approaching her. She asked:

Who is that in a long white robe?

And then, turning to the little closet by her, she said:

O! it is Hildegarde! I have two relics of her, one large, which I do not often find, and a smaller one that is always coming to hand. The large one is less luminous. It belongs to a less noble part, for bones differ in dignity. So too the garments worn by Magdalene before her conversion shine less than the others. The members lost by a saint before his second birth are relics, since all humankind, even before the coming of Jesus, were redeemed through him. The relics, the holy bones of pure, chaste, courageous souls are firmer, more solid, than those of persons agitated by passions; consequently, the bones belonging to the simple old times are firmer and more attractive than those of a later period.

The pilgrim brought Anne Catherine a little box containing about fifty fragments of relics all lying together. As she was at the moment perfectly conscious—in the waking state—he remarked that it would be a good time to sort and arrange them. She assented and set to work earnestly, putting the particles of the same body by themselves, and even designating to what members they belonged. She said, as she picked up some scraps:

These were once in fire. I now see people hunting for them in the ashes. These were in the city church, and I see how they cleaned and prepared them. Those there are very brilliant, these less so; and there is one (pointing to it) that sheds around a particularly beautiful golden red light.

Here she fell into contemplation, from which she soon returned with the words:

I see an old palsied man lying on a bed in an open square. A bishop, with a crosier resting on his arm, is leaning over him, his head upon his shoulder, while his attendants stand around with lighted torches.

And she pointed out the relic with the beautiful light as connected with this scene, naming it Servulus. She also named Quirinus in connection with one of these relics.

The pilgrim then brought her a small package of relics belonging to the castle of Dülmen. It contained eight scraps of old stuff, which she laid aside with the words:

It was once worn by a saint. It is a piece of a stole, a vestment that touched a holy thing.

When asked how she knew that, she answered that ever since the package entered her room she had seen four saints by her clothed in this stuff. They had cut and touched it, and again they appeared to her as she was picking out the shreds. The pilgrim inquired if she did not see Thekla, whose relic lay by her. She answered:

Yes, I see her, now here, now there, in a vision, as if on the watch near the prison in which Paul is confined. Sometimes I see her gliding along by a wall, sometimes under an arch, like a person anxiously seeking something.

Picking up then a splinter of brown wood wrapped in blue, she said:

This is a piece of the wood of which was made the cross Mary had at Ephesus. It is of cedar, and the scrap of blue silk belonged to a mantle that once clothed an image of Mary. It is very old.

On November 6, 1821, Anne Catherine found among her relics a scrap of wood which she gave the pilgrim, saying:

This was brought from the holy land long ago by a pilgrim. It was taken from a tree that stood in the little garden of an Essene. Jesus was carried up over it by the tempter at the close of his forty-day fast.

Then she handed another package to him:

Here is some earth from Mount Sinai. I see the mountain by it.

Taking up a bone, she said:

It belongs to a saint of July; his name begins with E. I saw him in prison with two others whom starvation forced to suck the bones of the dead. When led forth to martyrdom, he was—on account of his wonderful discourse on God—looked upon as a fool, and they wanted to free him. But one of the soldiers cried out: "Let us see if he can call his God down from heaven! He is as worthy of martyrdom as the others!" and the blasphemous wretch was immediately struck by lightning. Then I saw the saint celebrating divine service in a church, after which he was martyred.

History of a Reliquary

WHEN, *on November 8, 1819, the pilgrim visited Anne Catherine, he brought with him in his breast pocket an old cross containing relics that she had never seen. As he approached her bed, she cried out: "O here comes a whole procession!" and she extended her hand toward the cross, which he had not yet removed from his pocket. He handed it to her. Opening it eagerly, she exclaimed: "Here they all are, and one old man as upright as the Swiss hermit!" The pilgrim left the cross with her, and next day she related the following history:*

As this reliquary approached I saw, in the order in which the relics lie, the saints hovering in the air in the form of a cross. Below lay a wild, woody country with a mass of dense underwood. I saw also some people, among whom was one old man like the old Swiss hermit. Then I had a vision referring to the cross:

In a woody valley among mountains near the sea I saw a hermitage of six female recluses, and I beheld their whole way of life. They were all young enough to help themselves; they were very silent, retired, and poor—keeping by them no provisions whatever, but depending wholly upon alms. They lived under a superior and recited the canonical hours. They wore a coarse, brown habit with a cowl. In front of their cells were neat little gardens that they cultivated themselves; each had its own entrance and contained orange trees. Here I saw the recluses.

I saw them occupied also in some labor new to me. On a machine like a loom were stretched cords which they wove into various colored carpets, coarse but very neat; they also did beautiful basketwork out of fine white straw. They slept on the ground, on a plank with two coverlets and a poor pillow, and they ate scarcely anything cooked. They took their meals together off a table in which holes were hollowed out to serve for plates; on either side swung leaves that could be raised to cover these stationary plates. I saw them eating a brownish-looking stew of vegetables. The greatest simplicity reigned also in the chapel. Whatever there was beautiful in it was of plaited straw. I thought: "Here are golden prayers and straw ornaments; but we have prayers of straw and gilded ornaments!" The stone altar was covered with a beautiful straw matting, scalloped on either side and falling at the ends. In the center stood a small tabernacle on which was that same cross that the pilgrim has. Two wooden candlesticks and a pair of wooden vases, with bouquets very symmetrically arranged in the form of a monstrance, stood on either side.

The little convent was a square, stone building with a shingle roof. The rooms were partitioned off by a boxwood wickerwork, the openings about as large as one's hand, and they were of various heights. In the chapel they were higher than a man, though they did not reach the roof; but in the cells they were lower, the recluses could see over them. They were woven on rods fixed in the walls. The entrance faced the sea and led into the kitchen, which opened into the refectory with its singular table; behind was the chapel. To the right and left were three cells, before which lay the little gardens. The doors leading into them from the cells were in the form of an arch, low and narrow, and the windows were over the doors, so that the residents could not look out. Before the windows were straw mats that could be raised on sticks like screens. The straw stools had no backs, only a wooden handle to raise them. The chapel was covered with the coarse striped carpet that the recluses made themselves. They did not have mass every Sunday, but a hermit came from time to time to say it for them and give them holy communion. They kept the blessed sacrament, however, in their little chapel.

I saw them one evening at prayer in their chapel when they were attacked by pirates. They had short, broad swords, wore turbans on their head, and spoke a strange tongue; they often carried off people into slavery. They were very savage, almost like beasts. Their vessel was large and lay at some distance from the shore, to which they came in a small boat. They destroyed the hermitage and dragged off the recluses, but without offering them insult.

One of the religious, still young and robust, took the reliquary from the altar as a protection, fervently imploring God's assistance. Before the robbers reached the shore, they quarrelled over their prey and, during their struggle, the young girl crept into a thicket, vowing to serve God in the wilderness if He would deliver her. The pirates sought her long, but in vain. At daybreak she saw them embark. Kneeling before the cross, she thanked God.

The wilderness lay in a narrow, deep valley, snow-capped mountains on either side, far away from any road; no people, no hunters, ever came there. The recluse sought long for a suitable place and found deep in the forest a little clearing surrounded by trees and thornbushes. It was sufficiently large for a small house. The trees almost entirely hid it overhead, and their roots spread over the ground. Here she resolved to serve God far away from humankind, destitute of both spiritual and human assistance. She built an altar of stones, placed upon it the cross, her only treasure, and arranged a little place wherein to take repose. She had no fire; she needed none, for it burned in her own heart. For nearly thirty years she never saw bread. High up in the mountains were animals like goats leaping among the crags, and around the dwelling of the hermitess were white hares and birds of the size of a chicken.

At last, a hunter in the service of a lord whose castle was some miles off came with his hounds into the neighborhood. (The castle was destroyed at a later period, only part of a moss-covered tower now stands.) The hunter wore a tight gray jacket, an embroidered belt as wide as one's hand, and a small round cap; he carried a spear in one hand and a crossbow under his arm. His dogs pressed barking into the thicket, in which the hunter saw something shining as he came up. It was the cross. Entering the enclosure, he began to call aloud but the solitary had hidden. She hoped to remain undiscovered; but finally, having no alternative, she made her appearance, bidding him not to be frightened at seeing one who no longer bore the semblance of a human being. As we looked at her—the hunter and I—we saw her surrounded by a bright light. She was tall, had a cincture round her waist, and her long gray hair hung over her breast and back; her feet were rough, her arms quite brown, and she walked bent down by years. In spite of her singular exterior, there was something very noble and imposing about her.

She seemed, at first, unwilling to disclose her story; but seeing in the hunter a good, pious man, she said: "I see that you are a servant of God," and then explained to him how she had come there. She refused to go with him but begged him to return in a year with a priest who would bring her the blessed sacrament.

At the time specified, I saw the hunter return with a hermit, a priest, who gave her holy communion, after which she asked to be left alone for awhile. When they returned, she was dead. They tried to bear away her body, but they could by no means move it; so they interred her on the spot. The hunter secretly took the cross as a memento of the affair. Later on, a chapel was erected over her grave in honor of a saint whom she particularly venerated and whom she had named; on all sides of it were doors. This virgin had lived a life of extreme poverty and entirely hidden in God. Before the pirates' attack she had had a dream in which she saw herself dragged into the water. In her dream, she made a vow to Our Lady of the Hermits to keep perpetual fast in solitude, if she were saved. Then she suddenly found herself in a canal or sewer, along which she crept until she reached the wilderness in which she afterward really lived, and where she was told she should remain. When she asked on what she should subsist, figs and chestnuts fell from the trees. As she gathered them, they turned to precious stones, the fruits of her penance and mortification.

As she related this prophetic dream to the hunter, I saw every circumstance of it. She was a Swiss by birth, and she had been just thirty years in the wilderness when the hunter discovered her. She told him that she was from Switzerland, as he might find on inquiry, and she named her birthplace.

She had always had great confidence in Our Lady of the Hermits, and from her childhood she had heard a voice urging her to leave her home and serve God in solitude. To this, however, she had paid little attention. At last, a youth appeared to her saying: "What! still here? Not yet set out?" and he led her away. She thought it all a dream; but on awaking she found herself in another country, far from her home. She entered the little convent of recluses, among whom she was well received.

The hunter kept the cross devoutly for some time, and then gave it to a man who lived in a town across the mountains. He too prized it very highly and always prayed before it. He attributed to it his own preservation and that of his property during a tempest that destroyed the whole town. At his death, it passed to his heirs and, at last, fell into the hands of a peasant who sold it with other effects; but misfortune followed this transaction, for the man lost all that he possessed. Then I saw the precious cross thrown aside with all sorts of things among people who thought little of the fear of God. A stranger, with no fixed principles of faith, purchased it from them, not through piety but through pure curiosity. He knew not the treasure he acquired, and yet it brought him great good.

Here the pilgrim makes the following remark in his journal:

"This last incident refers to the pilgrim himself who, at a time in which he lived in deplorable blindness, purchased the reliquary at Landshut from an old-clothes' dealer. Anne Catherine knew nothing of this by human means; therefore, if her last remark is beyond questioning, why should we hesitate to receive as authentic all that refers to this singular story?"

Then, as if deeply impressed by Anne Catherine's supernatural knowledge, he exclaimed:

"How wonderfully are all things preserved in the Treasury of God! Nothing is lost, nothing annihilated, nothing comes to pass without design! All is eternal in the Mind of God! Now do I understand why God must punish every idle word! The thought of my sins saddens me. Does this evil exist eternally? Are a man's sins visible after penance, after repentance?"

And Anne Catherine answers:

No, Jesus Christ atones for them; they no longer exist! I never see them, unless when they are intended to serve as an example; for instance, the sin of David. But sins that have never been expiated, sins that a man carries around with him shut up in his heart, I clearly see. The expiated are like footprints in the sand, which the next step, the step of repentance, effaces. The contrite confession of sin blots out sin!

An Infant-Martyr of Sachsenhausen

THE *pilgrim presented a relic to Anne Catherine, which she had already designated as belonging to a hermit. After a few days she related the following vision of a child, a relative of the old hermit, who had been martyred by the Jews:*

I have had an apparition of a child about four years old, surrounded by the martyrs' rosy aureola. There was something wonderfully attractive about him; his words were few, but full of wisdom. I went a long journey with him, and I was deeply impressed on seeing the little boy so brilliant with light, so grave, and so wise! We passed over a city, and I was instantly conscious of its state; I felt that its pious souls were few. The child led me over a bridge and showed me the house in which he was born, a tolerably large, old-fashioned dwelling. All was still within. On our approach, the occupants thought of the little boy—a faint remembrance of their history recurred to them—and I was told that the sudden remembrance of the dead often arises from their proximity.

The child showed me that, as the union between the soul and the body never ceases, not even after death, so the influence of a holy soul never ceases to be exerted over all belonging to it by ties of blood. A saint continues his influence over his family and, in proportion to their faith and piety, do they profit by it. He told me also of the salutary influence he had exercised over his relatives, and that he had attained by martyrdom to that perfection to which he would have arrived, if his life had not been cut short by man's wickedness; yet more, his relatives had profited spiritually by the influence he would have exercised had he lived, instead of being snatched away in his fourth year.

Evil happens not by the will of God, but only by His permission, and the accomplishment of good, prevented by another's sin, is not wholly frustrated; it is effected most surely, but in a different way. Crime in its essential consequences attacks its author only. As to its innocent victims, martyrdom leads them all the more speedily to perfection. Though sin against another be an act directly opposed to the law of God, yet the designs of God are never frustrated, since all that the victim would have achieved during life, he accomplishes spiritually and with the same freedom of will.

Then I saw the history of the martyred child. His parents were very pious people who lived about three hundred years ago, at Sachsenhausen, near Frankfort. They had a near relative in Egypt, an anchorite, whom they regarded with great affection and veneration. They frequently remarked, as they looked on their child, how happy they would be if he too would one day lead a holy life and serve God in solitude. Surely, parents who could form such a desire for an only child, still in his first year, must have been persons of more than ordinary piety!

When the child had attained his first year, one of his parents died. The other married again, and, still in the new family, continued to speak of the hermit and of the child's following his example. The little fellow was often entertained with this plan for his future. At last his only surviving parent died, and the little boy was now an orphan. The hermit continued to be spoken of in the family and the child, now four years old, earnestly longed to see him. (He told me that he was a beautiful child, but by no means so beautiful as I now beheld him, and that, had he lived, he would have been very good, perhaps a hermit.) His stepparents, who saw in him an heir of the family, were nothing loath to get rid of him. They secretly encouraged him in his desire to walk in his pious relative's footsteps; and, when not quite four years old, they entrusted him to some foreign Jews who were journeying to Egypt. This they did to make away with him; the plea of sending him to his relative was only a cloak for their treachery. Although this step led to his martyrdom, yet the child ever loved his family and country.

A feast was going on in the old-fashioned house. I thought it was a wedding, but the child told me it was a local festival. I saw numbers of brilliantly lighted apartments filled with elegantly dressed people dancing and feasting. "Thus they make merry," said the child, "over the bones of their ancestor who, by his piety, laid the foundation of their affluence." Then he took me to a walled-up vault where lay a white, well-preserved skeleton on a neatly arranged couch in a double coffin—the inner one of lead, the outer of some kind of dark wood. This was the progenitor of the family and a near relative of the child. He had been a very pious man and had amassed great wealth, without detriment to his piety. When the church in which he had been interred was destroyed, his children deposited his body in this vault, where he now lay wholly forgotten. I went through the whole house.

In this city I saw numbers of sacred bones in vaults over which had once stood convents and churches, but whose sites were now occupied by dwellings. The child told me that the city would soon decline, for it had now reached the summit of pride. Then he left me.

I traveled far across the sea into a hot sandy country where he again joined me in a ruined city whose houses seemed to be toppling down on one another. In a cave under a hill he showed me the place of his martyrdom: it looked like a slaughterhouse. In the walls were iron hooks from which the Jews had hung the child, as from a cross, and slowly bled him to death. On the ground yet lay the bones of many other martyred children, shining like sparks. It seemed as if no one knew of this place, and the martyrdom of the child had never been discovered or punished. There were no Christians there, only a few hermits who lived in the desert and occasionally visited the city.

Then I went into the desert and again met the child-martyr under the palm trees by the hermit's grave, in the same spot in which he had lived. He had died before his young relative had left Frankfort. His remains were luminous. Several others were buried in this desert, and around in the white sand lay pieces of some kind of black stuff, like broken pottery.

Here the child again left me and I was taken over the sea to another place, to a hill near the city which contains the *martyr-place* (Rome). On one side stand houses with grape vines here and there, and under it is a spacious vault upheld by columns. The entrance is closed; no one knows of its existence. As I entered, the child-martyr again appeared to me and I found a rich treasure of holy bones; the whole cave was lighted up by them. There were entire bodies in coffins standing against the walls and numberless bones in smaller caskets. I set to work to dust and open them. In one of them I found a body whose winding sheet was perfect wherever it had touched the holy remains, while all the rest was fallen to dust; and in others the bodies were thoroughly dried up and as white as snow.

I saw by my visions of the life of these saints that most of them belonged to the early ages. Some had been martyred for making offerings to Christian priests and, I think, they were denounced by their pagan relatives. I saw them going along with little birds under their arms. I saw multitudes who had become religious by the vow of chastity, and married couples who, for the love of Jesus, had lived in continence. I turned to a square shallow casket to which I was irresistibly attracted. I felt as if it belonged to me, for there I found all my own saints, all whose relics I have here. I wanted to bring it away with me, but the child said no, it must stay where it was, and so I covered it with a blue veil. The relics were all arranged on little cushions. The child told me that they had lain there concealed since the early ages and that there they were to stay. But the time will come when they will be brought to light.

Relics Belonging
to Churches in Münster

(Sent by Dean Overberg)

DEAN *Overberg had sent to Münster at various times packages of relics, some encased and labelled, others without either label or wrapping. Anne Catherine had first a general vision of them and afterward, as the feasts of the different saints occurred, received more particular information concerning each. She says:*

When I received those relics from Dean Overberg, I saw in vision with what solemnity they had been brought from Rome to Münster, mostly by bishops, and with what veneration they had been received and distributed. I saw devout women assembling together to fold and ornament them, and I saw the priests who divided them. To be allowed to share this labor, one had to be most pure and holy. The relics were glued, surrounded by embroidery and flowers, and arranged in pyramids. The first time they were exposed for veneration was a grand festival; the whole city rejoiced. I saw that many sacred relics were put into the altars of the Überwasser church. I saw devout canons of the cathedral who, whenever they heard of a saint, or holy person, tried to get a relic of the same. This they honored as a great treasure. When the church was rebuilt, the relics of the different altars were mixed and the members of several of the holy bodies were scattered; thus it was that the remains of the holy maiden of whom I have a bone were discovered. The great blessings diffused around by relics I saw withdrawn when they are treated with neglect. It was not by chance that these bones fell into Dean Overberg's hands. Without knowing to whom they belong, he gave them the honor due them.

How wonderful are the ways of God! remarks the pilgrim. He willed that these relics should be scattered that they might fall under the supernaturally enlightened eyes of her who knows so well their value.

One day, having taken up the box of relics—"her church," as she called it—the apostle Thomas appeared to her, and she had a full vision of his journeys and apostolic labors in the Indies:

He went from kingdom to kingdom, wrought many miracles, and uttered many prophecies. He set up a stone at a great distance from the sea, made a mark on it, and said: "When the sea flows this far, another will come to propagate the knowledge of Jesus!" I saw that he referred to Francis Xavier. Thomas was pierced with a lance, buried, and afterward disinterred.[1]

I think Matthias and Barsabbas are among those relics, for I had a short vision of their election to the apostleship. Matthias, though more delicately constituted, had more strength of soul, and he was therefore preferred [as a replacement for Judas] by God to Barsabbas, who was young and vigorous. I saw many things concerning the latter. I had also a vision of Simeon, a blood-relative of Jesus. He became bishop of Jerusalem after James and suffered martyrdom when over a hundred years old. There must be a relic of him here.

The following day Thomas's relic was pointed out to her in vision. She labelled it and wrapped it in paper:

---

[1] For a full account of Anne Catherine's visions relating to Thomas's apostolic journeys, see "Thomas" in *People of the New Testament II.*

I had visions of his journeys. I saw them as if on a map, and the bones of Simon and Judas Thaddeus, his brother, were shown me. Then I saw the whole family of Anne. She had three husbands. Joachim died before the birth of Jesus. After his death Anne married twice and had two daughters. I was greatly astonished to hear of these marriages, but I was told the reason of her contracting them. Then I thought of the prophetess Anna, whom I at once saw, as well as all the lodgings of the widows and virgins in the Temple. Anne's first daughter was Mary Alpheus [later, Mary Heli] who herself, at the birth of the Most Holy Virgin, had a daughter, also named Mary, afterward the wife of Cleophas, by whom she had four sons: James the Less, Simon, Judas Thaddeus, and Joseph Barsabbas. I have bones of the last three. In the presence of their relics I felt that they were united to Jesus by consanguinity. I had also a vision of Judas Thaddeus going to King Abgar, in Edessa. He carried a writing in his hand which Thomas had given him. As he entered I saw a radiant apparition of the Savior at his side, before which the sick king inclined, taking no notice of the apostle, whom he saw not. But the latter laid his hand upon him and cured him. After this he preached in the city and converted all the inhabitants.

I have again had visions of different saints. I saw the martyrdom of one Evodius who, with Hermogenes, his brother, and a sister, suffered in Sicily. I saw also many pictures of a holy white-robed nun, the Cistercian Catherine of Parcum. I saw her still a Jewess, reading from rolls of parchment things relating to Jesus, which deeply affected her. Some Christian children told her of the child Jesus, of Mary, and the crib, to which they took her secretly, and she was still more drawn to Jesus. She received instructions privately and, in consequence of an apparition of Mary, fled to a convent. I saw many other touching things concerning her, especially her longing to be despised.

This saint's relic was firmly sewed in red velvet, and when Anne Catherine took it to label and wrap, she saw—being in contemplation—that it contained a scrap of stuff that touched the Savior's crib, some splinters of the same, and a ticket on which all was marked.

This relic of the crib was the one that had belonged to St. Catherine herself and had been particularly honored by her, for she had seen in a vision the infant Jesus lying in his crib, and she often had the honor of holding him in her arms. All the above Anne Catherine related to the pilgrim before opening the little package. Judge of his satisfaction, then, when on removing the covering he found just what she had described, some scraps of wood, wrapped in a piece of brown stuff, with the inscription: De proesepio Christi [*that is, the nativity scene*].

Anne Catherine had fallen into ecstasy and, when the pilgrim offered her the scraps of wood, she took them smilingly, saying:

Ah! these belong to the crib of our Lord. The little nun used to venerate them!

The pilgrim, seized with a feeling of veneration for the favored being before him, made a movement as if to kiss her hand, but she suddenly withdrew it with the words:

Kiss St. Clare's relic. That is no longer of this earth! This (raising her hand) is still earthly.

At these words he was still more astonished, for he had in his breast-pocket a relic of St. Clare, which he had not yet shown her. He now presented it to her; she kissed it, exclaiming:

O there is Clare beside me!

When returned to consciousness, she said:

I had a little vision of St. Clare. War was raging around her convent, and although she was ill she had herself borne to the gate. She carried in her hands the blessed sacrament in an ivory box lined with silver. Here she knelt with all her nuns invoking God, when she heard an interior voice bidding her not to fear, and I saw the enemy departing from the city.

One day the pilgrim drew near her bed with a relic from the casket which she had not yet seen. She exclaimed joyously:

Afra! Here we have St. Afra; I see her bound hand and foot to a stake! O how the flames dance around her! (She turns her head to look.)

And with these words Anne Catherine seized the relic, which she kissed and venerated as belonging to St. Afra.

Toward dusk that same day the pilgrim opened another of the little parcels on which were inscribed the words: From the clothing of a saint, *and which contained also a bone and a label. It was almost dark and the objects were so very small that he did not imagine Anne Catherine noticed his action. To his surprise she called to him:*

173

Take care of the label! The relic shines; it is authentic!

He handed her the particle of bone, at which she instantly fell into contemplation. On returning to herself she said:

I have been far away to Bethany, Jerusalem, and France. The bone belongs to Martha; the clothing, to Magdalene. It is blue with yellow flowers and green leaves, the remnants of her vanity, which she wore under a mourning mantle in Bethany at the raising of Lazarus. This dress remained in Lazarus's house when he and his sisters went to France, and pious friends took it as a memento. Some pilgrims, when visiting their tomb in France, wrapped this relic in a part of the dress, thinking both belonged to Magdalene; but only the clothing is hers, the relic is Martha's.

When the pilgrim closely examined the inscription, he indeed found: "Sancta Maria Magdalena."

Among these relics of Dean Overberg's, Anne Catherine recognized a bone of Pope Sixtus VIII and another of the third pope after Peter. She appeared pleased at having been able to decipher the numbers, but next day she said:

When I again saw the saints to whom the relics belong, it was said to me: Not the third, but the *thirteenth*. His name signifies "Savior."

The pilgrim exclaims: "How wonderful! The *thirteenth* pope is Soter, the Greek for Savior!"

One day the pilgrim drew Anne Catherine's attention to the fact that St. Teresa's feast was at hand, adding: "We have a relic of her here, also one of Catherine of Sienna. There they lie among several others," whereupon she began and named in their order the saints whose relics hung in a cross at the foot of her bed:

I see their names, either at their feet or by their side, and I see, too, their attributes. There is Ediltrudis with the crown she resigned, and there are Teresa, Radegoncla, Genevieve, Catherine, Phocas, and Mary Cleophas. The last named is taller than Mary, but dressed in the same style; she is the daughter of Mary's eldest sister. And there I see Ambrose, Urban, and Silvanus!

The pilgrim asked: "Where is Pelagia?" *and she answered:*

She is not by me any more, she is there—pointing to the pilgrim's breastpocket, where indeed the relic really was, he having taken it to fold and label as one already recognized. The same was the case with another that he still had about him for a similar purpose.[1]

On February 11, 1821, as Anne Catherine lay in ecstasy, the pilgrim dropped from a prayer-book a little picture of Jesus crucified, which fell on the coverlet of her bed. She seized it quickly, her eyes still closed, ran her fingers over it several times, and exclaimed: It must be venerated! It is very precious! It has touched some sacred object; it shines brilliantly!

Then, laying it on her breast, she said: It has touched Christ's robe, on the neck of which is a stain of the precious blood of which no one knows!

On April 8, 1823, she said: I have had to perform a wearisome task connected with relics of the earliest ages, in a country beyond the holy land where the priests do not dress exactly like Catholic priests. They wear very antique vestments, something like those I saw on Mount Sinai. It seemed to be in the country I always see next to that of the three kings; the city in which was the old book of prophesies on copper plates (Ctesiphon)[2] lay to the left of it. Here I had much to do with the blood of Christ, and I had to discover a treasure of relics to the priests:

I saw seven old priests digging under ruined walls in an underground cave; they first propped the wall up for fear of its falling in. There they found holy relics sealed up in a great stone seemingly of one piece, but really formed of many three-cornered pieces skillfully put together. When it was opened, there first appeared a thick hair-cloth under which reposed the treasure, the principal relics of the passion and the holy family, all preserved in three-cor-

---

[1] At this point, Anne Catherine begins giving more extended accounts of the saints whom she saw in connection with relics, which are offered later in the section "Relics and Blessed Objects," along with other visions regarding them at other times, not always in connection with relics. When, later, Brentano recommences his report of visions more particularly related to relics, the first one, entitled "A Relic of the Precious Blood and of Our Lord's Hair," soon turns into an extraordinarily extended and detailed account of a married couple, Datula (the wife) and Pontianus (the husband), which may be read in full at the end of this volume.

[2] See "Ezra and the Canon" and "The Holy Book of Ctesiphon • Zoroaster" in *Mysteries of The Old Testament*.

nered vases placed side by side: sand from the foot of the cross, moistened and tinged with the blood of Jesus; and, in little phials, some of the water from his side—clear, consistent, no longer liquid; thorns from the crown; a piece of the purple mantle of derision; some scraps of the Blessed Virgin's clothing; some relics of St. Anne, and many others. Seven priests were there at work while deacons held torches, and I think they placed the blessed sacrament above them. I had much to do there, and many poor prisoners—that is, poor souls—to deliver, in which work the precious blood helped me. I think the apostles had to say mass in that cave.

Longinus and the
Effects of the Sacred Lance

IN *July, 1820, Anne Catherine's confessor, Father Limberg, received some relics without labels that had once belonged to the house of Dülmen; among them was a particle of the sacred lance. When he presented it to her, she exclaimed: "It pricks! that's a sign! I have received a thrust!"—and the wound in her side became red. Then she had the following vision of Longinus:*[1]

I saw the Lord dead on the cross. I saw all the people standing around in just the same position as on Good Friday. It was at the instant in which the legs of the crucified were to be broken. Longinus rode a horse or mule, but it was not like our horses; it had a thick neck. He dismounted outside the circle of soldiers and went in on foot, his lance in his hand. He stepped upon the little mound at the foot of the cross, and drove the lance into the right side of Our Lord.

When he saw the stream of blood and water, Longinus was powerfully affected. He hastily descended the mountain, rode quickly to the city, and went to tell Pilate that he looked upon Jesus as the Son of God, and that he resigned his appointment in the army. He laid down his lance at Pilate's feet and left him.

I think it was Nicodemus whom he next met, and to him he made the same declaration, after which he joined the other disci-

---

[1] For a more complete account of Longinus and the sacred lance, see "Cassius • Longinus," in *People of the New Testament III.*

ples. Pilate esteemed the lance dishonored, inasmuch as it had been used as an instrument of punishment, and I think he gave it to Nicodemus.

Here Anne Catherine laid the relic away in the little closet by her bed; but after some time she turned to it in ecstasy, saying:

There are the soldiers with the lance! Some of Christ's lance is in there! That is St. Victor. He carries a particle of it in his lance, but only three know of it.

That evening she lay insensible from excess of pain; she was in such a state that neither her confessor's benediction nor command seemed to have any effect upon her. Later, she related what follows:

After midday, I felt that the cross of Jesus was laid upon me and that his sacred body lay dead on my right arm; at some distance lay the lance, first a large piece, then a tiny particle. Which should I choose for my consolation? I took the holy body, and the lance was taken from me. Then I could speak again.

Again she exclaimed: I still saw the sacred lance sticking in my right side, and I felt it passing through to my left ribs. I held it in the wound to direct it through between the ribs.

Anne Catherine, on this occasion, vomited blood and her side bled freely.

A Particle of the True Cross

DR. WESENER'S *journal contains the following, dated Oct. 16, 1816. It is the first fact reported by an ocular witness respecting Anne Catherine's power of recognizing relics:*

"I found the invalid in profound ecstasy. Father Limberg was in her room. I showed him a little case I had found among some objects left me by my mother-in-law, lately deceased. Among other relics it contained two tolerably large particles of the true cross. Father Limberg made no remark, but took the case. Approaching to within some distance of the bed, he held it out to Anne Catherine. She arose instantly, eagerly stretched out her hands toward it and, on obtaining possession of it, pressed it closely to her heart; whereupon Father Limberg inquired: 'What is that?' 'Something very precious! some of the holy cross!'—she answered and, when withdrawn from her ecstasy by a command from the priest, she expressed her astonishment on finding that the relic was mine. She thought it had come among some pieces of old silk sent her from Coesfeld for her poor, and she wondered much that the pious donor had not taken better care of the precious case."

Five years later, the pilgrim writes: "Today they presented to Anne Catherine a piece of the true cross, belonging to Dr. Wesener. She grasped it eagerly." *She then exclaimed:*

I, too, have that! I have it in my heart and on my breast! (She always wore a relic of the true cross sent her by Dean Overberg.) I have a piece of the lance also. On the cross hung the body, in the body was the lance! Which shall I love the more? The cross is the instrument of redemption, the lance opened a wide door to love. O yesterday, I was far, far in! (The yesterday alluded to was a Friday.) The particle of the true cross renders my sufferings sweet, the relic chases them away. I have often said to our Lord, when the particle of the true cross sweetened my pains: "Lord, if it had been so sweet for Thee to suffer upon this cross, this little piece of it would not now make my pains so sweet!"

In August, 1820, Anne Catherine was moved to other lodgings, and the particle of the true cross was lost in the confusion consequent on such a change. She was greatly distressed; she prayed to St. Anthony of Padua and had a mass said in his honor for the recovery of her treasure. On returning from vision a few days later, she found it in her hand and exclaimed:

St. Joseph and St. Anthony have both been with me, and St. Anthony put the cross in my hand!

Relics of Mary
Relics of the Blessed Virgin's Clothing

ON *July 30, 1820, Anne Catherine said:* In the little package of relics that my confessor gave me I have more than once come across a small piece of brownish stuff belonging to a garment of the Mother of God. I had, in consequence, a vision of Mary. I saw her, after the death of Jesus, living with one servant in a small house off by itself. In a glimpse at the marriage feast of Cana I saw that Mary wore this dress there; it was a holiday dress. When she lived alone with her servant, she was frequently visited by

John, or some other apostle or disciple—but no man lived in the house. The servant provided the little that was needed for their support.[1]

The country around was still and tranquil; a forest stood not far from the house. I saw Mary in this dress following a road she herself had laid out near her dwelling in memory of the last sorrowful journey of Jesus. At first, she went all alone, measuring each step of the dolorous passion, which she had so often retraced in spirit since the death of her Son. Wherever anything remarkable had happened to Jesus, there she set up a memorial with stones, or made a mark on a tree if one stood near. The road led into a little thicket that contained a hillock in which was a grotto, and here was represented the tomb of Jesus. When she had thus laid off the different stations, she went from one to the other with her maid in silent contemplation, sat down at the places marked, meditated upon the mystery it recalled, prayed, and often arranged things still better. I saw her engraving on a stone with a stylus the particular circumstance of each station, or something of the kind.

She and her maid cleaned out the grotto and made it fit for the tomb and for prayer. I saw no pictures nor crosses, but only monuments with inscriptions, all very simple. This first attempt of Mary to perpetuate the remembrance of her Son's sufferings became, in consequence of frequent visits and improvements, a very beautiful road to which long after her death pious Christians went to pray. Here and there they used to kiss the ground. The house in which Mary dwelt was, like the house of Nazareth, divided off by light partitions.

The garment to which the relic belonged was an upper one; it covered only the back, where it fell in a fold down to the feet. A piece passed around the neck from one shoulder to the other, where it fastened by a button, thus forming an opening for the neck. At the waist it was confined by a girdle; thence it descended to the feet over the brown underskirt and turned back at the sides to show the striped red and yellow lining. The relic does not belong to the lining but to the outside stuff. It seemed to be a

---

[1] See *The Life of the Virgin Mary.*

holiday dress of ancient Jewish style. Anne had one like it. She wore an under robe, the bodice shaped like a heart. The front and sleeves were not concealed by the upper robe; the latter were narrow and gathered in around the elbows and wrists. The hair was concealed by a yellow cap that fell on the forehead and was caught in folds at the back of the head; over this was a veil of black stuff which fell halfway down the back.

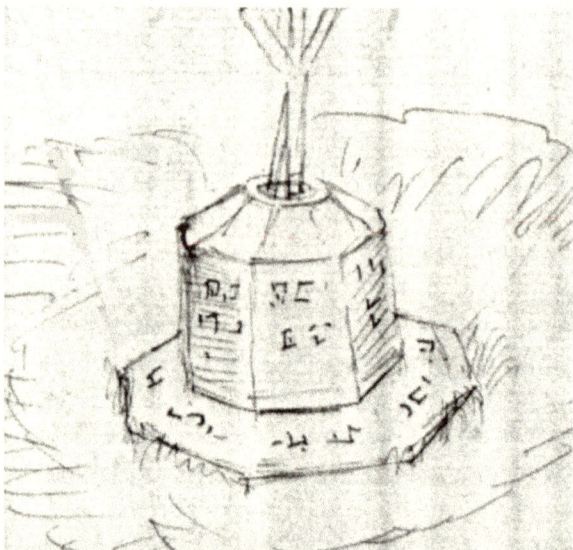

A Station of Mary's Own Way of the Cross in Ephesus,
drawn by Cl. Brentano, after Anne Catherine

I beheld Mary in her last years, making the way of the cross in this robe. I know not whether she wore it because it was a holiday dress, or because she had worn it at the time of Christ's crucifixion under the mantle of prayer and mourning that completely enveloped her. She was at this time advanced in years, though there was visible in her no other sign of age than an ardent desire for her transfiguration. She was remarkably grave. I never saw her laugh, and the older she grew, the fairer and more transparent became her countenance. She was thin, but I saw no wrinkle, no trace of decay about her; she was like a spirit.

I have examined the relic; it is a piece of stuff about the length of one's finger.

Other Relics of Mary
and the Holy House of Loreto

I MADE my usual journey into the holy land and to many places in which I saw all sorts of relics of Mary and learned their history. I was also in Rome with St. Paula. It appeared to be on the day of her departure for the holy land, and she visited the holy places with me. I know not why I saw so many relics of the Blessed Virgin.

I have been to that place (I think Chiusi) where was once the ring of Mary that is now at Perugia.[1] They still exhibit there a white stone in a vase, but the ring is gone. Of this ring I still remember that a youth before his burial arose in his coffin, declaring that he could not rest until his mother, a worldly woman named Judith, would give to the church Mary's wedding ring, which she had in her possession. After these words he lay down again.

I have been some place. I know not whether it is the same in which the house of Loreto first stood,[2] or whether only the vessels I saw came from it. They were not in an orthodox Christian church; the people looked like Turks. There were bowls and earthen vessels like those in the holy house when it came to Loreto, but I know not whether they were genuine, or only the models that St. Helena had made. There are still many of them at Loreto, but Helena had both the original and the copies covered with a thick coat of glazing to preserve them. I think those at Loreto are genuine. Those that I saw in the place of which I speak were carefully kept under an altar.

I saw also in a Greek church somewhere in Asia a piece of faded blue stuff, a part of Mary's veil. It was once very large; but so

---

[1] See "Mary's Wedding Ring" in *The Life of the Virgin Mary.*

[2] The Basilica della Santa Casa (Basilica of the Holy House) is a shrine of Marian pilgrimage in Loreto, Italy. The history of the house dates from at least the close of the crusades. The town of Loreto has been a popular pilgrimage site since the thirteenth century. Local lore recounts that the house in which the holy family lived was miraculously flown from Palestine to Loreto by four angels just before the final expulsion of the crusaders from the holy land. According to this narrative, the house at Nazareth in which Mary had been born and brought up, received the annunciation, and had lived during the

much had been given away that only this small piece remained. Through John's influence it was presented to the church in which I saw it. I saw in a vision people disputing its authenticity. One rash man, attempting to seize it, boldly reached out his hand, which was instantly paralyzed. His wife began to pray earnestly for her husband's cure. Luke, who was present, proved its authenticity by laying it on the man's hand, which was instantly cured. He also gave them something in writing concerning it that is still preserved there. He spoke to them of his own life, of his travels, of his having frequently seen Mary when he was with John at Ephesus, and of his own connection with the liberal arts. He mentioned the portraits he had painted.[1]

I went also to a place where was preserved an undergarment of Mary. I think it was in Syria, near Palestine. The garment was one that Mary had given to two women before her death. The people of the country were not Roman Catholics, but Greeks, I think; they held the relic in high veneration and were very proud of it. I think Francis of Assisi went there once and wrought a miracle in confirmation of its authenticity. I saw, in the place in which are Mary's veil and Luke's writing, a letter written by the Mother of

---

childhood of Jesus and after his ascension, was converted into a church by the twelve apostles. In 336, Empress Helena made a pilgrimage to Nazareth and directed that a basilica be erected over it, in which worship continued until the fall of the kingdom of Jerusalem. The tale further states that, threatened with destruction by the Turks, the house was carried by angels through the air and initially deposited in 1291 on a hill at Tersatto (now Trsat, a suburb of Rijeka / Fiume, Croatia), where an appearance of the Virgin and numerous miraculous cures attested its sanctity. These miracles were confirmed by investigations made at Nazareth by messengers from the governor of Dalmatia. In 1294, angels carried it again across the Adriatic Sea to the woods near Recanati; from these woods (Latin: *lauretum*; Italian: *Colli del Lauri*)—or from the name of its proprietress (Laureta)—the chapel derived the name, which it still retains (*sacellum gloriosæ Virginis in Laureto*). From this spot it was afterwards removed to the present hill in 1295, with a slight adjustment being required to fix it in its current site. It is this house that gave the title Our Lady of Loreto, sometimes applied to the Virgin. The miracle is occasionally represented in religious art wherein the house is borne by an angelic host.

[1] See "Luke as Painter" in *People of the New Testament III*.

God. It is very short, but not even slightly discolored by age. I heard it read, and perhaps I shall remember some of it. John wished her to write it to the people because they were incredulous about many things concerning Jesus.

I had a vision of the cincture of Mary and the swathing bands of Christ, which were once preserved in a magnificent church at Constantinople. Where they now are, they are not known. I had another great vision of a pilgrim bringing from the holy land all sorts of relics of Mary, her clothing and also some of her hair. He was attacked and wounded by robbers who cast the sacred objects into the fire. But the holy man afterward crept to it, found the relics uninjured, and was healed.

Where Mary's house at Ephesus stood, there still lies hidden under the ground a stone upon which both Peter and John used to say mass. Whenever they went into Palestine, they visited the house of Nazareth, and offered there the holy sacrifice on an altar raised where the fireplace once was. A little stand Mary had used stood on the altar for a tabernacle. Anne's house was in the country about half a league from Nazareth. From it one could go, by a short cut and without being remarked, to the house of Mary and Joseph, which stood near a hill—not on the hill but on the opposite side, a narrow path running between it and the house. Though it had a small window on that side, it was dark.

The back of the house was, like that of Ephesus, triangular. Here, in this corner was Mary's sleeping apartment; here she received the angelic message. Her room was cut off from the rest of the house by the fireplace which, like that at Ephesus, was provided with a pipe terminating in a tube above the roof. At a later period, I saw two bells hanging from it. Right and left of the chimney were doors opening into Mary's room. In the chimney walls were niches in which were placed the dishes. Mary's sleeping place was on the right; a little wardrobe stood on the left and also an oratory with a low kneeling-stool. The window was opposite. The rough walls seemed to be covered with large leaves over which hung mats. The ceiling appeared to be woven out of sapwood. In the three corners shone a star, the largest in the middle one. When Mary went to Capernaum, she left the house beautifully adorned as a sacred oratory. She often returned to visit the scene of the Incarnation and pray there. Time rolled on, and more stars adorned the ceiling.

I remember that the rear of the house, the chimney, and the little window were transported to Europe and, it seems to me when I think of it, that I saw the front in ruins. The roof was not high and conical, but level in the center and sloping toward the edges—not so much so, however, that one could not take a turn on it. There was no turret, only the chimney and projecting pipe covered by a little roof. At Loreto I saw many lights burning. At the moment of the annunciation, Anne was sleeping in an alcove to the left near the fireplace.

Spurious Relics of Mary's Hair

ANNE *Catherine had received from the convent of Notteln, through one of her former fellow-religious, some hair said to have been brought into the country by St. Ludger as the hair of the Blessed Virgin. It was not long before she had the following vision concerning it:*

From the foot of my bed there to the right, an uncommonly lovely maiden approached me. She wore a shining white robe and yellow veil; the latter fell down to her eyes, and through it I could see her golden hair. The whole room was suddenly lighted up around her, not as by reflected light, but as if by a sunbeam. Her whole appearance and her surpassing loveliness reminded me of the Mother of God; and, as this thought passed through my mind, she addressed me pretty much as follows:

"Ah! I am far, far from being Mary, though I sprang from her race about thirty or forty years after her. I am of her country but I did not know her, nor did I ever visit the places of her sufferings, for I could not make known my religion at a time in which the Christians were very much persecuted. But the memory of the Lord and his mother was so greatly revered in my family that I strove in every way to imitate their virtues. In spirit I followed the footsteps of the Savior as other Christians do the way of the cross. I received the grace of realizing Mary's secret sufferings, and that formed my martyrdom. A successor of the apostles, a priest, was my friend and guide (here she told me the name, but I have forgotten it; it was not one of the apostles, nor is it in the

Litanies—it is an ancient, foreign name which, it seems to me, I have heard more than once).

"This man was the cause of my being known; but for him, I should have remained wholly unknown. He sent some of my hair to Rome and a bishop of the country obtained possession of it. He brought it here with many other things, but the circumstance has long been forgotten. Many relics of my time were sent to Rome, though no relics of martyrs."

This is about all I learned from the apparition. The way in which such communications are received cannot be explained. What is said is singularly brief, though one single word then imparts more knowledge than thirty would at another time. One sees the speaker's thoughts, though not with the eyes, and all is clearer, more distinct than any ordinary impression. The recipient experiences such pleasure as is produced by a cool breeze in the heat of summer; but words cannot express it! Then the vision disappeared.

Blessed Objects

I NEVER saw miraculous pictures shining, though I have seen before them a beam of light from which they receive the rays that fall upon those praying below. I never saw the crucifix of Coesfeld shining, but only the particle of the true cross in the upper part of it. I have also seen rays darting from the relic toward the devout suppliants kneeling before it. I think every picture that recalls God or one of His instruments may receive the power of working miracles by virtue of prayers said in common and with lively confidence. In this, faith triumphs victoriously over the weakness of nature.

One day the pilgrim presented Anne Catherine an Agnus Dei, which she took with the words:

This is good and endued with strength. It is blessed. But here, in these relics (she was at the time arranging some) I have strength itself.

Of a blessed crucifix, she said: The blessing shines upon it like a star! Keep it reverently. But the consecrated fingers of the priest (turning toward her confessor) are still holier. This crucifix is perishable, but the sacerdotal consecration is ineffaceable; it will last for all eternity, neither death nor hell can annihilate it! It will shine forth in heaven! It is from Jesus, who has redeemed us.

Someone brought her a little picture of the Mother of God that had been blessed:

It is blessed! Keep it carefully. Do not let it lie among profane things. He who honors the Mother of God is honored by her before her Son. It is good in time of temptations to press such things to our heart. Keep them carefully!

Another little picture given her she laid on her heart, saying:

Ah! the strong woman! This picture has touched the miraculous picture.

St. Benedict's Medal

THE *pilgrim gave Anne Catherine a reliquary inclosing a medal on a scrap of velvet; she said:*

This is a blessed medal of St. Benedict, blessed with the benediction that Benedict left to his order by virtue of the miracle that took place when his monks presented him a poisoned draught. The glass fell to pieces when he made the sign of the cross over it. It is a preservative against poison, pestilence, sorcery, and the attacks of the devil. The red velvet on which the medal is sewed is also blessed; it once rested on the tomb of Willibald and Walburga, the place where oil flows from the bones of the latter: I saw the priests carrying it there barefoot, and then cutting it up for such purposes as this. The medal was blessed in that monastery.

One day the pilgrim laid near Anne Catherine's hand a small picture of St. Rita of Cascia that some time previously had been moistened by a drop of blood from her own stigmata. She took it, saying:

There, I see a sick nun without flesh or bones! I cannot touch her.

On July 11, 1821, while Anne Catherine was relating something she had seen in vision, the pilgrim quietly slipped into her hand a book opened at a page stained with her own blood. Instantly a bright smile played over her countenance and she exclaimed:

What a beautiful flower! Red and white streaked. It has fallen from the book into the palm of my hand.

Again the pilgrim laid the same leaf in her hand with the question: "Has is touched anything?" She felt it a moment and answered:

Yes, the Wounds of Jesus!

In October, 1821, a lady sent her from Paris a little picture that had touched the bones of St. Bobadilla. Anne Catherine was at the moment suffering from intense headache. She raised the picture to her forehead, when the saint appeared to her, relieved her pain, and she saw the whole scene of his martyrdom.

As she lay in ecstasy one day, the pilgrim offered her a broken silver ring blessed in honor of Blessed Nicholas von der Flüe,[1] at his tomb in Sachseln. When returned to consciousness, she said:

I saw how Brother Klaus separated from his family and how, in his conjugal union, by suppressing the material, he rendered the spiritual bond so much the stronger. I saw the mortifying of the flesh figured by the breaking of a ring, and I received an instruction on carnal and spiritual marriage. The ring which brought me this vision was blessed in honor of Brother Klaus.

Petrified Bone:
A Glance at Paradise

ON *February 13, 1821, as Anne Catherine lay, as usual, absorbed in ecstatic contemplation in the presence of Father Limberg and Christian Brentano, the brother of the pilgrim, the latter entered the room with a piece of petrified bone in his hand. It was about the size of an egg and had been found in the river Lippe. He laid it gently on her bed. Still in ecstasy, she took it into her left hand and held it for a few moments; then she opened her eyes and looked steadily at the pilgrim, who fully expected to receive a rebuke for having given her the bone of a brute animal instead of a holy relic. But still absorbed in contemplation, she exclaimed:*

How did the pilgrim get into that wonderful, that beautiful garden into which I can only look? There he is with that great animal! How can it be! O how beautiful is all I see! I cannot express it, I cannot describe it! O God, how wonderful, how incomprehensible, how powerful, how magnificent, how lovely art Thou in all Thy works! O here is something far above nature! For here there is

---

[1] See "Nicholas of Flüe" in the present volume.

nothing touched by sin! Here is nothing bad, here all things seem to have just come from the hand of God!

I see a whole herd of white animals, with hair like masses of curls falling over their backs; they are much taller than men, and yet they run as lightly and nimbly as horses. Their legs are like pillars, and yet they tread so softly! They have a long trunk which they can raise and lower and turn on all sides like an arm, and long snow-white teeth protrude from their mouth. How elegant, how clean they are! These animals are enormous, but so handsome! Their eyes are small, but so intelligent, so bright, so mild—I cannot describe it! They have broad, hanging ears, a tail fine as silk, but so short, they cannot reach it with their trunk. O they must be very old, their hair is so long! They have young ones which they love tenderly; they play with them like children. They are so intelligent, so gentle, so mild! They go together in such order, as if on some business.

Then there are other animals! They are not dogs—they are yellow as gold and have long manes, and faces almost human! O they are lions, but so gentle! They catch one another by the mane and frolic around. And there are sheep and camels, oxen and horses, all white and shining like silk, and wonderfully beautiful white asses!

Words cannot say how lovely it all is, or what order and peace and love reign here! They do no harm to one another, they mutually help one another. Most are white, or golden; I see very few dark ones. And what is most astonishing is that all have abodes so well arranged, so beautifully divided off into passages and apartments—and all so neat! One can form no idea of it. I see no men; there are none here! Spirits must come and put things in order— we cannot imagine that the animals do it themselves.

Here Anne Catherine paused as if attentively regarding something, and then exclaimed:

There is Frances of Rome! And there is Catherine of Ricci! High over the beautiful garden floats something like a sun in whose rays the saints are hovering and looking down; there are ever so many of them up above me, and the sun is dazzlingly white. Its rays look like a great white silken carpet on which the saints float, or it is like a great white silk cover shining in the sun's rays. The saints are standing on it and looking down—O now I know it all! All the water comes from up there, and the lovely garden is the garden of paradise![1]

---

[1] The rest of this vision will be found in "Paradise" and "The Mountain of the Prophets" in *First Beginnings*.

Some Other
Persons Described

Datula and Pontianus

(And a Relic of the Precious Blood
and of Mary's Hair)

IN *June, 1822, the pilgrim received from a suppressed Carmelite convent
of Cologne a little package inscribed: "De Cruore Jesu Christi," which he
hid, unknown to Anne Catherine, in the closet at the head of her bed.
The next day she said:*

I have had a very uneasy night, I was in a most singular state! I
was attracted in this direction (pointing toward the closet) by a
sweet feeling of hunger, a feeling of thirst, an insatiable longing!
It was as if I were forced to fly thither while drawn at the same
time in a contrary direction. In this excited state, I saw numerous
successive scenes. I saw over there the whole of Christ's agony in
the garden of Olives. I saw him kneeling on the rock in the grotto
and sweating blood. I saw the disciples sleeping near, while the
sins of humankind were crushing their Lord. I saw the rock sprinkled with the drops of congealed blood, which were in time completely hidden by the overlying dust and earth. It seemed as if
that covering had been removed, that I might see those drops. I
seemed to see it all in the far, far past. Then I had a vision of the
Blessed Virgin who, while her son agonized in the grotto, knelt
on a stone in the courtyard of Mary Mark's house. She left upon
it the imprint of her knees. She suffered the agony of Jesus with
him; she became unconscious and her friends supported her.
These two scenes were presented to me at one and the same
time. Then I had a vision of Mary's hair, and I saw again that it
had been divided into three parts and that the apostles cut some
off after her death.

Here the pilgrim produced the little bag with the above-named relics, which Anne Catherine regarded devoutly for a few moments.[1] *She then said*:

I see it again, and that is really the blood of Christ! There are three tiny particles, and they exert an influence totally different from the bones of the saints. They attract me most wonderfully; they excite in my soul a sweet, longing desire! Other relics shine with a light which, compared to this, is as a fire compared to the splendor of the noonday sun.

At intervals, she repeated: It is the blood of Christ! Once before I saw some that had flowed from a host. This is truly some of the blood of Christ that remained on the earth. It is not the substance of blood, but it is like it in color. I cannot explain it. I saw the

---

[1] With this relic was the following document: "I, John Verdunck, Chamberlain and Master-of-the-Robes to His Electoral Highness Maximilian, Duke of Bavaria, etc., hereby attest that his Most Serene Princess and Lady, Countess-Palatine of the Milne, Duchess of Upper and Lower Bavaria, etc., *née* Duchess of Lorraine, having died in the convent of Randshofen, bequeathed her effects to her heirs. On the occasion of their being put in possession of them, the marechal of the Court of His Electoral Highness, Count Maximilian Kurz von Senfftenan, etc., presented some tokens of remembrance to many connected with the execution of said bequests, whereby there happily fell to me a golden *Agnus Dei* with diamond pendant, enclosing a relic of Our Dear Lady's hair. I know not whether the countess was aware of its containing this relic, but I kept it carefully and reverently, and gave it to my daughter Anne of Jesus, Carmelite religious, on the day of her profession in the convent of Cologne. Three or four years after, my gracious master, His Electoral Highness, after the birth of his heirs by his second wife, caused the holy relies to be exposed. Among them was a large piece of the *Terra madefacta Sanguine Christi*, of which he put three particles into an *Agnus Dei*, for Madame, his Countess, and the two young princes respectively. On the paper on which it had been divided there still remained two or three particles, so small that His Highness could not pick them up. He ordered me to burn them for fear of desecration. I folded them in the fine paper, but did not burn them as ordered. I preserved them most honorably and, at the request of my dear daughter, Anne of Jesus, I gave them to her. This I attest upon my conscience and as I hope for salvation! I declare the above statement true and exact, and in proof of the same, I have marked the relics with my private seal. I have written the above, I sign it, and I affix thereunto my seal, given at Munich, the 30th day of May, AD 1643.

L.+ S. Johm Verdunck,
Electoral Chamberlain and Master-of-the-Robes

angels gathering up only what flowed to the earth during the passion and on the road to Golgotha.

And now Anne Catherine received repeated visions upon the discovery, the worship, the whole history of this relic. She related them at intervals, as follows:

✝ ✝ ✝ ✝ ✝

I SAW a devout princess in pilgrim's garb going to Jerusalem with a numerous train. She belonged to the Isle of Crete. She was not yet baptized, though she ardently sighed for that grace. I saw her first in pagan Rome in a time of peace just before a persecution; for the pope, who instructed her, dwelt in an old ruined edifice, and the Christians held secret assemblies here and there.

The Christians were tolerably secure in the holy land, though a journey to Jerusalem was attended by many dangers. The city was very much changed: hills had been leveled, valleys filled up, and streets built over the principal holy places. I think, too, that the Jews were confined to one quarter of the city, and only the ruins of the Temple were to be seen. The site of the holy sepulcher was near Golgotha and still beyond the city limits, but it could not now be reached—the road leading to it had been closed, and buildings had been raised over and around it. There dwelt in caves hard by many holy personages who venerated the sacred spot and who seemed to belong to a community established by the first bishops of apostolic times. They could not visit the holy sepulcher in body, but they often did so in spirit. Few of the inhabitants seemed to trouble themselves about these Christians. They could, by using some precautions, freely visit the holy places around the country. They could also dig in search of, and collect, precious things. It was at this period that many bodies of the saints of the early ages were found and preserved.

The pilgrim princess, while praying on the Mount of Olives, saw in vision the precious blood. She pointed it out to a priest of the holy sepulcher. With five companions he went to the spot indicated, turned up the earth, and found part of the colored rock, upon which Jesus had knelt, sprinkled with blood. As they could not remove the whole stone that formed a part of the solid rock, they detached from its surface a piece as large as one's hand. Of this the princess received a part, as also some relics of the garments of Lazarus and the old Simeon, whose tomb not far from the Temple lay in ruins. I think the princess is inscribed in the calendar, although she is not known among us. The piece of stone was three-cornered, with various colored veins. At first it was placed in an altar, and afterward in the foot of a monstrance.

The father of the princess was descended from the Cretan kings, but Crete was at this time in the hands of the Romans. He still had vast possessions and lived in a castle near a city in the western part of the island, Cydon, or Kanea (or something of the kind),[1] where grow quantities of yellow, ribbed fruit, broad at the stem and flat at the top.[2]

Between the city and the castle was a great arch through which one could see right into the former. A long avenue led to it. The father had five sons living. The mother had died while the daughter was still young. The father had been to the holy land and Jerusalem. One of his ancestors had been an acquaintance of that Lentulus[3] who had loved Jesus so much and who had been a friend of Peter, from whom he had learned the doctrines of Christianity. Hence it was that he was not unfavorable to the new religion. Once he was in Rome with his daughter's future husband. They conversed together of Christianity, the young man expressing his hope of one day embracing its teachings. It was on this occasion, I think, that they agreed upon the marriage or, at least, became acquainted. They received from a priest more detailed instructions. The affianced, a count, was in fact of Roman extraction, though born in Gaul.

The Cretan prince became increasingly estranged from paganism. His daughter and other children, whom he had reared as well as he knew how, often heard him lauding Christianity. He had a claim over the labyrinth of Crete which, however, owing to the change in his sentiments, he resigned to his son-in-law. The laby-

---

[1] The city's name was similar to that of a city in the holy land (Cydon = Sidon, Canea = Cana); Canea is the former Cydon, by which Knossos is meant. CB

[2] Doubtless she meant quinces, known as *malum Cydonium*.

[3] See "Lentulus" in *People of the New Testament IV*.

rinth and temple were no longer used as formerly. Men were no longer brought there to be torn to pieces by wild beasts, though idolatry was still practiced. Numbers flocked to them out of curiosity, and they were the scene of many shameful observances. At a distance, the labyrinth looked like a verdant mountain.

The verdant mountain was covered with all manner of trees, walls, and idolatrous temples from which one might be lowered down, though it was possible also to ascend thereto from below. There were intricate passageways and large rooms, greater in length than breadth. One came often into round chambers illuminated with lamps. These chambers were open above, and plants and trees could sometimes be seen along their perimeters. When men approached, the wild animals crept into their lairs, only to spring forth upon them, then, from such hiding places. Lewd women were kept there also. In the middle was a great plaza upon which many idols were assembled in the form of a pyramid. There was some sort of structure built above the plaza, though it was still possible to see through to the opening and trees growing upon the distant mountainside.[1]

When the young princess was in Rome to be instructed, she may have been seventeen years old; and when in the following year she made her pilgrimage to Jerusalem, it seemed as if her father was dead and she was her own mistress. She carried the precious blood on her person in a richly embroidered girdle in which were several little pockets. All the pilgrims wore such girdles, crossed on the breast.

She returned to Crete, but it was not long before the count took her away again. They embarked in a ship for Rome, where they stayed until secretly baptized. The papal chair had long been vacant, for there had been confusion, a schism, and a secret massacre of Christians. From Rome they embarked for Gaul with a numerous retinue of soldiers, having lived about six months after

---

[1] It seems this arrangement was not the same as the labyrinth of old, but perhaps rather like that of which students of Apollonius of Tyana sometimes spoke, perhaps constructed in association with idolatrous temples, underground passageways and gardens, the like of which Diodor Siculus and Pliny the Elder discovered already destroyed in their own time.

their marriage, partly in Rome and partly in Crete. The count now wore the precious blood in a girdle, for the princess had given it him as a pledge of her fidelity. His castle was on an island in the Rhone about seven leagues [hours] from Avignon and Nîmes, near a little village later known as St. Gabriel's. It owed its origin to a miracle by which a man had been saved during a storm on the lake. Tarascon and Martha's Solitude were not far off, Martha's monastery being situated on a mountain lying between the Rhone and a lake.

We find here in Brentano's notes that Anne Catherine described in further detail the location of Martha's monastery in connection with a hand-drawn map (which unfortunately has gone missing):

It lay among rocky mountains east of a little river, between a small lake and a larger hook-shaped lake communicating with the sea. It was here that Martha gathered together many pious women. She also traveled further north [upriver?] to Avignon, where she taught and healed a drunken youth.

On this occasion Anne Catherine quite precisely pointed out on her map the town of Marseilles [Marsilia] where, as she said, Martha [and the others] had made landfall [after their miraculous journey from the holy land]. She added also that there was at that time in the wilderness around Tarascon a dragon wreaking havoc among the people, which Martha slew by making the sign of the cross.[1] She then said further:

There were at that period in Nîmes some Christian catechists living together secretly, and the count received from time to time the visit of a holy hermit, a priest. The precious blood was, at first, preserved in a dark, underground vault whose entrance lay through many others, in one of which were stored plants and provisions—in winter even green trees were there preserved. It was kept in a vase like a chalice on an altar that had a little tabernacle with a locked door. Before it burned a lamp. I often saw the count and his lady praying before this tabernacle.

---

[1] Anne Catherine added: "Magdalene also slew at her hermitage a dragon obstructing the entrance to her cave. She took hold of it and cast it down. It must surely have been a spectral dragon." See also "Dragons" in *Inner Life and Worlds of Soul & Spirit*, and both "Magdalene" and "Martha" in *People of the New Testament V.*

I saw that, at a later period, they lived apart like hermits and at a distance from their castle. They went to it only to make their devotions before the precious blood. Once they heard a voice enjoining them to place the relic in a chapel, whereupon they prepared a suitable place for it near the dining hall. Their devotion toward it ever increased, though they continued to venerate it only in secret. The relic was afterward transmitted to their heirs with numerous precautions and duplicate documents.

I saw at this time something connected with Trophimus of Arles, but I can now recall only the names. Before the count's marriage, some Christians had immigrated to that country from Palestine; they were supported by him and they lived there in little communities.

The countess's father had concealed his sentiments from his eldest sons, whose ideas differed from his; but the younger ones held the same faith as their sister, and I think there were martyrs among them.

On another occasion, while thinking of the precious blood, I had a glimpse of the altar in the count's castle, and then I saw the countess herself, first as a maiden with her father on the Isle of Crete, then with her husband in Rome. At the same time I saw the holy monk Moses in Rome. I saw him as a boy eight or ten years old, giving all kinds of nourishment to the Christians, sick and in prison. I saw the count and countess with other Christians in a subterranean vault, lit by lamps, where priests seemed to be instructing them from rolls of writings. There were at that period many distinguished personages secretly baptized in Rome; there was indeed no open persecution, but from time to time one or another of the Christians was seized.

I have said the Christians from Palestine had already settled near the count's domains, and that with them he kept up secret communications. They did not have holy mass at first, only prayer and reading; but later on a hermit came about every six weeks, and afterward a priest from Nîmes to offer the holy sacrifice. The faithful at that time were still allowed to carry the blessed eucharist to their homes.

When the count and countess separated to live in solitude, they had grown children, two sons and a daughter. Their caves or hermitages were about half a league from each other and the same distance from the castle. They were, however, on its lands. To reach them, one had to cross a bridge over a small stream. Other Christians throughout the country lived in the same way, mutually assisting one another. At one time it was like a monastery. They did not end their days there, however, nor were they martyred; but when danger threatened, they fled.

✚ ✚ ✚ ✚ ✚

A SHORT *time later, Anne Catherine designated a relic as belonging to Pope Anacletus, saying that he had been the fifth pope, had succeeded Clement, and had been martyred. At the same time she remarked, in allusion to the relic of the precious blood:*

The priest who searched for the precious blood was the saintly Bishop Narcissus, of the race of the three holy kings, with whom his ancestors had journeyed to the holy land. It was perfectly light when he dug that night upon the Mount of Olives, and the young princess was present. Narcissus was dressed like the apostles.

Jerusalem was then scarcely recognizable, for when it was destroyed, valleys had been filled up and hills leveled. The Christians still had a church at the pool of Bethesda between Sion and the Temple. They had had one there even in the apostles' time, but it was not now in existence. They dwelt around it in huts, and although perfectly isolated from the other inhabitants, they were obliged to pay a tax for the privilege of entering their own church. A man and a woman sat at the gate to receive from the faithful five small pieces of money as toll. This regulation lasted some time.

The pool of Bethesda with its porches was no more, all was closed up; but there was a covered well whose waters were regarded as sacred and used by the people in time of sickness, just as we use holy water.

The count's name was the same as that of one of Augustine's friends, Pontianus; that of the countess was Tatula, or Datula—I cannot give it correctly. There is such a saint toward the close of May, or the beginning of June.

Several days thereafter Anne Catherine suddenly exclaimed:

There was a man here just now, a cardinal, the confessor of a holy queen named Isabella. He was a very able director of souls.

He told me that I must accuse myself of the good I neglect to do, and do penance for the sins of others. He showed me Datula, who possessed the relic of the precious blood. For its sake she had abandoned all her wealth and retired with her husband to grieve over their sins. The cardinal was called Ximenes, a name I never heard before. He is not canonized.

One day, having seen several things in Martha's life, Anne Catherine pointed out more precisely the abode of Pontianus and Datula:

The island with the castle lay at the mouth of the eastern branch of the Rhone and was about half a league in circumference. Pontianus had soldiers under him; his castle looked like a strong fortress. Seven leagues further up river lay the city of Arles, and at about eight leagues distance was Martha's monastery, in a rocky, mountainous district.[1]

Several more days later, Anne Catherine had a vision, occasioned by what, or referring to what, she did not know. She recounted it with all the simplicity and astonishment of a peasant girl beholding the march of a grand procession. She constantly interrupted her recital to give expression to her admiration at the magnificence, order, and propriety displayed in every part of it:

Crete is a long, narrow island, with numerous indentations, the center traversed by a mountain ridge. The castle of Datula's father was a very handsome, spacious building, apparently terraced out of a marble rock. On the different terraces were colonnades and porticoes, on top of which were gardens. After embracing Christianity, Datula's father had built these porticoes and hanging gardens as a screen to cut off his home altogether from the abominable, idolatrous temple and its labyrinths. He was a very skillful man; he could do almost anything; and he constantly superintended the architects and workmen himself. He was bald and stooped in the shoulders, but still very active and

---

[1] Anne Catherine notes also that in Martha's time the region was much wilder than at the time of Pontianus: "It was mostly forest, with here and there a fortified castle, or fortress. In those days there were also more islands at the mouth of the region than later on." She recalled also a bridge built over the river, on which trees grew. There is reference in the notes to a map, which however has not been discovered.

most benevolent. He owned other large properties on the island, and he also exercised some kind of authority. The wall mentioned above was built in terraces that were full of well-kept plants. They opened into rooms and passages.

Today is the anniversary of the day on which Pontianus led his bride Datula from her brothers' castle, the father being then no more. All night I saw the grand feast—so distinctly that I still have the servants and children under my eyes. Two of Datula's brothers lived in the castle with their respective families. There were many children, boys and girls, and crowds of domestics; for every child had, besides its tutors, several attendants, both male and female, each with a special duty. All the relatives of the family, with their children and servants, were then at the castle for the marriage. The road for half a league was adorned with triumphal arches and seats erected on either side, artfully twined with flowers and ornamented with statues and rich hangings. Here sat the young musicians. At the gate of the castle was a raised throne for the bride and her attendants.

Pontianus had arrived at a neighboring port the day before with a numerous retinue of ladies, soldiers, servants, and presents. He repaired to another castle at no great distance and there marshalled his procession. The joy of the bride's domestics and slaves was most touching. They had always been most lovingly treated and rewarded, and now they were all delight. They were stationed in order on the road, the highest grades nearest the castle, the children with their attendants on raised seats.

Pontianus appeared in sight with a grand cortège. Before and around him marched his soldiers, while servants in rich dresses lead asses and little nimble horses laden with baskets of clothing and pastry. Pontianus himself rode in an elegant large carriage, like a great canopied throne. It was surrounded by lighted torches set in stands transparent as glass, the canopy surmounted by a flambeau. The whole carriage was covered with gold and ivory, adorned with rich hangings, and drawn by an elephant. In Pontianus's suite was a long train of ladies.

All moved so orderly, so joyously, through the lovely country with its charming walks of golden fruits, beautiful flowers, and happy people—it was a real jubilee, but without any disorderly shouting. When the procession reached the first row of servants, clothing and flat cakes—some of the latter stuck full of little sprigs—were distributed to everyone by Pontianus's servants. And so they advanced, distributing gifts to the joyous crowd. When the bridegroom reached the seats of the children of the family, they stretched silken draperies with fringes and long streamers across the road before him, while the choir of children saluted him with music. Pontianus arose, presented them with gifts, and the procession moved on toward the brothers and sisters-in-law of the bride. At last it passed through an immense arched avenue of trees elegantly decorated, and across a bridge.

And now appeared between the magnificent buildings and gardens a kind of stage in tiers, covered with rich carpets and ornamented with garlands and beautiful statues transparent and glittering. I remember among others the representation of a whole chase, the eyes of the animals sparkling like fire. The procession took place in the daytime; but the throne of the bride was placed in a recess lit partly from behind, partly from the sides, by flambeaux such as surrounded the bridegroom's carriage. Around it was raised a semicircle of little balconies whence burst forth at the instant of Pontianus's arrival a chorus of voices accompanied by flutes—it was all wondrously charming!

But loveliest of all was Datula, the bride, seated high on her throne, below her arrayed in double rows her young companions and attendants all in white with long veils, their hair braided artistically around their head and adorned with rich ornaments. Datula wore a glistening white robe, I think of silk, which fell in full, long folds, and her hair was entwined with most beautiful pearls.

I cannot say how powerfully I was touched when I beheld through her clothing the gleaming of the relic of the precious blood. It lay on her heart in its richly embroidered girdle, shedding rays of celestial glory over the magnificent scene. Her heart was perfectly absorbed in the thought of the sacred object she bore about her. She looked like a living monstrance when her betrothed appeared before the throne, his attendants, male and female, in a semicircle around him. Upon a great silken cushion under a beautiful cover they bore presents of costly dresses, jewels, and ornaments of all kinds. The cushion was presented to the female attendants and then to Datula, who with her suite now descended from the throne. Veiling her face, she knelt humbly before Pontianus, who raised her up, lifted her veil, and led her by the hand first to the right and then to the left, the whole length of the semicircle, presenting her to his followers as their future mistress. It was a touching sight: the precious blood borne on Datula's person in the midst of these pagans! I think Pontianus knew of its presence, so respectful, so reverential was he. At last, they all entered the castle with the family.

No words can describe the order that reigned throughout the joyous multitude scattered in the chambers, the courtyards, the terraces and groves, or under tents, eating, singing, jesting. I saw no dancing.

There was a grand banquet in a spacious, circular hall into which one could see from all points. The bride sat by Pontianus at a table higher than those in use among the Jews. The men reclined on couches, the women sat cross-legged. Most wonderful-looking things were set on the table: great animals and figures with the meats in their sides, in their backs, or in baskets held in their mouth. It was droll and fantastic, and drew forth many pleasantries from the guests. The drinking vessels shone like mother-of-pearl. I gazed upon this scene all night.

But yet, I did not see any nuptial ceremony, though I saw Datula's departure with Pontianus. A great deal of baggage was sent on before to the ship, and amid tears and good wishes they proceeded in festal procession to the port. Pontianus, Datula, and several others rode in a long, narrow chariot on many wheels and built in sections. At the turns in the road, sometimes it wheeled so as to bring the occupants into a semicircle. It was drawn by little frisky horses.

I saw nothing disorderly during the whole feast, nothing even slightly improper; and although these people were not all Christians, there was nothing idolatrous about them. They seemed to be pleasing to God, as if all were inclining toward Christianity. The men were remarkably handsome, and I cannot forget those tall, beautiful, healthy-looking women and girls. Datula took some of them with her, among them her nurse, or governess, whose sentiments were very Christian. I did not see them embark.

Some weeks later, as Anne Catherine lay in ecstasy, the pilgrim dropped from a prayer-book a little picture of Jesus crucified, which fell on the coverlet of her bed. She seized it quickly, her eyes still closed, ran her fingers over it several times, and exclaimed:

It must be venerated! It is very precious! It has touched some sacred object; it shines brilliantly!" Then, laying it on her breast, she said: "It has touched Christ's robe, on the neck of which is a stain of the precious blood of which no one knows!

And on a subsequent occasion, she reported:

I have had to perform a wearisome task connected with relics of the earliest ages, in a country beyond the holy land where the priests do not dress exactly like Catholic priests. They wear very antique vestments, something like those I saw on Mount Sinai. It seemed to be in the country I always see next to that of the three kings. The city in which was the old book of prophesies on copper plates (Ctesiphon)[1] lay to the left of it. Here I had much to do with the blood of Christ, and I had to discover a treasure of relics to the priests.

I saw seven old priests digging under ruined walls in an underground cave; they first propped the wall up for fear of its falling in. There they found holy relics sealed up in a great stone, seemingly of one piece but really formed of many three-cornered pieces skillfully put together. When it was opened, first appeared a thick hair-cloth under which reposed the treasure—the principal relics of the passion and the holy family—all preserved in three-cornered vases placed side by side: sand from the foot of the cross, moistened and tinged with the blood of Jesus; and, in little phials, some of the water from his side—clear, consistent, no longer liquid; thorns from the crown; a piece of the purple mantle of derision; some scraps of the Blessed Virgin's clothing; some relics of Anne, and many others. Seven priests were there at work while deacons held torches, and I think they placed the blessed sacrament above them. I had much to do there, and many poor prisoners—that is, poor souls—to deliver, in which work the precious blood helped me. I think the apostles had to say mass in that cave.

---

[1] See "The Holy Book of Ctesiphon" in *Mysteries of the Old Testament*.

Vignettes From
Datula's Journey to Jerusalem

ANNE *Catherine beheld Datula in Jerusalem at the time Narcissus was bishop there, and reported the following:*

The men and women accompanying her were all clothed in masculine attire, though she herself was dressed as a woman. She was quite slender. She wore a long, wool-gray dress, and over a veil a small hat of this shape (see drawing), held in place by a ribbon fastened around her neck, which served also to hold it loose on her back should she care to remove it from her head. Panels of fabric hung from her arms. She looked most elegant.

At the time, Narcissus was resident at the church beside the pool of Bethesda, which still stood, though it had undergone renovations, having been redesigned with numerous compartments, latticed enclosures, and galleries. The pool of Bethesda was also much altered. The surrounding ambulatories had been blocked with rubble, so that there was not a trace left of the pool. Instead, to the side stood a structure covering a great spring-cistern that held what remained of the pool's waters. The circle of supports holding up this structure was formed both of old trees and newly-planted ones, which below were green. The roof was of thatch, the walls of wattling. The site served still as a place of baptism.

For a time, Datula lived together in this vicinity with some Christians. She undertook to visit all the holy sites. The holy sepulcher lay outside the city, buried in rubble, built over, and quite in ruins. The neighboring caves were inhabited by pious people.

Datula in Jerusalem in 190–200

The caves around Bethlehem, on the other hand, were still in relatively sound condition and much reverenced by the Christians. I watched as Datula prayed upon the Mount of Olives, where she was granted a vision of the holy blood. When she told Narcissus of this vision, that very night he, together with some anchorites of the holy sepulcher, went to the place and, after breaking away a piece of the stone where Datula had prayed and received the vision, presented her with a corner thereof.

I saw then that upon her return journey Datula visited the house of Mary in Ephesus, as also Mary's house in Nazareth, which was being maintained by some Christians.

Datula wore a wide-flowing dress of many folds, and over this a short, sleeveless outer garment open at the front. Such sleeves as there were—or rather, the lappets with which the arms might be wrapped—were attached to an undergarment whence they hung down from the shoulders like little mantles. Her hair was enclosed in a kind of coif covering the nape of her neck, over which was set her little hat. A veil lay around her neck, and she was girded with a wide belt of many laces [see drawing on preceding page].

Regarding Datula's Island

THE island lay not far distant from Montpelier. At an earlier time it had still been connected to the mainland. A city is now built upon it, lying west of the mouth of the Rhone. Further west is the site of Datula's death, and further still a place called Agatha[1] (which Anne Catherine believed to be a Spanish town). Toulouse lay to the northwest, along a river.

Anne Catherine recalled much of this story with wonderful clarity, illustrating just how much she could have related had she received the necessary encouragement and gracious support, especially from her religious guides:

Datula would often don men's garb when venturing from her wilderness retreat to help others. She was a very spirited and determined woman.

---

[1] This could be Agde.

*The pilgrim had read that at one time Montpelier had been called Aga-
thopolis, and so he asked Anne Catherine whether she knew this name.
She said:*

Yes, in Datula's time the city near the island was called by that
name, and is to be distinguished from another city further west
called Agatha.

*She further described the island as a long, narrow ridge lying along the
bank of the river (Rhone); and when the pilgrim inquired whether the
city may have been called Cette,[1] she said:*

Yes, it seems to me that that is the name by which it is now
called. The castle where Datula died lies perhaps two hours further to the west, on an island that was inherited by her daughter.

*Then she again described the natural features of the region, especially
its flora, with the utmost charm and precision:*

When Datula was still with her father, she was so enthused by
all she was told about Jesus that she would often say: "If only I
were where he so often journeyed, and might accompany him, if
but a little way." It was after this that she conceived such a yearn-
ing for the stone containing his blood.

Datula's Passing

ONE *day Anne Catherine beheld the day of Datula's death and said
that upon her baptism in Rome she had been given the name Mamille.
Then she related what follows:*

I have seen much of the life of Datula, and today beheld her
passing from this world, of which I can recall some things.

When she was in Jerusalem just prior to her marriage, she was
seventeen years old. Narcissus, the bishop of Jerusalem, died
about two years later. Datula herself died sixty-two years thereafter, so that she was approximately eighty-one years of age upon
her passing.

At the beginning, Datula led a secluded life with her husband
on her island by the mouth of the Rhone, as has been told. Later
she withdrew into the wilderness along with seventeen virgins,
there to live together as a community of anchorites, much as Mar-

---

[1] Known now as Sète.

tha had done. At that time there were men also living a similar life, among them some priests who went about discretely teaching and converting. These priests would bring the sacrament to Datula's community, and say the mass.

In this connection I saw much of Saturnin, the first bishop of Toulouse, who is often wrongly identified with the Saturnin who was a disciple of Christ and the apostles, and who came also to Toulouse as a captive, but was never bishop there.[1]

Much of what I beheld of this Saturnin, who was to become bishop of Toulouse I can no longer recall in detail, but I can say that as a youth of about twelve years he one day left his parents and—it seems to me with the support of Datula's family—received a religious formation. At the time of his death he was active as a priest, but I can recall nothing more of this, even though he became bishop of Toulouse.[2]

During the persecutions of the emperor Decius,[3] many Christians—men and women—were flushed out from their wilderness retreats and captured. However, Datula escaped and made her way to the home of her married daughter, a very old edifice with thick walls hard by the sea—indeed, it extended right out over the sea, so that water flowed beneath it. The region was densely forested and not far from Toulouse, where she would later die.

Many of Datula's former anchorite community were carried to Rome and martyred there, as were men from the neighboring monastic community. I recall the names of some of the martyred women: Agnes, Sybil, and Lillie (or perhaps Lillis or Lillit)—a

---

[1] See the extended article "Saturnin" in *People of the New Testament III*.

[2] Elsewhere Anne Catherine reports: "At the age of twelve, the pagan youth Saturnin left his flock of sheep and came running through Datula's community, and then also to the Christian priests hidden in the region. Later he went to Paris, where he was ordained a priest. It was after Datula's death, I believe, that Saturnin went to Rome, later returning to Toulouse. He died a martyr, but not in Toulouse—although I am not entirely certain on this point."

[3] Trajan Decius (Gaius Messius Quintus Decius Augustus, c. 201–June, 251) was Roman Emperor from 249 to 251. Decius, who was born at Budalia, near Sirmium in Pannonia Inferior (now Martinci and Sremska Mitrovica in Serbia), was one of the first among a long succession of future Roman emperors to originate from the Danube provinces.

beautiful, slender woman who had been a trusted maidservant to Datula. As for the martyred men, I recall the names Silvan, Azzo, and another that sounded something like Mammemas.

In time, Datula died a natural death while with her daughter, whose husband resided at the time further inland.

During her illness, Datula wore a portion of the relic of the holy blood in a heart-shaped locket upon her breast. Just before her death she received the holy sacrament from a priest named Mamerius (or Mamertus), who was later martyred by being dragged to his death.

Since Datula's end was near, this priest took into his possession her various religious objects, among them the locket of the holy blood. They were properly distributed, each trusted servant of her husband receiving some part in them. Those of Datula (or Mamille) herself later passed to a community rather like the Brothers of the Holy Cross,[1] who venerated them.

That Datula had died was first remarked by the appearance in her room a great brilliance. Anne Catherine beheld how the Blessed Virgin came to her and gathered in her soul:

Miracles were attributed to Datula's remains: a dead child laid upon her body was restored to life, and one possessed was healed. During her life, and especially during the time she lived withdrawn with her community of women, her good works were beyond enumerating. Truly, she is one of the dearest of all souls.

Datula died after Agatha,[2] for she knew of the martyrdom of Agatha, whom she venerated.

Anne Catherine then mentioned several other martyrs from this time, adding that the holy martyr Moses[3] died somewhat later.

Some Further Glimpses

DATULA had three sons and a daughter. One son became a priest, another died in battle, and after a long military career the

---

[1] Brentano places a question mark after this expression.

[2] See "Agatha" in this volume.

[3] Possibly Moses the Black (330–405)—known also as Abba Moses the Robber, the Abyssinian, the Ethiopian and the Strong—an ascetic monk and priest in Egypt in the fourth century AD, and a notable Desert Father.

third was touched by a miracle and thereafter became a priest also. But I have forgotten any further details regarding this.

After Datula's death, her daughter was not permitted to sequester herself as she would have wished, but in the end she died a blessed death.

Datula's husband predeceased her. After a period during which they had each lived in seclusion in the vicinity of their castle (occasioned perhaps by a persecution), he withdrew again, and perished while in this state.

There was a most vivid memory during Datula's lifetime of the presence [in their region] at one time, among the early, secluded Christians, of Lazarus, Magdalene, and Martha. Christians would gather at Magdalene's cave, and also places where Martha had been active, to hold mass—as also, I believe, at their graves. It is beyond credence to me that any doubt can remain that Lazarus, Magdalene, and Martha had been present there.

The earlier religious communities of Martha and Thekla were more regulated—having a specific rule—than Datula's later community, which was more of the nature of fugitive women living a withdrawn, common life in cave and forest. Their Christly task was to take in and serve the persecuted, poor, sick, and destitute— teaching and converting also. During the time their community endured, many were converted, some of whom later journeyed to Rome, others all the way to Jerusalem.

The castle wherein Datula died lay by the sea, or perhaps surrounded by the sea. It was a thick-walled, rounded, somewhat crude structure. On its landward side were many gardens and trees—in particular chestnut trees of astonishing size—encircled by pleasure seats or bowers spanned by interlaced greenery. There were also long rows of high, straight trees like poplars, but rooted in water.

While still living, Datula was already regarded as a saint, and worked many wonders among the sick who came to her. She healed the blood-flux of a woman who asked for her help.[1]

---

[1] Brentano adds: "Perhaps by means of the relic of the holy blood that she carried with her?"

While on her deathbed I heard Datula say that in a vision from God she was told to instruct her daughter to bring all the sick then with them to come and pray by her body after she had died.

Mamertus (or Mamerius), the priest who gave Datula the holy sacrament just prior to her death, came from a place quite distant. He was aged, and had survived a persecution at a time, I believe, before Datula had come to the region. He took from her breast the heart-shaped locket with the holy blood, along with other relics, when he took leave of her, setting out that evening in order to circumvent—as it seemed to me—certain dangers. Datula died that same night. At that time I saw how by her side a possessed woman was healed, and others with wounds or ruptures made well. Her body lay for a long time in the castle cellar.

Datula's story is exceptionally beautiful and touching. It only we had it in its entirety! She had been specially chosen already in her youth. I find nothing more touching than her time with Narcissus in Jerusalem, her visit to the grave of Mary in Ephesus (where she walked the way of the cross), the story of her meeting and travels with her husband, and especially her baptism.

At this, the pilgrim expressed his surprise, for nothing had yet been said of Datula's baptism:

No? I thought I had related the whole story. It was very moving. Perhaps it will come to me again another time. She was baptized by a pope, who confided in her also. He prophesied that she would make a good marriage. I saw all this in great detail, as also the whole story of her life and of some of her saintly companions.

Datula's Daughter

ON *another occasion Anne Catherine discovered and identified among her dusty collection a relic of the nurse of Datula's daughter, who had been married at the other extremity of the same island where Datula and her daughter had lived:*

This nurse had wed a trusted servant of Datula's husband Pontianus, who had accompanied her upon her journey to Jerusalem. This servant had three brothers, all of them pagan, who lived also on the island. One of these brothers occupied an important position and lived in a building that stood opposite the castle of Pontianus. The nurse's husband died, leaving her with a young son, who became heir of his childless uncle.

The uncle despised his sister-in-law [the former nurse of Datula's daughter], and under a pretext abducted the boy, telling his mother that he had gone missing.[1] Ever after, the mother harbored a secret hatred for and fear of this man, who then, pretending to want to effect a reconciliation, invited her to a meal where he clandestinely served her own murdered son as a prepared dish. After consuming some of this dish, she became unusually affected and inward, reconciled with her brother-in-law, and admitted that she had secretly entertained the thought that he may have murdered her son—and so she asked his forgiveness. The villain was so shaken by this experience that he afterward converted.

Anne Catherine related this story with many such details, some seemingly tangled in some confusion. She said that both were later martyred and mentioned Rome in this connection.

Next day, having to deal with the usual distractions and challenges of her health and household without adequate support, Anne Catherine returned to the same story, giving the name Blonda (or Blanca) as the name of the nurse, Seneca as the name of Datula's daughter, Thystus as the name of the murderous brother-in-law, and Aceo as the name of her deceased husband and father of her child. She added that Datula's daughter's name was pagan, and she had seen it in writing. She was of the opinion that a feast day must have been established for Blonda (or Blanca), adding that that very night she had seen a cloistered nun from whose mouth a glow emanated whenever she took the blessed sacrament.

The pilgrim then diligently researched the matter of a Blonda or Blanca, and discovered what is described below:

"In Roetz's *Sakramentalischem Jahrbuch*, Volume II (Cologne, 1751), page 192, we read that the son of a woman named Blonda was murdered, and his heart given her by the murderer to eat—and that she was so affected by this that love was awoken in her for the murderer, and also an intense desire to receive the sacrament and to become a nun in the Servite Order. In the introduction to

---

[1] Anne Catherine was not entirely certain on this point.

this account, however, we are told further that this story is very similar to that of the second tragedy of the pagan playwright Seneca, which centers upon the pagan Atreo and his brother Thyesten.

"Here we find Aceo in Atreo, Thystus in Thyesten, Seneca (spelled in the same way), and Blonda (not Blanca). It should also be noted that the very day of the vision, September 2, is the feast day of Blonda the Servite."

The pilgrim related this very striking discovery to Anne Catherine's father confessor with the request that he ask Anne Catherine to try to call to mind again, with utmost attention, the whole story of the nurse of Datula's daughter. The good man promised to do so, but in the end forgot, as he so often did.

And so the pilgrim took it upon himself to tell Anne Catherine what he had discovered and thereafter asked her to please take the relic again and see if she could unravel the story further. Anne Catherine then told him, quite unaffectedly, that she had seen the story of Blonda that same day on account of its similarity to that of the nurse of Datula's daughter—adding that nine years previously she had come upon the story [of Blonda] in a religious book, and it was perhaps owing to this that the names she gave had come into her head.

And so, day after day, she promised to search for the bone fragment [the relic that had occasioned the initial vision] and see if she could sort out how the names had been interchanged. But she neglected to do so, in the end forgetting her promise. The pilgrim must have asked twenty or more times, but she kept putting it off, saying she knew the matter well enough and felt certain she must have already related it several times.

Finally, after the pilgrim had asked yet again, Anne Catherine located the relic later that afternoon and gave a summary account of the story given above, but with some additional details—among others:

The brother-in-law had said: "I will have it so that the god-eaters (a derogatory pagan term for the taking of the holy sacrament) really do, for once, eat their own child.

She indicated also that it might have been that more children were dealt with in this way. He was said to have been brought later to Rome as a criminal, was converted, and confessed his conversion when he was brought before the court.

Anne Catherine said that the nurse, along with many others, was martyred in Gaul, after which their bodies were carried to Rome, and along with many others there interred in beautiful caskets in a vault. She maintained that she knew quite well the names of those interred there, but had difficulty distinguishing them from others, and that it was for this reason that, when trying to sort it all out, she sometimes confused the names and thereby gave a wrong one.

Judith of Africa

ON *the first Sunday of Advent, 1819, a poor old Jewess came begging alms of Anne Catherine for her sick husband; she was kindly received, and to a few silver pieces Anne Catherine added words that both touched and consoled her. On this occasion, she was also seized with such compassion for the poor Jews that she turned to God with ardent prayers for their salvation. And she was most wonderfully heard, for shortly thereafter she related the following vision, in which her task was assigned for the beginning of the ecclesiastical year—prayer not only for the poor Jewess, but also for her whole race:*

It seemed to me that the old Jewess Meyr, to whom I had often given alms, died and went to purgatory, and that her soul came back to thank me, as it was through me that she was led to believe in Jesus Christ. She had reflected that I had so often given her alms, although no one gives to the poor Jews, and she had thereby felt a desire spring up in her heart to die for Jesus, if faith in Jesus were the true faith. It was as if her conversion had already taken place or would take place, for I felt impelled to give thanks and to pray for her.

Now, old Mrs. Meyr was not dead. But her soul had been disengaged from the body in sleep, so she might inform me that, if she died in her present sentiments, she would go to purgatory. Her mother, she said, had also received an impression of the truth of Christianity, and she certainly was not lost. I saw the soul of her mother in a dark, gloomy place, abandoned by all. She was as if walled up, unable to help herself or even to stir, and all around her, above and below, were countless souls in the same condition. I had the happy assurance that no soul was lost whom ignorance alone hindered from knowing Jesus, who had a vague desire to know him, and who had not lived in a state of grievous sin. The

213

soul of the Jewess said that she was going to take me to the native place of her family, whence her maternal ancestors had been banished for some crime.

She would take me also to a city of her people, among whom some were very pious, but who, as they had no one to instruct them, remained in error. She said I should try to touch their hearts. I went with her willingly.

The soul was far more beautiful than the poor old woman, who is still living. My angel was at my side, and when the Jewess made little mistakes, he appeared to shine more brilliantly and corrected them. Then she appeared to see him too, for she would ask eagerly, "Who told you that? Was it the messiah?"

We journeyed over Rome and the sea and through Egypt, where I did not see any great waters—only in the middle of the country a great white river that often overflows and fertilizes the soil. All was sand and sand-hills, which the winds scattered around. In this desert are immense stone buildings—high, thick, massive—such as are nowhere else. They are not houses, but are full of great caves and passages where rest numbers of dead bodies. They are very different from the subterranean tombs of Rome. The bodies are all swathed like little infants, hard, stiff, dark brown, and tall; ungraceful figures are sculptured on the monuments. I went into one and saw the bodies, but not one was luminous. We went on further and further south over sand deserts, where I saw spotted beasts, like great cats, running nimbly, and here and there round buildings on high hills covered with straw, with towers and trees above.

We went up higher and higher over white sand and green stone polished like glass, into a region of steep and rugged mountains. I was surprised to see so many fertile places among the rocks. At last we reached a large, strange-looking Jewish city, like nothing I had ever seen before in the narrowness, obscurity, and intricacy of its streets and houses. The mountains and rocks appeared as if about to topple over. The whole place was pierced with caves, grottoes, and fissures over which one must either climb or go around them. It is less a city than an enormous group of mountains covered with houses, towers, square blocks of stone; and it is full of caves and excavations.

We did not touch the earth, though we did not go over the houses either, but moved between them along the walls, always mounting higher and higher. It seemed to me that it was all hollow and might cave in at any moment. There are no Christians, but on the distant part of the mountain are people who are not Jews. I saw on one side a high quadrangular stone building with round holes in the top covered with iron bars, which I took for a Jewish synagogue. Here and there were houses with gardens on shelving rocks lying above and behind them.

We entered the city near the gate through a long, narrow, dangerous court between two rows of houses that looked like an open street, but that really ended in an angle full of caves and windings leading into the heart of the rocks. All sorts of figures were cut out in them. I had a feeling that murders had been committed here and that few travelers left them alive. I did not go into them, they were too frightful. I know not how we got out of the court again.

The soul of the Jewess Meyr said that she would take me now to a very pious, almost saintly family, upon whom the people all looked as upon their hope; they even expect from them a deliverer, perhaps the messiah. "They are very good," she said, "and so are all their connections." She wanted me to see them. We crossed the mountainous city that we had entered at the north, and mounted toward the east till we reached a level place whence we had a view of the eastern side. There was a row of houses running toward the south, at the end of which stood a large, solid building overtopped by mountains and gardens.

The soul told me that seven sisters dwelt here, the descendants of Judith. The eldest, still unmarried, was also named Judith, and all the inhabitants of the city hope that some day she will do for her people what Judith of old did for their ancestors. She dwells in the large stone castle at the end of the place. The soul begged me to be kind to them, for they know not the messiah, and to touch their hearts as I had touched hers.

I forgot to say that it was night when we entered the city. I saw men sleeping in the caves and corners, and among them many good, simple-hearted people. They were like gold compared with lead or copper; still there was also a great deal of superstition, crime, horrible filthiness among them, and even something like witchcraft.

We went into the first house at the corner, which belonged to one of the seven sisters. We passed through a round vestibule and entered a square apartment, the bed-chamber of the owner. The soul of the Jewess again praised her excellent qualities, but whenever she said anything inexact my guide drew near—that is, he appeared and corrected it. She would then ask, "Was it the messiah who told you that?"' I answered, "No, his servant."

As I looked upon Judith's sleeping sister, I suddenly became conscious that she was not good. I saw that she was a wicked adulteress who secretly admitted strangers. She appeared aware of our presence, for she sat up, looked around in alarm, and then arose and went about the house. I said to the soul that now she saw that this woman misbehaved. She was greatly surprised and asked if the messiah had told me that too.

We went then into the houses of the other sisters, and all were better than the first. I cannot now remember how it was that I found them alone, for all were married and some had children. They wanted for nothing. Their houses were richly carpeted and furnished, beautiful shining lamps hanging in the rooms; but all lived upon their sister Judith's generosity.

The sixth sister was not at home. She was with her mother, who lived in a small house just in front of Judith's. We went in by a little round court and saw the mother, an old Jewess, at her window. She was complaining angrily to her sixth daughter that Judith gave her less than the others, that she even gave more to her bad sister, and had turned her, her mother, out of doors. It was horrible to see the old Jewess in such a rage.

We left them quarrelling, and went to see Judith herself in the castle, before which stretched a deep and broad chasm. I could not look down it steadily. A bridge with an iron railing spanned it, the flooring being only a grating through which at a frightful depth could be seen all kinds of filth, bones, and rubbish. I tried to cross, but something held me back. I could not enter without Judith, so I had to wait; such were my orders.

Morning began to dawn, and I saw that the side of the mountain on which we then were was more pleasant and fertile than the north side by which we had ascended, and I noticed that the castle gate was fastened by a huge beam shaped like a cross. This fact very much surprised me.

Suddenly Judith, returning from distributing alms in the city, stood before the bridge. She is about thirty years old, unusually tall and majestic. I never before saw a woman of such vigor and courage, so heroic and resolute; she has a noble countenance. Her whole person, her gestures, breathe something elevated, something extraordinary; but at the same time she is simple, pure, and sincere. I loved her from the first. She wore a mantle. Her dress from the neck to the waist was most proper, tight as if laced, especially over the breast; she looked as if she had on a stout corset under her long, striped, many-colored robe. She had something like a gold chain around her neck and large pearls in her ears. A kind of variegated turban was wound around her head, and over it was thrown a veil. A tolerably large basket hung in full view upon her arm, the rods of which were black, the hoops white.

She was returning home from one of her nocturnal expeditions when she caught sight of me on the bridge. She appeared startled, took a step backward, but did not run. She exclaimed: "O My God. What askest Thou of me? Whence is this to me?" But soon she recovered herself and asked who I was and how I came there. I told her that I was a Christian and a religious, that I had been brought thither because of some good people sighing for salvation, but who were without instruction.

When she found that I was a Christian, she showed surprise at my having come so far by a route so dangerous. I told her that curiosity had not impelled me, but that the soul by me had led me thither, in order to touch her heart. "This is," I said, "the anniversary of the coming of Christ, the messiah; it is a yearly festival." I added that she should reflect upon the miserable condition of her people and turn to the Redeemer.

Judith was deeply affected; she became gradually convinced that she was conversing with spirits. It seemed to me that she either said or thought that she would find out whether I was a natural or a supernatural being, and she took me with her to the house.

A narrow path led over the bridge which could, however, be enlarged. When we reached the huge crossbeam that barred the gate, she touched something, the gate flew back, and we passed through a courtyard into which several gates opened. All around stood statues of various kinds, chiefly old yellow busts. We entered an apartment in which some women were sitting cross-legged on the ground before a long, narrow table about as high as a footstool; they were taking something, and Judith thought that she would now put me to the test. She made me enter first. I did so and went around behind the women, who did not appear to see me; but when Judith entered, they arose and passed before her bowing slightly as a mark of respect.

Then Judith took a plate, passed around the women, and presented it to me, holding it against my breast for she wanted to find out whether I was a spirit or not. Now, when she saw me decline her offer and that none of the women appeared to see me, she became very serious and went with me into her own room. She acted like a person who half-believes herself alone, who wants to convince herself that it is so, but who at the same time doubts it. She spoke timidly, but not fearfully. She is, in very deed, a Judith, most courageous!

Her room was simple, some cushions lying around and several old busts on the wall. Here we conversed a long time. I spoke of her wicked sister. Judith was exceedingly distressed and desirous of remedying the disorder. Then I mentioned her mother, whom I had seen in such a passion, and she told me that on account of her temper she had had to build her the little dwelling adjoining the castle; that she was very angry at being sent away, and at her giving more to one than to another, for all shared her bounty, as she, Judith, was not willing that they should live by usury. She took them money every night.

Many others of the city lived at her expense also, for her father had left a great treasure of which no one living knew but herself. He had loved her tenderly and left her everything. The people built their hopes upon her. Her secret alms made them see in her something superhuman, for they knew not of the treasure. They had once been greatly oppressed by war, when she had done all in her power for them; and so her deceased father (as she called him) left her the treasure. All wished her to marry, hoping that a deliverer would be born from her, but she instinctively shrank from marriage. My appearance made upon her an impression such as she had never before known, and she felt that the messiah might indeed be already come in Christ. She desired to inquire further into it, and, if she were convinced, would strive to lead her people to salvation. She knew well that all would follow her, and she thought perhaps that was what they expected of her.

After conversing in this strain, Judith took a lamp, led me into a kind of cave by a secret trap-door in the floor of her room, and showed me the immense treasure. I never before saw so much gold. The whole cave was lined with it and there was, besides, an enormous quantity of precious stones; one could hardly enter without stepping on them. She then took me all over the house.

In one room were seated a number of old men, some of them Moors, wearing frontlets and turbans, their robes bordered with fur; they smoked long pipes, and were drinking like the women in the other room. In another room were both men and women. We went up to the second story and into a large apartment singularly arranged. Around the walls and over the doors were yellow busts of venerable, old, bearded men. The furniture was odd-looking, antique and artistically carved. In the middle of the room hung a large lamp, and I think seven others around it; and there was also something like an altar with rolls of parchment on it. The whole room was wonderful! Near it was another where lay numbers of decrepit men, as if being cared for.

Then we went up on the roof. At the back of the house on a terraced slope was the garden, with large spreading trees carefully trimmed. We went up on this side and Judith pointed out in the distance a ruined building with crumbling towers, remarking that it had been the boundary of her nation's possessions before they had been conquered by a neighboring people and driven back. They still feared a renewal of their misfortune, of which these walls stood as a perpetual memorial. I saw them and water also in the distance.

We mounted then higher across deep ravines and strange buildings, the rocks at times jutting out over one another, as if the trees and houses on them were about to fall. We went to another part of the city where rose a steep rock like a high wall. Steps were cut in it, and here and there gushed limpid springs. Judith told me that there was a tradition of this city's having suffered extremely from drought. A strange man, a Christian, came and struck the rock with his staff, when water gushed forth. It used to be conducted by pipes, but they were not now in existence. All the springs, excepting this one, had ceased to flow.

Judith left me by the fountain, after which she returned home and I continued my journey. We took no leave of each other. It was all like a dream to her, and she parted from me as if she no longer saw me.

My road went up, up. I saw trees with large yellow fruits lying underneath, fertile fields, beautiful flowers, and bees in hives different from ours: they were square, tapering upward, black, and smeared with something. I was now far past the Jewish mountain, and I saw men who lived under large spreading trees like houses. They had few movables. Some of them were spinning, and I saw, here and there, a kind of loom. Their flocks, animals like those of the three kings, grazed around. There were also animals like great jackasses, all very tame. Some of these people lived in tents; but they stayed not long in any one place, but were continually moving. Clambering over bushes and stones, I came to a large subterranean cavern in good condition supported by short square pillars on which were all kinds of figures and inscriptions; in it was something like an altar, a large stone, and above it and on either side great holes like ovens. I wondered why the people did not use this beautiful hall. They are good, simple creatures, and they doubt not that their faith is the right one. At last, I crossed the sea and returned home.

Last night I took another long journey to the high mountain city and Judith's castle. I did not find her sisters in the houses leading to the castle. I know not where they are. I know that she had promised faithfully to put an end to the disorders of one of them. All the rest was as before, only it was later in the day, and there were numbers of strange Jews upstairs praying in the synagogue.

I went to Judith, who was sitting in her room reading a book. There was something about her inexpressibly grand, noble, and touching. I gazed upon her with delight. I have no doubt that she will become a Christian, if God gives her the opportunity, and then the greater part of her people will follow her. I cannot look upon this woman in her beauty, her majesty, her courage, her tenderness of heart, her humility, without great love and hope. I saw her once more in my illness before the last, but I forgot to mention it. I have finished the journey that relates to her.

On another occasion Anne Catherine added some further details regarding Judith, as follows:

I was with Judith in the Mountains of the Moon, and I saw many changes there. The ravine and bridge leading to her castle have disappeared as if an earth-slip had filled up the former. A level road now leads to the house.

Judith looked much older. She seems to be much nearer to Christianity, if not really a Christian in heart. I do not think she has yet been baptized; but, were a priest at hand, it might be done immediately. In the room in which I once saw her taking coffee with several others stood something like a little altar; above it was the picture of an infant in a manger, below which was a cavity in the altar, cut out like a basin, in which lay a small spoon and a white bone or stone knife. Lamps burned around, and nearby were desks with rolls of writings. Judith knelt there in prayer with many younger than herself and an old man, her assistant. All seemed to be suddenly convinced that the messiah was already come; but I saw as yet no cross. In the upper room in which were the old busts, the aged Jews were still assembled.

The treasure in the cellar was greatly diminished, for Judith gave much to the poor. Her abode is very wonderful! Her house to the west faces a deep valley beyond which rises a mountain that shines and sparkles in the sun like stars; on the opposite side, far away in the distance, are seen strange high towers and long buildings on the mountains. They cannot be descried from the castle, but I saw them. I saw also the people on the Ganges. Their church is in beautiful order, and they have among them an old priest, a missionary, I think. [Brentano here adds in the notes: "Most probably these were Abyssinian churches."]

Mary of Agreda

BECAUSE *Anne Catherine felt she had forgotten some things regarding Mary's appearance to James the Greater at Caesaraugusta,*[1] *the pilgrim read to her one afternoon Mary of Agreda's account, as given in her City of God, of those events, including the miraculous image, the pillar carried by angels, and so forth. After listening awhile, Anne Catherine said she could not grasp how someone who had seen so much could use such garish expressions when describing what she saw:*

I can only say that neither Jesus nor Mary have I ever heard speak the way she describes. Mary is so unutterably simple, her whole being like a delicate white thread of silk. In the words you read to me, and in those I have myself read, there is no sense of devotion, only loud bluster and empty frills, as you might well expect from some plump, dolled-up madam.

She said these things with no air of presumption whatsoever, mentioning only that she had never experienced things such as had been described. On another occasion, when asked about Mary of Agreda, Anne Catherine said:

She surely saw a great deal, but it seemed that only the half of it had made it to the page, and what they[2] could not comprehend had simply been discarded, and the gaps filled in with stories of their own devising.

---

[1] Saragossa.

[2] Whoever took the notes, or perhaps later bishops.

www.ingramcontent.com/pod-product-compliance
Lightning Source LLC
Chambersburg PA
CBHW022006080426
42733CB00007B/490